The Ultimate
KOI

Edited by Nick Fletcher

RINGPRESS

This side view gives a perspective of body dynamics.

Photo: Dave Bevan.

Published by Ringpress Books Ltd,
Vincent Lane, Dorking, Surrey,
RH4 3YX, England
Designed by Rob Benson

First Published 1999
© Interpet Publishing

ISBN 1 86054 146 1

Printed in Hong Kong through Printworks Int. Ltd.

10 9 8 7 6 5 4 3 2 1

CONTENTS

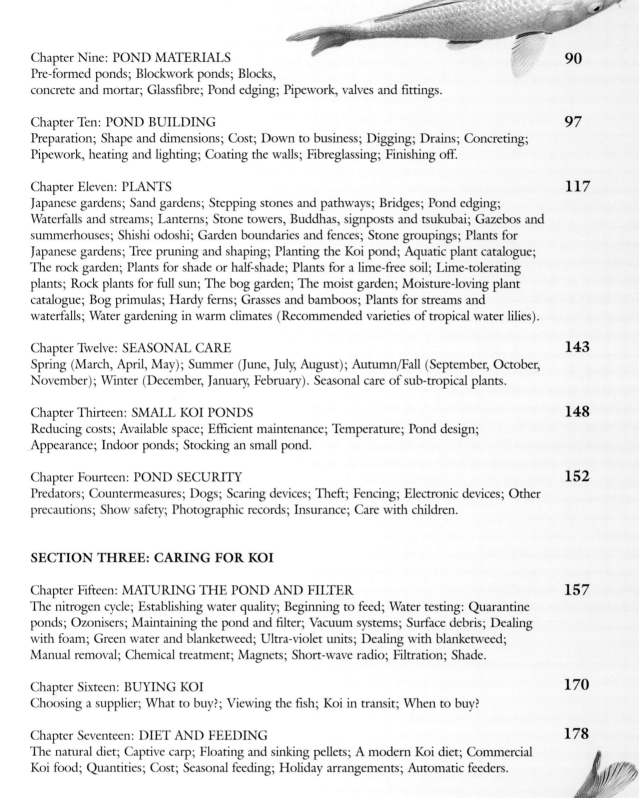

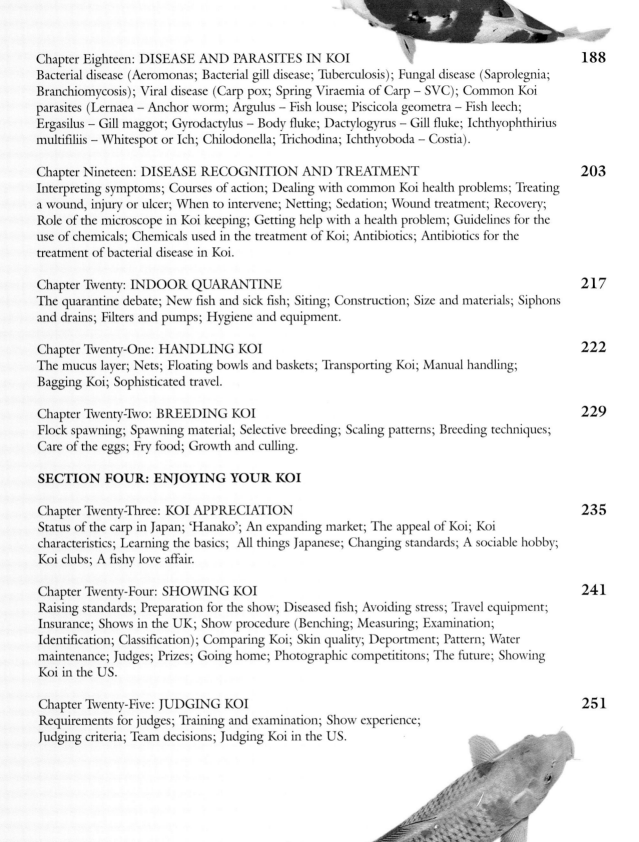

**This book is dedicated to the memory of Dr Keith Banister –
icthyologist, bibliophile, humorist, bon viveur and friend.**

CONTRIBUTORS

NICK FLETCHER (Editor): is a lifelong fishkeeper and angler with a specialist knowledge of Koi. A former editor of *Practical Fishkeeping*, Nick has worked on a number of fishkeeping magazines including *Angler's Mail*, *Angling Times* and *Trout and Salmon*. He is now a freelance writer and consultant, and is a trainee judge with the British Koi Keepers Society.

At home, Nick has a 3,500 gallon Koi pond. He also keeps tropical fish, specialising in Cichlids, and has an extensive collection of Bonsai.

DR KEITH BANISTER (1942-1999) was for many years an ichthyologist in the Fishes section of the British Museum (Natural History). He was an expert on sharks, barbs and blind cave fish, and had an abiding interest in sea monsters, in the existence of which he firmly (quite possibly) believed. Latterly, Keith spent some time in his beloved Africa, working on the Lake Tanganyika Biodiversity Project. A highly erudite and congenial man, his other great love was his collection of antiquarian books.
See Chapter One: Anatomy and Physiology Of Fish.

DEAN BARRATT is the aquatic centre manager at Stapley Water Gardens in Nantwich, Cheshire, and has been in the industry over 15 years. He has personally hand-selected fish from Israel for the past six years. He has written articles for a host of magazines, including *Practical Fishkeeping*, and was an original monthly contributor to the *Water Gardener*. Dean struggles to select a single favourite Koi variety, preferring to assess the merits of the individual fish. However, he regards Kohaku, Showa and Koromo as the class acts, but professes a soft spot for Doitsu, Hariwake, Kigoi and oddballs.
See Chapter Five: Israeli Koi.

VAL FROST has kept fish of many varieties all her life, peaking in the 1980s with a superb collection of disease-free Koi, kept in a 3,500 gallon pond, surrounded by a Japanese garden. A founder member of the British Koi Keepers Society, she held several official appointments in the society before becoming an honorary member. She is also a member of Nishikigoi International. A senior judge in the BKKS, Val is still active on the judging circuit. Now retired from Fleet Street, she maintains her interest in fish by travelling and scuba-diving around the world.
See Chapter Three: Koi Then And Now.

TERRY HILL is well known as a builder of Koi ponds, and he has a highly specialised knowledge of construction methods. He runs his own company, the Koi Pond Konstruction Kompany. Terry is married with three daughters, and his hobbies include Koi keeping, keeping tropical fish, collecting and renovating old juke boxes.
See Chapter Ten: Pond Building.

BARRY JAMES is a well-known authority on pondkeeping matters with several books to his credit, including one on Koi. He contributes to several aquatic magazines including *Aquarist and Pondkeeper, Practical Fishkeeping and Water Gardener*. For many years he ran the Everglades Aquatic Nurseries, near Cheltenham, where he gained an international reputation as an expert on water plants and water garden design. He currently lives in Southern Spain, working as a journalist, a garden consultant, and travelling the lecture circuit.
See Chapter Eleven: Plants; Chapter Twelve: Seasonal Care.

PAULA REYNOLDS BSc is an aquatic pathologist working as a fish health consultant. She runs her own laboratory and offers a full fish health service to Koi keepers, the veterinary profession and the aquatic industry. She is consultant to the British Koi Keepers Society Koi Health Forum, and writes in many publications including *Koi Carp* magazine.
See Chapter Nineteen: Disease and Parasites in Koi; Chapter Twenty: Disease Recognition and Treatment.

PAMELA SPINDOLA has been a Koi keeper since 1976, a hobby she shared with her late husband Robert. She currently maintains two ponds: one 5,000 gallon pond populated by 25 Koi, and another 2,500 pond, currently home to 30 Koi of all sizes. In the late 1970s, Pamela was a committee member orchestrating the start of Asssociated Koi Clubs of America, and she is now serving as president of her local Koi club in Santa Ana, California, where she has been instrumental in setting up and running many Koi shows. A prolific writer, Pamela is a regular contributor to *Pond & Garden* magazine.
See Chapter Three: Koi Then And Now; Chapter Twenty-four: Showing Koi; Chapter Twenty-five: Judging Koi.

TONY STADEN has had a lifelong interest in fishkeeping, and this has been channeled through his studies of science and biology which he has taught at college and university. He purchased his first Koi in 1974, and has owned and bred them ever since. He has travelled to both Israel and Japan to buy Koi and to find out more about them. Well-known as a writer on Koi and aquatic life, Tony also specialises in growing a wide variety of water lilies.
See Chapter Twenty-two: Breeding Koi.

INTRODUCTION

I saw my first Koi in 1975 – a quite accidental introduction to what subsequently became a consuming passion. It happened like this. Soon after moving from London to a new job in Peterborough, I met a near neighbour and mentioned to him that I had inherited a pond from the property's previous owners. It would be an ideal home, I said, for two stir-crazy goldfish that had shared a succession of cramped flats with me in the Smoke and richly deserved the outdoor life.

George said he would like to see the pond. We hacked through the undergrowth into my as yet untended back garden and there it was, a shallow bowl-shaped concrete pool that must have held all of 300 gallons. I had ambitious plans for it that included a fountain and a waterlily – after I had cut the grass, of course.

"Would you like to see my pond now?" asked George. "It might give you a few ideas." That was, at the very least, an understatement. The first clue was the nameplate by his front door – 'Kujaku'. I asked him what that meant. He replied: "It's Japanese for a Peacock, and that's my surname." Sneakily, he did not tell me it was also the name of a variety of Koi.

George introduced me to his wife Imelda, a lovely, houseproud Italian lady with a large collection of Capo di Monte porcelain and a taste for ornate crystal lampshades. But two very different cultures seemed to be struggling for supremacy in this household; on every wall were magnificent enamel plates of the most beautiful fish I had ever seen. There were Koi calendars, Koi clocks, quaint oriental statuettes and paintings of mountain scenery. Volumes on Koi (most of them in Japanese) filled the bookshelves.

On the kitchen table were spread what I took to be plans for a home extension. Only later did I learn that George was hoping to build a pond in the living room and link it to the one outside – but Imelda put her foot down over that, so it never got beyond drawing-board stage.

By the time I was ushered out to George's pond, I had a rough idea of what a Koi was, but nothing could have prepared me for the reality. This was a lake populated by technicolour dolphins, or so it seemed. Time plays tricks on the memory, but I now know the immensity of George's achievements, given that Koi keeping outside Japan was still in its infancy. His pond, though not very deep, was filtered – unheard of! – and stretched pretty much the entire width and half the length of the garden. The rest of the plot was taken up with a series of tanks for the rearing and growing of more Koi.

I was overwhelmed, the more so when George began talking of 'Sanke' and 'Kohaku' or his special pet, Pearl, who was an 'Ogon'. The terminology, technicalities and sheer alien nature of it all at once intrigued and intimidated me. So too, when I inquired, did the price of those fish. I duly went ahead with my own modest garden pool project, and it was not until several years later that I felt ready to take on the challenge of building my first Koi pond.

Back in the 1970s, Koi keepers like George were as much a curiosity as the fish themselves. The national body in the UK, the British Koi Keepers Society, had a membership of only a few hundred, and there were definitely no specialist dealers. The few Koi that did find their way into the country were occasional imports to special order. They were of low quality compared to those available today, and extremely expensive in real terms.

More to the point, most of them were doomed to an early death. Purchasers assumed that, because Koi resembled the familiar goldfish, they could be treated the same way. Accordingly, these pioneering fish found their way into small, shallow, planted ponds totally unsuited to their needs. First the plants would be uprooted, turning the

Koi-keeping soon becomes an all-absorbing hobby.

Photo: Dave Bevan.

water murky with silt, and then sooner or later – usually sooner – the Koi would succumb to stress-related ailments brought on by deteriorating water quality.

There were no readily available commercial filtration systems at that time, and most early Koi keepers anyway assumed that a fountain pump and perhaps a waterfall would keep the water sweet. It did not help matters that these would often be switched off at night, so as not to disturb the neighbours with the sound of running water.

Gradually, though, the veil of ignorance began to lift. Parties of BKKS members visited Japan and returned with information on the filtration systems and workable pond specifications they had seen. It was through contact with two of those forward-thinking folk, the late Eric and Hilda Allen, that George Peacock was able to keep his Koi alive – though he did lose his much-loved Ogon, Pearl, when his pond froze over one hard winter. Heated ponds, commonplace today, had not even been considered.

I still hear that Koi keeping is a hobby only for the rich. None of the early devotees I met were particularly well-off, but they were single-mindedly spending every spare penny on improving their ponds, foregoing holidays and trips to the pub to pay for their obsession. Most of them were extremely practical people, too – they had to combine the skills of builder, plumber, electrician and self-taught fish health expert, with varying degrees of success.

The picture is now entirely different. Virtually every aquatic store or garden centre with a pondfish section sells Koi, though relatively few of these originate from Japan. There are, however, dozens of specialist Koi dealers for those who want better-quality fish and are prepared to pay for them. The annual BKKS National Show attracts thousands of visitors, few noted for their obvious affluence. Outdoor aquatics is the fastest-growing garden leisure interest, and Koi are rapidly overtaking goldfish as the first choice for those who want fish, as opposed to just a water feature.

Much of the credit for this dramatic turn of events must go to the visionary Peter Waddington who, in 1982, founded Infiltration – the UK's very first specialist Koi outlet. Peter embarked on a steep learning curve, visiting Japan at every opportunity to buy direct from the breeders and discover what makes Koi 'tick'. Others, encouraged by his well-earned success, opened their own Koi-only outlets. Some were excellent, others less so, and the latter were run by people who imagined they were treading a rapid route to riches. These dealers tended not to last very long, but the damage they did to people's aspirations was incalculable.

In the early 1980s, building what is termed (for want of a better word) a 'proper' Koi pond could indeed gallop away with the money. Off-the-shelf filtration equipment was by then available, but production runs were small and tooling costs high. A bottom drain, for example, would be priced upwards of £50 ($80). Today, a similar item can be bought for £20 ($32) – a fifth of the cost, allowing for inflation.

At the same time, a filter revolution was taking place for ordinary pond owners with the advent of the 'black box' – otherwise known as the foam filter. These compact units process water both mechanically and biologically, and, though their use is decried in some Koi quarters, they did instil in the minds of the pondkeeping public the need for filtration. In my view, they enabled many people to take their first steps towards successful Koi keeping and, in today's larger and more sophisticated specifications, such filters have a valid part to play.

The third element of the burgeoning interest in Koi is, of course, the Koi themselves. Those that win shows, the high-grade Japanese fish, represent only a fraction of the total numbers sold worldwide. Most Koi now originate from Israel, America, China, Cyprus and even South Africa – places where the climate favours year-round mass production of ordinary-grade fish at attractive prices. This does not affect present demand for Japanese Koi. If anything, it works to the benefit of the top end of the hobby; there will always be a ready market for exceptional fish, and, as the Israelis refine their breeding techniques, the Japanese continually strive to retain pole position.

At the other end of the quality spectrum there are 'Ghost Koi'. These were originally Ogons crossed with common carp, but the term is now used more generally to describe pet fish of indeterminate parentage. Cheap and cheerful, 'Ghosties' have inspired many a garden pondkeeper to progress to Koi.

Whatever their pedigree, all Koi have great charm. They are not true shoal fish, but they love the company of their own kind; they are not super-intelligent, but they learn to recognise their owners and will feed from the hand. As they grow, they achieve a unique

*Knowledge of Koi
is spreading fast.*

Photo: Dave Bevan.

majesty of bearing. No two Koi are identical in either appearance or temperament. It is every Koi keeper's dream to own the perfect fish; it will never happen – though the quality of Japanese-bred stock is improving year on year.

The purpose of this book is to put present-day Koi keeping in perspective. There has never been a more exciting time to take it up and, in real terms, it has never been more affordable. A very competitive industry has grown around servicing the demand for Koi-related products, along with flourishing organisations whose members can pool knowledge and share in the social side of their hobby.

Unlike those early Koi keepers, the newcomer will find much of the work has already been done on his or her behalf. For example, instead of having to rely on garden peas, sweetcorn, prawns, boiled barley or lettuce, the Koi keeper now has available a whole range of specially formulated Koi foods, with the ratio of ingredients geared to the time of year these are fed. Besides basic diets, there are formulae to enhance growth rate and colour. Pellets are made in sizes to suit all Koi from fingerlings to metre-long jumbos, in floating and sinking varieties.

The understanding of what filtration should achieve, and how it can be put into practice, has changed radically in the last 20 years. Although many people still build their own systems, there are now relatively inexpensive modular units that demand only basic skills to install. The media they contain has changed dramatically, too – in fact, a mainstay of the modern hobby is a mechanical filter chamber holding no media at all, the vortex settler.

Knowledge of all things Koi-related is spreading fast, thanks to information technology. Many web sites on the Internet are devoted to Koi, while the UK society that started it all, the BKKS, now has thousands of members spread through its regional sections, and maintains links with Koi fans all over the world. Specialist magazines attached to the hobby sell well and provide an advertising platform for Koi dealers and equipment manufacturers. There is no sign of things slowing down.

This book will look at all the viable options in Koi keeping, even those which some purists consider to fall short of the ideal. One example is ponds built with a flexible Butyl rubber liner. In my view, it is unrealistic to dismiss Butyl when it is still the most popular construction material, but the drawbacks as well as the benefits of this and all other options in modern Koi keeping will be made clear.

Similarly, we shall not ignore the reality of smaller ponds, or Koi from sources other than Japan. After all, the fish have identical needs, whatever their pedigree.

Despite the commonsense maxim that it is best to create the ideal Koi pond at the first attempt, many people do not have the time, space or resources to do this. With suitable encouragement, though, and as their circumstances change, they will embark on successive projects until they arrive at their 'ideal' pond. Throughout the journey, I trust that keeping this book to hand will enable them to make the right decisions as they evolve through the many levels of Koi keeping. Chapters dealing with highly specialised subjects, notably fish health care, have been assigned to experts, and the information is bang up to date.

The pursuit of unattainable perfection is what makes this hobby so beguiling, and I hope that everyone who reads this book will be inspired to set out on their own personal quest for 'The Ultimate Koi'.

Nick Fletcher.

1 *ANATOMY AND PHYSIOLOGY OF KOI*

By Dr Keith Banister

Koi are merely selectively bred varieties of the common carp *Cyprinus carpio*. So it is not really surprising that their body structure and the way they respond to their environment are fundamentally the same as those of their wild ancestors. Any differences are superficial, and the colours and patterns of skin pigments belie an internal uniformity much more consistent than that of their cousin, the goldfish. Whether or not this consistency is innate or is yet to be fully exploited is hard to tell, since the Japanese do not even acknowledge the existence of the long-finned Koi so popular in the United States and the Far East!

BODY SHAPE AND SCALATION

In wild carp, the main variations occurring naturally are in body shape and scale cover. Carp from faster-flowing waters tend to be more slender-bodied, while those from still or sluggish waters are much more stockily built. These differences arise in response to the need for streamlining, and they help the fish get from A to B with the minimum of effort. In carp cultivated for food, body bulk is encouraged, irrespective of the needs of the fish, which is why the original Doitsu fish were deep-bodied, and why some scaleless Koi to this day have a tendency to revert to type and develop a fuller figure.

The reasons behind the natural variation in

A Kohaku: By tradition, Koi are assessed from above.

Photo: Nick Fletcher.

This side view gives a perspective of body dynamics.

Photo: Dave Bevan.

scale cover (degree of squamation) – from a full covering through to a reduced number of larger scales, or even none at all (leather carp) – are not so easy to interpret, although reduced scalation was probably bred into farmed carp to make them easier to prepare for the table. The skin of carp with reduced scales is thicker, and there is some evidence that Doitsu Koi grow faster than other varieties, which again would tie in with their food-fish origins.

In the original carp, the body is covered by approximately circular scales, with between 35 and 41 along the lateral line. As they are smooth-edged, they are called 'cycloid', as opposed to the rough-edged and toothed 'ctenoid' scales found in the perch family. Each scale lies in a pocket with the rear-facing third exposed and overlapping the

scale behind. In strains where scale cover is reduced (so-called 'mirror carp'), scales remaining along the back and the lateral line may be enlarged. The thin layer of skin on the exposed part of the scale may contain pigment cells (chromatophores).

Aside from damage, scale numbers stay constant as the fish grows, each scale enlarging through the more or less regular laying down of a ring around the circumference. On the outer surface, these depositions form ridges and troughs which show up as dark rings under the microscope (or to the naked eye if the scale is large enough). The ridges of these circuli, as they are called, are laid down at roughly regular intervals, so that the faster the Koi grows, the farther apart they will be. At times of slow growth – in the winter, during spawning, or

Anatomy And Physiology Of Koi

EXTERNAL FEATURES

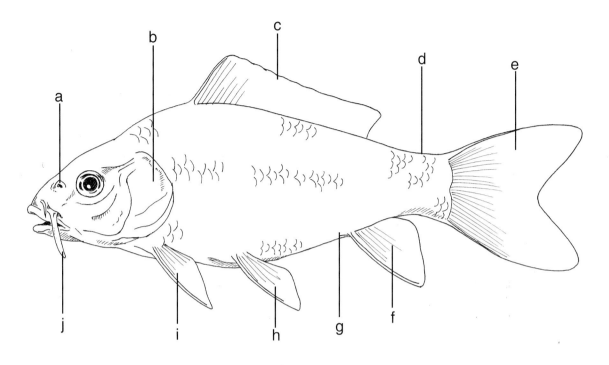

KEY

a. Nostrils
b. Operculum (gill cover)
c. Dorsal Fin
d. Caudal peduncle
e. Caudal fin

f. Anal fin
g. Vent
h. Pelvic, or ventral, fins
i. Pectoral fins
j. Barbels (two pairs)

when food is short – the circuli are closer together. These differences result in the separation of the circuli into 'tree rings'. A dark ring where the circuli are close together indicates a slow growth rate, while a pale ring with widely-spaced circuli indicates good growing conditions. Looking at these rings, the age of a wild fish can be fairly accurately assessed, but this does not work for Koi kept in heated, season-free pools where the growth rate is more constant and the fish never suffer famine.

COLOUR

The colour of wild carp is a standard dark green/khaki, the wild ancestor of the Koi being a deep bronze/black, but specimens occur naturally that lack one of the pigments. If, due to genetic factors, the black pigment is absent, a golden fish results. But it has taken years of selective breeding from such unpromising beginnings to produce the mosaic of colours that mark Koi out as special.

Artificial selection can produce colours that would never be viable in the wild, even though the potential always exists. Brightly-coloured fish are an easy meal for predators, hence the fry would be eaten before they could reproduce and pass on their genes. Only under the protective hand of the Japanese rice farmers were these genetic anomalies actively encouraged, resulting in the dazzling hues of today's Nishikigoi. Some

INTERNAL ANATOMY

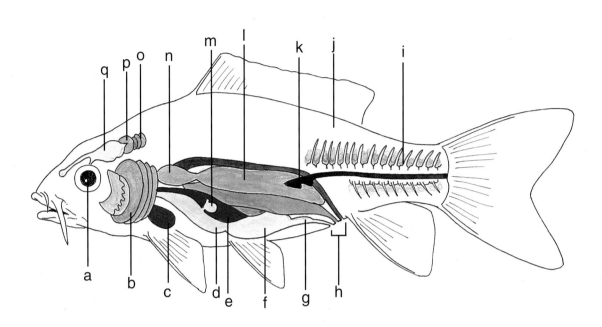

KEY

a. Eye
b. Gills
c. Heart
d. Liver
e. Spleen
f. Gut
g. Reproductive organ (ovary or testis)
h. Vent
i. Dark muscle
j. White muscle

k. Lateral line organ – this stretches from behind the gills to the tail, and is not a deep internal structure.
l. Swimbladder
m. Gall bladder
n. Kidneys
o. Weberian apparatus
p. Inner ear
q. Brain

of the naturally-occurring pigments of Koi will even fluoresce under ultraviolet light, but, below the surface, our pond pets are still *Cyprinus carpio*. The only reason they are not as hardy as their wild ancestors is that they are bred for colour, not durability – a parallel would be between a wolf and a Chihuahua, the one being a perfect hunting machine and the other a pampered pet.

FINS
The fins of Koi are distinctive. The dorsal is long-based, with three or four spines at the front, the leading one serrated along its posterior face. These are followed by from 17 to 22 branched rays. The word 'spines' does not properly convey the properties of these fins, as they lack the sharp, pointed tip and independent freedom of action of those of

THE SKELETON

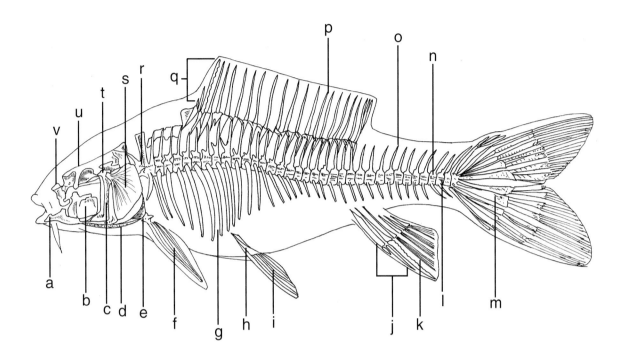

KEY

a. Lower jaw
b. Suspensorium of lower jaw
c. Preoperculum
d. Branchiostegal rays
e. Pectoral girdle
f. Pectoral fin
g. Ribs
h. Pelvic bone
i. Pelvic fin
j. Unbranched rays
k. Anal fin

l. Haemal spine
m. Hypurals (caudal fin bones)
n. Vertebral column or spine
o. Neural spine
p. Dorsal fin
q. Unforked rays
r. Weberian apparatus
s. Operculum
t. Hyomandibular bone
u. Skull
v. Upper jaw

true spiny fishes like the perch. Their main function is to act as a cutwater, and they are equipped only with muscles to raise and lower them. The last, and largest, of the spines (at the leading edge of the fin) has a serrated posterior edge in common with the dorsals of goldfish or crucian carp. The degree of serration varies, and the purpose of it (if there is one) is unknown. Other members of the carp family happily do without it.

All fin rays are bilaterally symmetrical, as can be seen from their basal articulation with the underlying supporting bones, but the visible part of the ray can take one of several forms, according to the fin's position and function. Maceration (by boiling up the fins of a dead carp in potassium hydroxide solution – do not try this at home!) shows that the exposed parts of the spines are not one strong unit, but are made up of two lateral halves held together by ligaments. More detailed studies show each lateral half to be formed by the coalescence of a series of nodules. Traces of this origin are not easily visible in the spine, but remain clearly so in the branched rays, where they are known as the 'articulations'.

The soft rays in the dorsal fin, behind the spines, all show their articulations at their stem, and this aids flexibility. Towards the fin margin, each of these soft rays branches several times. As the fibres of the fin rays are stronger than the membrane of the fin, the branching both strengthens the otherwise vulnerable fin margin and gives greater control over its movement; the membrane acts merely as a sail, with no muscular control of its own.

Fins will repair themselves when damaged (providing any underlying infection has been dealt with), but the nature of regeneration means that the original elegance is likely to be lost. After damage, a type of scar tissue forms to seal the wound, minimise the likelihood of further infection, and reduce blood loss (much as in humans). The arteries and veins temporarily re-establish themselves, joining up if necessary with their undamaged neighbours. This has to be the first move, as tissue cannot regrow without the food and oxygen supply brought to it by the blood system. The damaged ray then starts to regrow the outer segment (the nodule mentioned earlier). When this is done, growth continues inwards, joining with the undamaged, lower part of the fin ray. The whole then strengthens and sorts itself out. Finally, a definitive blood supply is established, as the temporary one is now redundant. This patching-up mechanism works the opposite way to the natural growth of the fin ray, so errors can occur in

fin shape – which concern the Koi's owner much more than the fish.

These general comments on the rays apply throughout the finnage, but the fins themselves have different functions, degrees of mobility and means of attachment to the underlying skeleton. Although fins are used for locomotion, they are not the main means of forward progression – this is the prime function of the trunk muscles. Fins come into their own in stabilising the fish, turning, reversing or exaggerating the thrust of the body. Look closely at a Koi swimming forward and you will see how it spreads its caudal fin to maximise the force of the propulsive sine wave passing down its body.

MUSCLES
If you skin a dead carp (or examine a cod fillet) you will find that the body muscles show a pattern like a warped 'W' on its side. Each W-shaped section is called a myotome, and is a band of muscle at once joined to and separated from the adjoining myotome by a band of tough tissue called a myoseptum. This ingenious arrangement is only part of a remarkable mechanical structure. If you now cut across the skinned fish to produce a steak (which, if you live in Japan, will probably end up grilled), the myosepta show up as a series of whorls, because each W-shape is an elaborate cone, stacking with the one in front and the one behind.

The end effect of this elaborate arrangement is to mould the muscles into a series of long tubes running the full length of the body. These enable the fish to produce forward thrust by alternate serial contractions of each flank. Bear in mind that muscle fibres can work only by a straighforward contraction (in this case using the elastic backbone as a foil); sideways working, or working around corners, is impossible. So Koi have found a splendid solution to the problem, which can best be appreciated by lightly boiling your cod fillet and gently trying to separate the muscle blocks. There is nothing gruesome about this, and it will give you a new appreciation of the hidden majesty of the internal design of the fish in your pond.

On a freshly dead fish you will notice two kinds of separate and distinct trunk muscles – red and white. In Koi, as in most fish, the white muscle predominates. Each colour has its own function. The red muscle fibres have a higher concentration of the oxygen-carrying blood pigment myoglobin and are used for cruising, because they are fuel-efficient. The white muscles, by contrast, have a poor blood supply but work anaerobically, using internal fuel stores, and are brought into play for sudden surges of speed which cannot be sustained for long periods. This is why 'chasing' a Koi with a net is so stressful to the fish and should be avoided.

So, the basic locomotive force comes from waves passing from head to tail along the body. The tailwards face of each wave presses on the incompressible water, pushing the fish forward. In relatively stocky fish like Koi it is difficult to appreciate that the body is thrown into waves, as each is incomplete due to the wavelength being longer than the body. Looking at an eel swimming will clarify how it works. As the forward gear is provided by the body, the fins can be used for the more delicate tasks of braking, steering, close manoeuvring and reversing. Carefully watching your Koi will soon show, for example, the paired fins working in synchrony to position it as it comes up for its floating pellets.

KOI SENSES

SMELL

Where the Koi wants to be is dictated by what its senses tell it. Koi have a particularly acute sense of smell, as wild carp very often live in murky water where sighting food is impossible. The nostrils, positioned either side of the snout, each have two openings which allow a current of water to flow over the sensory lamellae located in the olfactory pit. From each olfactory organ (which looks a bit like a leaf skeleton) Koi have two bundles of nerve fibres running straight to the brain. One bundle feeds the information received by receptors at the front of the olfactory organ, the other feeds stimuli from the posterior receptors. It is presumed that different information is perceived by different parts of the olfactory organ, in much the same way that our tongue detects four separate 'flavours' at different points on its surface.

All fish in the carp family possess a 'flight reaction' from danger; when injured or alarmed, they secrete a chemical from the skin which, as soon as it is detected in the water, causes other fish to get out of the area as fast as possible. The speediest way of detecting these alarm molecules is via the olfactory system, but the taste buds also respond to very similar molecules.

TASTE

From a practical viewpoint there is very little difference between the senses of smell and taste in a Koi. It was originally thought otherwise, but now it is realised that there is a great deal of overlap between the two. Both detect chemicals dissolved in the water, the major difference being in where this detection occurs. There is some evidence that the system of smell is more sensitive than the taste buds, generously located on the barbels and around the mouth. It is also thought that the taste buds are more sensitive to noxious substances, such as carbon dioxide, whereas the olfactory lamellae home in on pheromones. Whatever the case, Koi can distinguish between the same four sensations that our tongues detect – acid, salt, bitter and

Taste buds are located on two pairs of barbels on the lips of the Koi.

Photo: Keith Allison.

sweet – as well as other exudations from fish skin.

VISION

Koi have binocular vision in front of them where the fields of vision of the two eyes overlap, but only monocular vision to the side. It is thought that, as Koi grow, they become better at detecting smaller prey, as the angle between adjacent cones in the retina becomes smaller, and visual acuity increases. Despite our knowing this, it is difficult to guess exactly what the fish perceives. Some work suggests that the upper margin, or edge, of a shape is a more important recognition feature than is the lower. But this could be down to the fact that light enters from the water surface, better illuminating the upper surface of a figure.

Studies on some carp showed that they could barely distinguish between four and seven stripes occupying the same area. Points, sharp edges and acute angles are more readily picked out than curves or obtuse angles.

Anatomy And Physiology Of Koi

Food is engulfed by means of suction.
Photo: Dave Bevan.

Incidentally Koi, like most fishes, can see objects overhead, outside the water, providing they are within an angle of 97 degrees – the 'fish's window'.

Not a great deal is known about the colour vision abilities of Koi. They have visual pigments that selectively absorb at particular wavelengths, but this aspect of vision is far from fully understood.

TOUCH

The sense of touch is not developed in fish in the same way as in mammals. Generally, they lack specialised touch receptors in the skin (although there are some exceptions). However, as by 'touch' we mean the detection of pressure, the Koi can do this without actually touching anything – which

is very clever. The lateral line of the fish is represented by a series of perforated scales running along the mid-line of the flanks from head to tail. Each little perforation leads into a jelly-filled canal running below that row of scales. Pressure waves in the water are transmitted into this canal, where they are detected by mechanosensory receptors called 'neuromasts'. The lateral line system also extends on to the head, enabling the fish to detect the approach of obstacles when its visibility is impaired. The lateral line system is remarkably sensitive, and can effectively replace the eyes as a detector of obstacles and disturbances in the water – it has been called 'the sense of distant touch', and explains why even a blind Koi can still feed and move freely around the pond.

NUTRITION

Fish senses are there to enable the Koi to survive and they are concentrated around the head because, to all animals, the intake of food is the essence of survival. In the Koi, there are taste buds on the four barbels that stem from the upper jaw, and on the lips – there are fewer on the inside of the mouth. The carp is toothless, but a relatively uncritical feeder. Within sensible limits, size alone determines whether a food item is taken or rejected. Food is engulfed by suction – the mouth closes, the jaws then expand, and the mouth opens again. If they are small enough, food items will then be syphoned into the mouth on the inhalant current. Larger items are grasped as well.

The absence of jaw teeth is no drawback, as all cyprinids (members of the carp family) have pharyngeal teeth which make short work of the toughest prey. Pharyngeal teeth and bones are modifications of one part of the gill arch, and the shape of the bone and teeth and their relative positions are unique to each species. To better understand this, we need to look at the structure and function of the gills, whose other function is that other necessity for life, respiration.

RESPIRATION

Breathing in water relies on the extraction of dissolved oxygen and the elimination of the waste carbon dioxide. This exchange is most efficient if there is a constant stream of water flowing over a large, semi-permeable surface. This is where the gills come in. In evolution, they formed as a series of slits in the sides of the pharynx, and water flowed in through the mouth and out through these slits. The walls of the slits later became strengthened by the gill arches, and were finally covered and protected by a large bone, the operculum or gill cover. This mobile plate is hinged at the front and has a flap of skin on its posterior margin to give a good seal. To prevent the backflow of water, there is a one-way oral valve just inside the mouth. Now the water can be sucked or pumped over the gills, a function that helps both breathing and feeding.

CIRCULATION AND DIGESTION

The heart of the Koi, positioned in the chest just behind the gills, has two chambers – the atrium, which is uppermost and collects blood from all over the body, and the ventricle, which pumps it forward. There is no great blood pressure in fish, and what little that does exist is needed to push the blood upwards through tiny blood vessels in the gill filaments. Here, separated only by a thin layer of cells from the surrounding water, the blood takes up oxygen and gets rid of carbon dioxide.

Above the gill arches, the blood vessels collect together and form the dorsal aorta, which runs backwards along the fish just below the vertebral column. With so little blood pressure, there is no pulse above the gills, and the blood is circulated by muscular movement. As the gill slits perforate the sides

of the pharynx, along which the food passes, the delicate lamellae are protected by a series of stout bars called gill rakers. These lie across the internal entrance to the gill slit, and are supported by the gill bars. Gill rakers not only stop particles passing through the gill slits but, in trapping these particles, make them available as food. This is why fish that feed on fine particles have many slender gill rakers. Carp (Koi), feeding on larger morsels by choice, have between 20 and 30 stout gill rakers on the first gill arch.

In the archetypal fish there are five gill arches. In the carps, which lack teeth in the jaws, the fifth is modified into the very strong, tooth-bearing pharyngeal bone. This is roughly sickle-shaped, expanded in the middle where the teeth are supported. The teeth point inwards and upwards, and grind food against a gristly pad on the base of the skull. Strong muscles, a development of the usual gill muscles, provide enough strength to smash snail shells. The shape of the pharyngeal teeth gives a clue to the diet of the fish – those of Koi are molariform, showing that it grinds up relatively massive food items; it would be interesting to know if the pharyngeal apparatus of the Koi is powerful enough to crack wild almonds, as one of its Middle Eastern relatives is able to do.

The abdominal cavity contains the internal organs, of which the digestive tract and liver occupy most space. There is little development of a conspicuous stomach part of the alimentary canal, as the pharyngeal teeth make such a good job of breaking up food. The liver is a three-lobed structure, the most important function of which is to store energy derived from food to keep the fish going over the expected period of sluggishness during the winter.

THE SWIMBLADDER

At the top of the abdominal cavity, just below

the backbone, is the silvery sac of the swimbladder. In Koi this is a two-chambered structure, the front and rear chambers being linked by a narrow neck. In all bony fishes there are two types of swimbladder – closed (physocleistous), in which the gas pressure is maintained by a gland in the wall of the bladder secreting or absorbing the gas as necessary, and open (physotomatous), where the gas pressure is adjusted by taking in atmospheric air via a tube leading from the pharynx. Koi have this latter type, with a narrow tube leading from the top of the pharynx into the front of the rear chamber. This means that, as fry hatch, they must get to the surface to fill the swimbladder if they are to maintain station in the water column. Carp fry have 14 days in which to do this and fill up with air – if they fail, they are literally 'sunk', as fish tissue is denser than water!

The swimbladder does more than just keep the fish neutrally buoyant and provide a source of isinglass for the wine industry – it also acts as the Koi's ears. The real ears are located well inside the skull, and comprise three semicircular canals, arranged at right angles to one another. They are primarily organs of balance, the position of the fish in relation to gravity being detected by sensors attached to three calcareous otoliths – literally, 'ear stones'. All of this is the equivalent of our own inner ear. The Koi's 'ear drum' is the wall of the swimbladder, which picks up soundwaves and, by an ingenious system of little levers formed from parts of the anterior vertebrae, transmits the soundwaves to be interpreted by the brain. These little levers glory in the name of the Weberian Mechanism, in honour of the anatomist who discovered their purpose.

In effect, your Koi is rather like a Rolls Royce – not just pleasing to look at, but a superb piece of engineering (and cheaper to maintain than the car).

2 HISTORICAL BACKGROUND

The development of Koi keeping from a pastime enjoyed by a lucky few into a worldwide industry is a tale for our times – and, like many success stories, it had a most unlikely beginning. For, while Japanese cultural icons are traditionally associated with the ruling warrior classes and the trappings of Shinto Buddhism, the first coloured carp were raised by humble peasant farmers who little thought that a supplementary food crop would bring their descendants great wealth and international status.

Nishikigoi today are revered, not only for their beauty, but for engendering the spirit of friendship between nations. Japan, with her turbulent recent history, has much to thank these fish for in helping to heal the rift with her former enemies.

ORIGINS OF KOI
Nobody can rival the experience of the Japanese in Koi breeding, but it is a myth that these wonderful fish have evolved over many centuries. Only in the past 100 years have Koi worth the name been developed, and only in the last 30 has their breeding attained real refinement – though the foundations were laid well before then. It all began when the ancestral carp arrived in their adopted homeland with Chinese invaders before the birth of Christ.

Carp are hugely adaptable fish and are now spread all over the world, though their original range was Eastern Asia, around the Black, Aral, Caspian and Azov Seas. They supposedly arrived in Britain with the Crusaders around 1550 AD, and Sir Richard Baker's *Chronicle* records the event in a memorable couplet:

"Hops and turkeys, carps and beer
Came into England all in a year."

Linking *Cyprinus carpio* so closely to items of food and drink was no accident, for, in the Middle Ages, orders of monks who could eat no meat on a Friday resorted to fishing for carp in specially built ponds in their monastery grounds. These religious gentlemen were the pioneers of modern aquaculture, some of their ponds being so cleverly built that they could be drained down at will. The removable sluice boards that made this possible are known to this day as 'monks'.

The earliest written record of carp was in China in the 5th century BC, when, supposedly, the philosopher Confucius named his son after a fish presented to him by royalty. As in Japan today, carp were venerated for their strength and endurance, but they were nevertheless almost exclusively a food crop. Any colour mutations that arose were regarded as no more than curiosities – the Chinese preferred the selective breeding of goldfish.

INTRODUCTION TO JAPAN

Invading Chinese forces brought carp to Japan where, presumably, they established themselves in lakes and rivers. The Japanese call them 'Magoi', meaning 'black carp'. The words 'Koi' and 'Goi' are interchangeable, and can refer to all *Cyprinus carpio,* including the ornamental varieties. This may explain the very early references to Koi keeping in Japan, for example the account of an Emperor's pond given over to them soon after the fishes were brought into that country – probably they were kept for curiosity value rather than any inherent beauty. The proper and unambiguous Japanese term for Koi as we understand them today is 'Nishikigoi', meaning 'brocaded carp'.

THE 'HOME' OF KOI

Niigata prefecture, high in the mountains, is the 'home' of Japanese Koi, and still the district where the finest fish are bred. It is a farming region, the main crop being rice, and at some time (probably in the 17th century) Magoi began to be cultured as a source of protein to tide the peasants over the long, hard winters. Communication with other parts of Japan was impossible once the snow fell, and dried and salted fish provided essential protein to sustain the inhabitants.

These Magoi were not reared in the rice paddies themselves, but in the terraced irrigation reservoirs built into the steep terrain, which, every spring, filled with snow-melt water. The fish had only six months to grow before cropping, and only the carp needed for spawning the following season were retained alive. The reservoir ponds were not suited to housing them; instead, smaller ponds were dug in the villages, sometimes

adjacent to or even inside the farmers' homes, to hold the precious parent fish.

This practice was first identified early in the 19th century, but had almost certainly been going on much longer than that; the social history of the simple peasant classes was of little consequence to their feudal landlords, and so was not recorded.

It was some time in the mid-19th century that colour mutations in their carp were first spotted by the rice farmers – nothing dramatic at first. Mutations occur sporadically in all wild fishes, which have sets of pigment cells known as chromatophores. In cyprinids, the melanophores (black cells) and xanthophores (red/orange cells) usually combine to produce what is known as cryptic coloration – a dark back and pale belly – which makes the fish less visible to predators. Absence of the melanophores will bring about a highly visible fish that is snapped up early in life, before it has a chance to pass on its genes to another generation. But, in captive populations, these 'sports' will survive. The first 'Koi' were probably dark fish with a few red scales or patches of white, and, by keeping these back and breeding the oddities with one another, the abnormalities became fixed.

The Japanese farmers were soon enjoying these coloured carp among themselves, a closed hobby in a closed society, and thus it remained until their culture methods improved to the point where surplus stocks of cured fish could be sold to merchants from the big cities. In this way, the secret of Koi began to leak out, and keeping them became a status symbol among a few local dignitaries.

FAME SPREADS

The turning point was the 1914 Tokyo Taisho Exhibition, which was staged to promote trade and culture from all regions of Japan. The farmers of Yamakoshi, Niigata,

The commercial exploitation of Koi, and their export to the west, got under way in the late 1940s.

Photo: Dave Bevan.

brought along 27 of their best coloured carp, which by then were recognisable as ancestral Kohaku, and after the event some of these were introduced into the moat of the Emperor's palace.

It was the food-fish connection that made these early Koi more readily available throughout Japan, for, after the exhibition, the salt-fish dealers purchased a few and sold them on as pets to business colleagues and friends. The rice-farmers were by then realising the commercial possibilities, and the culture of Koi gradually achieved the status it enjoys today – helped, of course, by improved communications, travel and transportation methods following World War II. The first Koi post-war exports were to Hawaii, in 1947, and some spectacular public

ponds can be seen there to this day; the arrival of Koi in Britain is given a chapter to itself.

VARIETIES
The time-scale in the development of the various Koi varieties is a little uncertain, but there is no doubt that the first to appear was the Asagi, from a strain of Magoi showing dark bluish scalation. Shusui, the Doitsu version, arose six years after the importation of mirror-scaled table carp from Germany in 1904.

Sanke can be pinned down to the Taisho Era (1915 onwards), hence their full name. The first Kohaku have variously been attributed to the early 19th century and any time in the following 100 years. This

KOI VARIETIES

Shusui/Asagi: One of the early varieties.

Photo: A. McGill.

Kohaku: Its roots go back to the early 19th century.

Photo: A. McGill.

Utsurimono: Developed in the 1920s.

Photo: A. McGill.

Showa Sanke: Bloodlines are not yet fixed on the Showa variety.

Photo: Keith Allison.

Yamabuki Ogon.

Photo: Keith Allison.

confusion hinges on how the word is defined – the first red and white fish were so far removed from the clearly-patterned Koi we know today that they barely merit the name. Hi patterns, such as they were, were confined to small areas of the body, sometimes just single scales, and were highly unstable. The 'Kanoko Kohaku', with dappled hi (red coloration), survives today in Kawarimono to remind us how far Japan's most favoured variety has come in modern times. But the true Kohaku bloodline was not stabilised until 1930.

Non-metallic Matsuba arose from dark-brown/black Magoi in the early 1900s, and, when crossed with Asagi, gave rise to the red and yellow carp 'Higoi' and 'Kigoi'. Utsurimono followed in the 1920s, but the first Showa as we know them, a cross between Ki Utsuri and Kohaku, did not appear until 40 years later. Originally insipid, the hi on this variety has improved immensely in the past two decades by crossing back to Sanke and Kohaku parents, although there are still no fixed bloodlines.

Metallic Koi arose spontaneously from Magoi parentage, the forerunners of today's Ogon being the so-called 'helmeted Koi', Kin-Kabuto and Gin-Kabuto. Crossing with the brown Chagoi resulted in the first Matsuba Ogon which, back-crossed with Higoi to lose the well-defined scale reticulation, became the yellow metallic fish we know as Yamabuki Ogon.

The more colours in an artist's palette, the richer the picture – so it has been with the development of Nishikigoi. The number of new varieties appearing has slowed, most breeders concentrating on what they know best and improving, rather than diversifying, their stocks. Showa were developed during the reign of the Emperor Hirohito; the succession of his son, Akahito, heralded the Heisei era, but the variety bred to celebrate this event, a Doitsu metallic three-coloured Koi known as 'Heisei-Nishiki', has yet to achieve widespread distribution or popularity. Another Koi known as Kikokuryu, basically a metallic Kumonryu, has been exported since the mid-1990s; this one, again, is in the early stages of development and it will take many more years before the variety achieves its full potential.

CURRENT DEVELOPMENTS

The current challenge among Japanese Koi farmers is to produce the first genuine metre-long Go-Sanke – a substantial reward awaits the successful breeder. The fish will not have to be a good example of its variety, merely be recognisable as a Kohaku, Sanke or Showa. At the time of writing, the breeders are within just three centimetres of this goal!

Koi farming is no longer the exclusive preserve of the Japanese; fish for the mass global market are produced elsewhere in the Far East, in South Africa, America, Great Britain, Cyprus and especially Israel. Long-finned Koi (whose barbels are also elongated) are a popular mutation among general pondkeepers, but mercifully will never find favour with real aficionados. Since Israel switched from mass production to more selective breeding, their Koi have come the closest in quality to Japanese fish and are spawned from high-quality Japanese parentage. But the home of Nishikigoi always seems to rise to the challenge and stay several steps ahead.

With cloning much in the news at the moment, the prospect of being able to purchase Koi that are replicas of their parents is no longer in the realms of science fiction. True Koi-lovers can only hope that it never happens.

The appeal of Nishikigoi lies in their uniqueness – every single fish is different, and it would be a shame indeed if clones of Grand Champions ever became available.

3 KOI THEN AND NOW

By Val Frost

When approached by Nick Fletcher to write a chapter for this book "giving pictorial examples of top grade Koi of thirty years ago and those of the present day, with text to show how Koi have improved over the past three decades," I viewed the task with some trepidation.

The first problem was how to condense such a complicated evolution into a few thousand words – another was from what angle to approach it. Besides, the quality of film and photography has improved so much during the period that it would be very difficult to find acceptable examples to publish from the early days.

TWO PIONEERS

As far as I am aware, though, I am the only living Koi keeper to have seen and purchased Koi from the first two UK Koi importers in the mid-1960s, so I decided to approach the subject from a personal angle.

Living in Tunbridge Wells, Kent, England, I was blessed (some might say cursed!) to be only a few miles away from Frank Gooding, who had a farm in Copthorne near East Grinstead, in Sussex. As a businessman, Frank had seen Koi on his trips to Japan. Struck by their beauty, he not only wanted to purchase some for himself, but had scented the possibility of commercial success associated with their importation. His farm has a very

high water table, so it was comparatively easy to bring in a JCB and scoop out six very large holes which quickly filled with water to become six very large lakes.

The lovely, eccentric Frank then approached the equally eccentric Colin Roe – of the original Shirley Aquatics near Birmingham – to assess the viability of marketing Koi in the UK. The first 'official' importation of Koi subsequently arrived from the Japanese-based Koi breeder Mr Kamihata, and was quickly followed by many others. The best examples of Koi were then selected for sale at Shirley Aquatics, with the very best going on show in Colin's large exhibition pond.

Val Frost with her first 'big' Koi purchase from Friday Farm made in July 1969. Her obsession began with a couple of two-inch proto-metallic Koi.

Photo courtesy: Val Frost.

LEFT: Phil Searle in 1976 with his show winners acquired on the first-ever BKKS trip to Japan. (Note the 'classy vat.')

RIGHT: When an understanding of the needs of Koi was still rudimentary, they shared shallow ponds with planting baskets which soon ended up plantless... Photo courtesy: Val Frost.

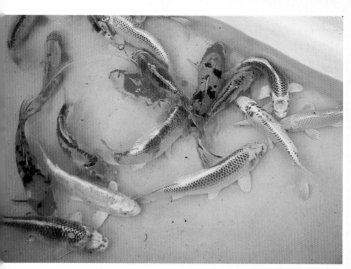

LEFT: Colin Roe's finest Koi, 1971. Metallic fish were much in vogue, but note the Go-Sanke and 'true blue' Shusui. Photo courtesy: Val Frost.

RIGHT: A lake at Frank Gooding's Friday Farm in 1968. Niigata may be the birthplace of Japanese Koi – but Sussex is where it all began for British Koi keepers. Photo courtesy: Val Frost.

It is worth noting here that Colin Roe was an aquarist held in very high esteem by his contemporaries. He was a qualified botanist specialising in aquatic plants, and all his beautifully maintained aquaria at Shirley contained luxuriant growths of both freshwater tropical and coldwater species, amid which swam myriad shoals of rainbow-hued fish. Many of these he had spawned himself.

When saltwater fish were first introduced to UK aquarists, Colin was the first to set up living coral reefs in association with them, and was shortly breeding Anemone Clownfish – a rare occurrence even today, when we have the benefit of modern techniques and equipment.

Prime Koi specimens from the first imports also found their way into Frank's personal pond close to his lovely farmhouse in Copthorne. The remainder were put into his lakes to grow on, while Colin Roe used his own extensive natural ponds to both grow on and attempt the breeding of Koi. I will not try to tell the fascinating story of Colin's first breeding attempts in this short chapter, but the growing-on was a success in both men's cases. Purely by accident, they had discovered the best way to keep Koi successfully – in mud ponds with green water and lots of natural food, topped up with extra helpings of fish pellets.

Both men were astonished at the growth rate of the fish, having previously kept only goldfish, shubunkins and orfe. Colin was the first to advertise Koi for sale from his premises at Monkspath. They were billed as 'Living Jewels from Japan' on his regular back-page advertisement in *The Aquarist* magazine; a mouthwatering list of unpronounceable names followed, with prices and English colour descriptions.

Still a schoolgirl, but a long-term keeper of coldwater, tropical and marine fish, I endeavoured to get myself one weekend from Tunbridge Wells to Birmingham using a complicated system of buses and trains, only to find that Colin had sold practically all his stock. All that were left were a few Gin- and Kin-Kabuto (silver and gold helmet) metallic Koi.

Until that moment I had considered a shoal of large golden orfe to be the ultimate in pondkeeping, but this was true love at first sight. So a two-inch example of each type travelled all the long way home with me on my lap in an air-filled plastic bag. After I had floated them in my back garden pond, they were released with no adverse effects to join the shoal of orfe – and thus was triggered my undying passion for Koi.

Shortly after this momentous trip, I became aware of Frank Gooding living locally. Like Colin Roe, he would only have you on his land if he liked you. Fortunately, both men instantly recognised me as a fellow 'nut' and we all remained firm friends until their respective deaths.

Frank came to love his Koi so much that he was reluctant to sell more than a few whenever they literally began to outgrow their living space. I will never forget my first walk with him down the centre path between his lakes on Friday Farm. Frank banged on the side of a bucket full of pellets he was carrying and a

tidal wave of colour converged from all sides – an unforgettable experience.

'LIVE JEWELS'
At this time there were no reference books in English, and the illustrations of Go-Sanke and other fully-scaled patterned Koi varieties we saw in Japanese books were thought to have been 'touched up' – surely no such colours could possibly exist in nature! Imported Kohaku were silver and orange (not chalk white and red); Sanke were silver, orange and grey (not white, red and black), and so on. It was not until the British Koi Keepers Society was formed in 1970 and organised the first-ever trip to Japan in the spring of 1975 that we saw correctly coloured examples of these varieties for the first time, and a mind-blowing experience it truly was, to lay eyes on these beauties.

Until then, metallic Koi were favoured – particularly Ogon, Kujaku and Hariwake – and the unheard-of red and blue colour combination of Shusui (Doitsu) and Asagi (scaled) was also highly prized. Battles were fought over Doitsu Matsuba Ogons, but it was mainly Shusui that made us aware of the importance of water quality, as the peacock blue and red coloration quickly changed to slate blue and rust red in most water areas of the UK.

A few copies of *Live Jewels* arrived in Britain around 1969-70 containing, for the first time, a little English text alongside the Japanese calligraphy. We also had access to Takeo Kuroki's exciting coffee-table book, with lots of pictures but text entirely in Japanese, called simply *Koi*.

From this, with painstaking but hit-and-miss interpretation, we were gradually able to unravel the mysteries of pond filtration (totally new to us), pond construction, and the importance of adequate depth, bottom drains, aeration and so forth.

IMPORT/EXPORT OF KOI

Ken Fawcett, of TFH Imports and Publications, Reigate, Surrey, had also started importing Koi into the UK by this time. To an experienced importer of all kinds of coldwater, tropical freshwater and marine fish, Koi were a natural progression. It would be true to say, though, that his inspiration came mainly from America. Holding the UK franchise for the American TFH Publications, he was responsible for sending out the monthly copies of *Tropical Fish Hobbyist* magazine to subscribers here, and articles on Koi occasionally appeared in these.

It is now a well-known fact that there is a large indigenous population of Japanese living in California. Most are emigrés from Hawaii, or internees and their descendants from the Second World War. They found themselves in a climate ideal for Koi keeping and breeding, and began to develop their favourite hobby of fancy coldwater fishkeeping. This was quickly picked up by the hobby at large, and soon imports of superior Japanese Koi were arriving on America's West Coast on a much shorter route from Japan than those reaching the UK – that is, straight across the Pacific.

Long-haul jet flights were a dream of the future, and the exporting of Koi to such distant shores as the British Isles was still at the experimental stage. No 'over the Pole' route then existed, and Koi had to be literally flown around the world, stopping once or twice for refuelling, maybe in desert or icy temperatures. Starved for a week, then crowded into large plastic bags (numbers according to size), anaesthetised in a small amount of water, the bags filled up with oxygen from cylinders and boxed up, it was very much in the lap of the gods as to the condition in which the Koi would arrive. Any major hold-up or extreme change of temperature and they could easily arrive dead or dying.

I remember one occasion when an early and valuable import of 'special' Koi to Aquatic Nurseries (close to Heathrow Airport) arrived during a particularly cold spell in November. The boxes were left on the runway by the Heathrow handling staff while they unloaded

Special imports from Japan raised awareness of 'proper' Koi. Dave Hollom was the lucky owner of these rather fine Kohaku and Matsuba, pictured in the mid-1970s.

Photo courtesy: Val Frost.

The first Koi show staged outside Japan was in Peter Waddington's back garden in the spring of 1975, when Roland Seal's Purachina Ogon scooped the pool. These days, metallics rarely figure among the top prizewinners.

Photo courtesy: Val Frost.

the rest of the cargo, and, by the time they reached their destination, all the beautiful fish were frozen into solid blocks of ice. None survived.

Unfortunately, many Koi that were dying as a result of their transit traumas were taken home by dealers for sale to the public. Either they never recovered from the stress and strain of travelling, or their internal organs were fatally affected as a result of swimming for endless hours in their own effluent.

All livestock routinely passes through the RSPCA units at UK airports before being allowed into the country, and I recall accompanying Colin Roe to Heathrow to meet a shipment of 'super' Koi back in the early 1970s. I was horrified to see him run a stream of fast-flowing water, straight from the tap (faucet), into the bags until the anaesthetised fish started to come round. He then gradually diluted the solution until it was clean, fresh water and then undertook to re-bag the Koi for their three-hour journey to Birmingham – the motorway system was far from being joined up at that time, so it was A4-A34 from London!

After a rest and a short quarantine period, the Koi were then sorted out into 'breeding pairs' and priced up individually in separate tanks. A 'breeding pair' consisted of any two fish which looked vaguely alike – and they sold like hot cakes!

In view of the above, is it any wonder that most early Koi keepers found it difficult to keep their fish alive?

Fortunately, though, help was on the way. The inspired Ken Fawcett advertised in fish magazines for all interested Koi keepers to meet at the Royal Horticultural Hall in Victoria, London, and the British Koi Keepers Society was formed, with Ken as president, in 1970. At last, like-minded people could compare notes and learn how to successfully keep these fish alive and well in the UK – but that is another story.

Once Koi shows started in the mid-1970s, and more and more Koi dealers jumped on the bandwagon, the quality of Koi imports improved progressively alongside pond design, filtration and water quality. Nowadays, the sky is the limit. Anyone with a deep enough pocket can purchase, and keep successfully, beautiful Koi of the quality you see in these pages, but one can still dream of the successful Tategoi – although the famous story of the rusty bicycle and Peter Waddington's Showa does seem a long while ago now!

THE HISTORY OF KOI IN THE US
Pamela Spindola

Precisely where and when Koi keeping began in the US is somewhat controversial. Some believe that Dr Herbert R Axelrod was the first to bring Koi to America in the 1940s. Dr Axelrod went on to breed them on a fish farm in Florida. Others contend that the Koi hoby got its start in California. Notably, the 1941 World's Fair in San Francisco displayed a huge Koi pond in the Japanese Pavilion. It is said that Japanese breeders during Word War Two hid their Koi stock in mountain caves for safety.

Support for the theory that California is where it all began can be found by tracing the story of the Akiyama family. In the 1930s, the Akiyamas lived in the then rural town of Westminster, a suburb of Los Angeles. They had many mudponds raising Koi and goldfish. They sold fish from their backyard for many years. In the early 1970s Joe Akiyama opened a retail establishment offering the largest selection of Koi and goldfish available anywhere. His prices were reasonable and clearly marked. In one corner of the shop was a beautifully landscaped pond which was often visited by school children and Boy Scout troops. For a dime, they could buy a handful of Koi food to distribute to the pond. It was great fun to visit his shop for the thrill of the hunt. Often the fish were not sorted and, with patience, one could find a potential show winner at a discounted price. This shop recently changed ownership, as Joe retired in 1998.

In the 60s, in Gardena, a suburb of Los Angeles, Seiji Kaneshiro, and his son, Eddie, opened E & S Pet Shop, specialising in goldfish and Koi. This shop became the gathering place for all who shared the love of Koi. Hobbyists would gravitate towards the rear outside of the store where there were about six sunken ponds holding Koi of varying qualities and sizes. It was the cultural centre for all interested in Koi, and Seiji was the teacher.

Also in the town of Gardena, the Nakamuru family opened Asahi Koi, Inc in 1968. In that same year "Mits" Nakamaru, originally from Hawaii, had travelled all the way to Japan to enter his three step Kohaku in the first All Japan Koi Show and brought home the flag for the top prize. This Koi shop was considered the premier shop for everyone. There were several vats brimful with Ogon for the beginning hobbyists. As one walked further back in the shop, the quality and the prices increased. The very best were behind gates. What a thrill it was to be taken behind the gates to see the jumbo Koi and the really special show Koi! These were the fish one only dreamed of owning. Mits Nakamaru and his wife were always very gracious, serving steaming hot cups of "ocha" or green tea.

Mits, according to his son, Henry, who now runs the business, "was a Koi hobbyist first and foremost. You could always find him at a Koi show looking hour after hour at Koi. Whenever we travelled to Japan, he would want to bring home every Koi he saw and fell in love with. He was always forgetting people's names but he never forgot the Koi people bought. He tried to teach people about the Koi so they could enjoy and appreciate them even more. With his help, we saw the quality

of the Koi keeping rise to what it is today."

Today, Asahi Koi, a family-run business, upholds its reputation of handling some of the finest Koi in the country.

In Falbrook, an agricultural community north of San Diego, is California Koi Farms, a ten-acre spread on a hillside, established in 1974 by the Adachi family. Mr Yoshihiko Adache was a Koi breeder in Japan in the early 50s, but moved to California in the early 70s. His son, Takemi, now runs the business in the US as his father returned to the Adachi Koi Farm in the Yonado Prefecture. According to Takemi, the elder Adachi's grandfather was raising and breeding fish in the 1800s in Japan and acted as their mentor. Because of the beautiful rural setting, many clubs planned weekend outings to view the California Koi. The terraced ponds and lush countryside gave the feeling of being in Niigata, Japan. Visiting the farm was always an educational adventure for the Koi hobbyist as one could observe spawning techniques, culling and seining. Usually several clubs gathered at the farm for an auction and picnic as well as to purchase fish. Traditionally, many excellent prize-winning show Koi are from California Koi Farms.

Until fairly recently, the climate of different parts of America dictated how easy (and hence popular) the Koi hobby was. Keeping Koi in California was far simpler than coping with the long, cold winters of Montana, for example. With the advent of pond-heating, however, keeping Koi in intemperate climates became easier and the hobby grew in popularity.

The Associated Koi Clubs of America had just 12 clubs listed at its first annual meeting in 1981. Today, the AKCA has more than 80 member clubs across the country. One of the largest organisations on the east coast is the Mid-Atlantic Koi Club, which has hundreds of members, not only spanning the eastern seaboard, but across the nation.

4 KOI VARIETIES

Judging classes for Koi are divided between non-metallic (the majority) and metallic. Each class contains anything from one to dozens of varieties. For example, the Karwarimo class contains all non-metallic and fully-scaled fish that do not fit into any other class. Therefore a Koi variety could be deemed a 'brand' of Koi, and a variable number of brands could go to make up a class.

KOHAKU
Kohaku, with Sanke and Showa, form the group known as 'Go-Sanke' from which most show winners are drawn. Of the three varieties, the Kohaku (translating as 'red and white') is the favourite of the Japanese and is appreciated by Koi connoisseurs the world over; the scarlet markings (hi) setting off flawless white skin can be laid down in endless permutations that give every fish its unique character. Some Kohaku are flowery and feminine, others bold and 'in your face'. Perfection in simplicity is impossible to achieve, but its pursuit has captivated Japanese breeders since the now extinct Gosuke lineage was established more than 100 years ago.

Modern Kohaku are bred from four main bloodlines and combinations thereof – Manzo, Tomoin, Sensuke and Yagozen, all with their own distinct trademarks. Breeder

Kohaku: White with red markings.

Photo: A. McGill.

bloodlines (such as Dainichi and Matsunosuke) derive from the same quartet of genetic building blocks, assembled through time and experience to maximise desirable traits passed down by parent Koi.

Bloodline will determine how body shape, colour and pattern develop, and so some Kohaku will look stunning even as youngsters, while others only begin to impress when they are five or six years old. Obviously, in order to tell a late developer from a 'never will', some knowledge of a Kohaku's ancestry is desirable, but bloodline should be only one consideration when purchasing a fish. High-born parentage is no guarantee that anything but a tiny percentage of a given spawning will make the grade, and buying on the basis of bloodline alone is a sure route to disappointment.

Judging standards for Kohaku used to be quite inflexible. Traditional stepped patterns and evenly-placed head markings that did not intrude over the eyes or too far down the face were favoured over the avant garde. The old pattern designations remain (Nidan = two-step; Sandan = three-step and so on), but symmetry is no longer necessary or even desirable as long as the overall effect is pleasing. The one trait still frowned upon is lack of Ojime (an area of white separating the tail from the end of the red pattern), but the modern trend is to accentuate the positive attributes of Kohaku, rather than pick faults.

Most important is impeccable milky skin, deep and even red (hi) markings going sharply into the area of white, a full (though not obese) body shape and, in larger fish, a dignity of bearing. Unlike some metallic Koi, a Kohaku has 'nowhere to run' and no flashy livery behind which defects can be masked.

It is a mistake to buy young Kohaku that look finished – better to go for those that appear rather 'hi heavy'. As the Koi grows, its skin stretches and pattern usually breaks at one or more points along the body. But

'Ippon hi' (an uninterrupted block of red running from nose to tail) makes for a boring and worthless Koi.

Two types of hi predominate – orange-red and purple-red. The latter looks the more immediately impressive, but orange-red can be brought on to deep scarlet with the proper colour feeding and pond conditions. Many breeders use no colour food at all, and their best Tategoi Kohaku can look insipid upon first arrival at the dealer's.

As with all Koi, female Kohaku grow imposing with age and command a higher price than males. Doitsu Kohaku look very beautiful, but are regarded as two-dimensional by the Japanese and rarely take top awards.

SANKE

Sanke are white Koi with a red and black pattern – take away the sumi (black) in your

Sanke: White, with a red and black pattern.

Photo: A. McGill.

mind's eye and you should be left with a passable Kohaku. Bloodlines can be traced back to the 1920s (Torazo) from which was developed the Jinbei strain. The Sanba line followed 30 years later. As with Kohaku, top breeders have made bloodlines all their own, and Toshio Sakai's Matsunosuke Sanke are now reckoned the best in the world. Evolution continues, notably with Shintaro's work on that famous bloodline which is producing Koi with incredible future potential.

Sanke have come a long way in a short while, as a glance at any older illustrated book will confirm. The 'old-fashioned' standard was for fish with equal percentages of the three colours, resulting in Sanke which look sumi-heavy to today's Koi keeper. The trend now is towards smaller areas of strategically-placed sumi which accentuate, rather than dominate, the areas of red and white and rarely extend below the lateral line. Two types occur – Tsubo sumi lies over white skin and the less desirable Kasane sumi over the hi. In Aka Sanke the red predominates.

Sumi is not always present in the pectoral and caudal fins, but, when it is, it takes the form of parallel stripes following the line of the fin rays. Sumi is quite permissible on the heads of modern Sanke, but its configuration is quite different to that found on Showa.

Depending on bloodline, young Sanke can display little or no sumi, or the black markings can appear early, vanish again and then re-emerge and stabilise. So knowledge of bloodline in high-grade fish is important if the purchaser is to make an informed guess as to how they will develop over the years.

SHOWA

Showa are the Koi that satisfy the gambling streak in us all. No other variety exhibits so many pattern changes, or can delight or exasperate to such a degree as it develops from good to better or (more usually) from

Showa: There are numerous pattern permutations within this variety.
Photo: A. McGill.

bad to worse. If there were such a creature as a top-grade Koi that somehow managed to escape the notice of its breeder to be sold as part of a cheap job lot, that fish would be a Showa.

Showa are a recently-developed variety, originally the result of a Kohaku x Ki Utsuri cross (Ki Utsuri are now almost never seen). There is no stabilised bloodline, but back-crossing to Sanke and Kohaku parent Koi has improved the hi and sumi no end since the 1960s.

Showa are black fish with a red and white pattern, while Sanke are white fish with a red and black pattern. Not surprisingly, the two varieties are frequently confused, and the trend towards Kindai Showa (predominantly white Koi) has not helped. Some fish start life being legitimately judged Sanke, only to cross over into equally valid Showa territory.

Bekko: Sanke lacking the red

Photo: A. McGill.

Gin Rin Bekko.

Photo: A. McGill.

Showa sumi is often called 'wrap-around' and can extend down into the belly area as well as extensively over the head and face, where it typically forms a lightning-like pattern known as Menware. Ideally, sumi on the pectorals is concentrated around the fin root (Motoguro), but a common fault in Showa is over-heavy sumi on one or both fins. Absence of pectoral sumi, particularly in Kindai Showa, is now acceptable.

Further common demerits are patterning strong at the head end of the Koi which then tails off disappointingly, or too much sumi drowning out small patches of hi.

Showa do not yet have any recognised bloodlines and are especially prone to genetic defects, such as mouth deformities and poor head shape. A truly accomplished, large Showa is therefore a very valuable Koi indeed.

BEKKO

Bekko were once a popular Koi variety but are now less often seen. They are non-metallic Koi with white, red or yellow skin overlaid with Sanke-type sumi. The Shiro Bekko (white and black) could almost be described as a defective Sanke without hi, and many Koi bought as Sanke later lose their red entirely to become Bekko. Excellent Shiro Bekko are now being produced in Israel as well as in Japan.

Aka Bekko (with a red base colour) are frequently confused with Aka Sanke. If there is any white visible on the body, the fish is Sanke. Common faults with Bekko are yellowing of the head, or sumi markings moving down over the face – though, as with Sanke, these can actually enhance the fish's appearance as long as they are not over-intrusive.

Ki Bekko are predominantly yellow Koi, and very rare.

In all Bekko, good skin quality without shimis (black or dark-brown spotting) is paramount.

Shiro Utsori: Simple black and white chic.

Photo: A. McGill.

Hi Utsuri: A Showa lacking visible white markings.

Photo: A. McGill.

UTSURIMONO

Unlike Bekko, the base colour of all Utsuri Koi is black, with white, red or yellow patterning. The most commonly seen, the Shiro Utsuri, is often thrown from Showa spawnings, although many Japanese breeders now specialise in this variety. Shiro Utsuri are regarded as 'honorary' Go-Sanke, and good examples win major show awards.

Confusingly, as with Showa, the most predominant colour in today's Shiro Utsuri is white, but the sumi markings again wrap around the body in blocks, rather than remaining above the lateral line in tortoiseshell blotches.

If there is any red at all on a fish claimed to be a Shiro Utsuri, it is in fact a Showa – even if the hi is on the very edge of the lips and all but invisible. Similarly, if any white appears on the body of a 'Hi Utsuri', that too is Showa. Ki Utsuri, like Ki Bekko, are comparatively rare fish and when they do appear it is unusual to find them with a clear yellow pattern unmarred by shimis.

Good-quality Shiro Utsuri bought young can be unprepossessing – often the sumi will be grey and washed out and the skin yellow, especially on the head. The variety shares all the common potential pitfalls of Showa, and the sumi markings are just as unpredictable as they develop. The old standard was for fish with black and white in equal proportions, but modern taste is for a Koi that resembles a Kindai Showa without the hi. Ideally, Motoguro appears on the pectoral fins.

ASAGI/SHUSUI

Asagi were the first Koi variety developed from the ancestral Magoi. They are Koi with blue backs showing pale scale reticulation, and hi on the belly and fins in varying amounts. If this red covers much of the body above the lateral line, the fish is a Narumi Asagi; those with dark blue backs are Konjo

Shusui.

Photo: Keith Allison.

Asagi.

Photo: A. McGill.

Asagi, while those blue-grey in colour are Mizu (Mouse) Asagi.

The variety is enjoying something of comeback, as all subtly marked Koi are tending to do. Good examples must have a clear head, well-defined scale reticulation, and evenly distributed hi. It is quite difficult to obtain good volume in Asagi, and if they are kept in hard water the blue areas revert to grey or black.

Shusui are the Doitsu form of the Asagi, although the two fish look completely different. Here, the ideal is a light blue back with evenly-placed darker blue dorsal scales and hi positioned as in Asagi – sub-varieties are Hi Shusui (a predominantly red back) and Hana Shusui (where the red occurs in patches over the blue above the lateral line).

Shusui are unusual in that they are the only Doitsu fish to be assigned their own judging variety – under BKKS rules, all other Doitsu Koi must take their chance with fully-scaled fish. For example a Doitsu Showa would be judged in Showa. As Asagi/Shusui is an under-represented variety at most Koi shows, there is some feeling that Asagi should be moved into Kawarimono and Shusui into a separate Doitsu class, which would give all Doitsu fish a better chance of the appreciation they deserve.

KOROMO
Koromo simply means 'robed', and these fish are basically Kohaku with another colour (deep blue or black) overlaying the body hi only. Aigoromo, the most valued among this group, have blue scale edging, while if the secondary colour is black the fish are Sumigoromo.

A Budo Goromo has a purplish overlay, the result of blue and black combined. Pattern conformation is supposed to resemble bunches of grapes.

If the blue and/or black markings extend out of the hi and over the white base colour,

Koromo (Goshiki).

Photo: A. McGill.

Goshiki.

Photo: Keith Allison.

the fish becomes a Goshiki – a variety formerly judged in Kawarimono but now moved back, under BKKS rules, into Koromo.

Young Ai Goromo can have such faint pattern overlay that they resemble Kohaku, and it can take some years for the full robed effect to develop. The pitfall with these is that the blue markings can later move into the white areas; from this point the fish will be Goshiki.

Modern Goshiki are a far cry from the rather sombre and indistinctly patterned fish that tended to darken almost to black in the winter months. Like some Showa and Shiro Utsuri, they have 'lightened up' and the white areas are thrown into relief by the other four colours – black, red, blue and purple. A Goshiki known as 'Polo', imported

into Britain by Shirley Aquatics of Birmingham, was acknowledged to be the finest example of the variety ever seen on these shores.

KAWARIMONO
All non-metallic Koi, Doitsu or fully-scaled and not in any other variety, are judged in Kawarimono. They include the popular, fast-growing and friendly brown Chagoi and its variants: the Soragoi (grey) and Ochibashigure (brown and grey); self-coloured Koi (Kigoi=yellow, Benigoi=red and Shiro Muji=white); and variants of the ancestral Magoi under the general heading of 'black Koi' which are classified according to the distribution and colour of additional markings. Hence we have Hajiro (black with white on tail and pectoral fin tips only);

Chagoi.

Photo: Keith Allison.

Hikarimuji (single-coloured metallic Koi).

Photo: A. McGill.

Yamabuki Ogon.

Photo: Keith Allison.

Hageshiro (with the addition of a white head); and Karasu, or 'Crow Koi' (a velvety-black fish with a red belly). A very popular Koi is the Doitsu fish known as a Kumonryu, black with white patterning giving the effect of a Chinese dragon painting.

The Matsukawabake is a black and white fish whose markings are said to transpose from summer to winter, though this is an oversimplification. Suminagashi are Koi with black scales, reticulated in white.

Named after the liqueur Midori, Midorigoi are Doitsu Koi that can vary in colour from a luminescent yellow to true green. They occur as rare sports, and good examples are much sought after.

Others included in Kawarimono are Go-Sanke with Kanoko (dappled) hi which resembles the spotting on the flanks of a fawn; and obvious crosses between non-metallic Koi, for example Showa-Shusui.

The 'catch-all' Kawarimono class embraces some truly unique Koi.

HIKARIMUJI

This is the first of the metallic Koi varieties, and includes the very popular single-coloured fish collectively known as Ogon. Confusingly, Matsuba Koi are included too – these are metallic fish with 'pine cone' reticulation of the scales which could rightly be construed as a second colour.

Yamabuki Ogon (gold), Purachina (platinum), Hi (red) and Orenji (orange) Ogon should all have a high lustre and a clear, broad head. Ogons are prone to obesity and the pectoral fins are frequently out of proportion to the body, so that otherwise good fish are spoiled. A good indication of quality in young examples is an almost bubbly ('Fuji') gleam on the head.

The same applies to Matsuba which, in addition, must have even reticulation with each scale picked out in clear relief. Kin

(gold), Gin (silver) and Orenji (orange) Matsuba are the commonest examples.

HIKARI UTSURI

These are metallic Showa and their derivatives, once a very popular show variety but now less often seen because all but the very best examples can appear 'washed out'. In metallic Koi, hi and sumi are toned down by the lustre, and so good kiwa and sashi are particularly important.

There is no such fish as a Gin Showa; irrespective of whether the metallic lustre is gold or silver, all Showa in Hikari Utsuri are termed 'Kin Showa'.

The metallic equivalent of a Hi Utsuri is a Kin Hi Utsuri; likewise Kin Ki Utsuri (black

Hikari Utsuri.

Photo: A. McGill.

with yellow), and Ginshiro (a metallic Shiro Utsuri).

Lustre should spread across all the fins as well as the body.

HIKARIMOYO

'Moyo' means 'many', and Hikarimoyo are metallic Koi of more than one colour, with the exception of Hikari Utsuri. They include Hariwake, silver fish with gold pattern very popular with beginners for their brazen beauty and, at the other end of the appreciation scale, Kujaku. These are metallic five-coloured Koi which should have well-defined scale reticulation on their backs and clear, unblemished heads. The fish most likely to cause confusion in this variety is the Sakura Ogon, which is really a metallic Kohaku. Its Doitsu equivalent is the Kikusui.

The Yamatonishiki is a metallic Sanke; all the Sanke appreciation points should apply to this fish, but the hi can never approach the richness of that of the non-metallic Koi. Metallic Shusui, Koromo (known as Shochikubai) and Bekko are included in this class, as is the recently developed Kikokuryo, effectively a metallic Kumonryu which has silver patterning over a black, brown or maroon base colour.

Hikarimoyo.

Photo: A. McGill.

Doitsu Kikusui (classified in Hikarimoyo).

Photo: Keith Allison.

Kin Gin Rin Kohaku.

Photo: A. McGill.

Tancho Kohaku.

Photo: A. McGill.

Gin Rin Hi Utsuri (classified as Utsurimono).

Photo: Keith Allison.

KIN-GIN-RIN

Gin-Rin and Kin-Rin are silver and gold reflective scales which can appear on all varieties of Koi, including metallics. However, for show purposes, only Kin-Gin-Rin Kohaku, Sanke, Showa and Utsuri are entered into the Kin-Gin-Rin class.

For a Koi to be classed Kin-Gin-Rin, there should be too many of these reflective scales to count; a few on an otherwise matt Koi can highlight areas of pattern and add to its charm.

There are different types of Kin-Gin-Rin and Kin-Rin scalation, including Beta-Gin, Kado-Gin, Tama-Gin (Pearl Scale), and Hiroshima Nishiki, where the reflective pigment radiates out from the scale pocket to the leading edge in a fan shape.

TANCHO

True Tancho Koi are Kohaku, Sanke or Showa where the red pigment is entirely confined to a head marking. Any other hi appearing at all, and the fish are shown under their respective varieties. Tancho-type markings can appear on almost any Koi, but unless they are Go-Sanke this will not affect where they are benched – so, for example, a (Tancho) Goshiki would still be entered in the Koromo class.

The Tancho Kohaku, especially, is valued by the Japanese. The (ideally circular) head marking is reminiscent both of their flag and the graceful Tancho crane.

Without the head hi, a Tancho Sanke would be a Shiro Bekko, and a Tancho Showa a Shiro Utsuri. In Tancho Showa, but not Tancho Sanke, it is permissible and desirable for head sumi to cut across the head hi.

The classic Tancho has a centrally placed marking as near as possible to a perfect circle, but other conformations (such as oval or heart-shaped) are more acceptable than they used to be. With such a simple pattern,

Tancho Koi have to approach perfection in skin quality and body shape if they are to find favour.

TATEGOI

'Tategoi' is a word simply defined but much misunderstood. The literal meaning of the Japanese word translates as 'a Koi that will, in time, become good, or better' – in other words, one with potential for continued improvement.

Many of us have personal experience of such fish, usually purchased young and 'unfinished'. As they grow, quite dramatic changes can take place in pattern, body volume and depth of colour, so that what starts out as an unprepossessing Koi transforms into an imposing and beautiful creature. If entered into shows, it may well win awards, although the chances of this happening immediately are slim – Koi are (or should be) judged on their appearance on the day, not how they might look in the future. This capacity for change year on year applies particularly to Go-Sanke (Kohaku, Sanke and Showa), to the extent that it is sometimes difficult to believe that they are the same fish – although, realistically, the metamorphosis is by no means always to the good.

The full potential for change will not be realised if water quality is not 100 per cent, or if the Koi are being fed an inferior diet. But the type of hobbyist who buys fish at the top end of the price scale is unlikely to neglect the basics – Tategoi represent an investment in the future.

If you have Koi that are 'special' in this way, be sure to keep a photographic record of their development over three-monthly intervals; seeing them on a daily basis, you might otherwise miss the subtle changes taking place. Your photographs (they need only be Polaroids) will also give you some idea of how future purchases from a particular bloodline may turn out – although an endearing quality of Koi is their unpredictability.

CHAMPION KOI

The word 'Tategoi' is used broadly to designate high-grade Koi with potential. However, for practical purposes, it undergoes a subtle shift in meaning, depending on whether it is applied to fish inside or outside Japan. Koi which sweep all before them in shows in Europe and America are still – in the view of the Japanese – some way behind the quality of fish to be found at the All-Japan Show. Just occasionally a special (and very expensive) Koi is purchased in Japan on behalf of a hobbyist elsewhere in the world, grown on by the breeder and entered into the show with some success, but such occurrences are exceptional.

Every Japanese breeder's ambition is to produce Best in Size or (the ultimate dream) Supreme Champion at Tokyo's annual showcase event. The motivation behind this is part personal pride and part hard economics, since winning a major award will enhance a breeder's reputation: his top fish will command higher prices in years to come.

With that in mind, every one of the millions of fry spawned each year is viewed at some point by its breeder as Tategoi. In the very early stages of life, for the great majority of Koi, that accolade is short-lived. When the fish are only days old, the obviously deformed fry and those which, to a practised eye, will not develop true to variety, are culled out. This is a painstaking task, involving usually only the breeder and his immediate family. In the case of Showa, only the black fish are retained; true Kohaku fry are yellow. Fry which appear much larger than their brothers and sisters, known as 'Tobi', leave the arena at this point, as it is presumed that their fast growth rate is due to cannibalism.

Subsequent culls are equally ruthless, though once the 'rejects' reach saleable size they are disposed of through brokers on to the mass market, for those who are content with pretty pondfish. The remainder are kept back and overwintered indoors, to be grown on the following Spring in mud ponds. After each subsequent October pond harvest, the potential of each fish is reassessed, and the breeder decides if he should retain it for another year or more, or sell it. The questions he asks himself are: Will this Koi increase in value sufficiently to make it worth my while accommodating and feeding it? Has this Koi the potential to reach the very top?

That is not to denigrate the one- and two-year-old high-grade Koi destined for export or sale within Japan. Some will not necessarily have reached their full potential – they are still Tategoi in the generally accepted sense, and their price will be high. Others will be Tategoi only in the eyes of the buyer, who may still occasionally secure a real bargain. There is always a slight risk that the breeder will let a fish go too early, only to see it improve beyond his wildest expectations; equally, buyers of Tategoi have no yardstick other than bloodline precedent as to how their fish will progress. There are many instances of breeders selling a Koi, only to buy it back at a later date and at a greatly increased price, to develop it to its full potential.

RECOGNISING TATEGOI

So-called 'Tategoi' are frequently the subject of one-off sales at unlikely venues. People are attracted to these, imagining they will have the chance to purchase fish out of the ordinary. But if these Koi are really exceptional, why have the Japanese breeders not held them back, or else asked a realistically high price? The buyer should be especially wary of 'Tategoi' sales organised by so-called dealers who do not have their own fish-holding premises and who hire a school or village hall to display their wares. The Koi on offer may indeed be from top breeders, but a designer label does not mean anything in isolation – you will be paying for the name, not the quality of the fish.

While it is true that almost any Koi is for sale at the right price, a true Tategoi in the Japanese sense of the word would be out of reach of all but the wealthiest of hobbyists. True aficionados travel to Japan to seek out their own Tategoi, or they appoint agents on their behalf who know exactly what to look for. Sometimes these prized fish are left with the breeder to grow on and improve for a year or more in their mud ponds, but the price is fixed at the time of purchase – the Koi will then command a 'boarding fee' which, in itself, is more than most Koi keepers would be prepared to pay for a fish, let alone its upkeep.

Such special Tategoi would certainly not be available as part of a job lot, either in Japan or elsewhere, though still-improving fish of lesser quality from the same breeders are more freely available.

Known bloodlines and respected breeders do not guarantee Tategoi. They can be no more than good starting guidelines. The 'Tategoi' mentioned above may indeed have such a pedigree, but in the breeders' eyes they have reached their best economic potential, and so it is time for them to be sold.

To the average Koi keeper, the subtle differences between very good Koi and Koi of exceptional quality are academic until it comes to paying for them. Then it may seem to him that the price difference is not justifiable. The truth is, at the top of the Koi ladder of excellence, a fish deemed to be ten per cent better than its neighbour may cost three or four times as much. The cheaper fish may still improve, but only if kept under ideal conditions.

Beginners (who anyway tend to buy small fish) are drawn to scaled-down versions of the top Koi they have seen in books or at shows. This is a mistake, as a pattern which complements a young fish can become sparse as the Koi lengthens and fills out. Sumi on Sanke, and particularly on Showa, can develop to the point where it becomes too heavy, whereas the hi you see is the hi you get – unless, as often happens, it fades. Also, young Koi which appear finished are likely to have reached their full potential too early.

Tategoi are 'late developers' and rarely look anything like finished Koi. Pattern is often uninspiring, because elements of it have yet to come through. Black markings (sumi) can take years to stabilise, coming and going in varying degrees of intensity. The hi can be orange or even yellow, a long way from the deep red of a finished fish, but this is often simply because the breeders have not been using colour-enhancing food. Young Tategoi Kohaku can carry a pattern that looks heavy and dull. Careful examination will show where it is likely to 'break' into more interesting elements.

SKIN QUALITY

The main quality that sets a Tategoi apart from the rest is the subtle element of fine skin. This can be appreciated only by a close encounter in full daylight, never from photographs or video footage. It helps, too, if the Koi is viewed against others which, at first glance, appear to be just as good – the difference then becomes apparent.

A Tategoi is not necessarily a young fish – as long as it retains the capacity to improve it will remain such. Nor is the term restricted to Go-Sanke – any Koi can be a Tategoi, even unpatterned varieties like Ogon or Chagoi. Here, skin quality is even more important, though other elements must not be forgotten – an unblemished head, good body shape and deportment, and well-shaped fins in proportion to the rest of the fish.

Unpatterned Tategoi of the highest quality are exported relatively frequently because the varieties that win the premier awards at major Japanese shows are almost invariably Go-Sanke. The only reason an Ogon would be held back is if it were felt it could reach a size where it could compete in the Jumbo class – the only one where the biggest fish invariably wins.

PRICES AND DEALERS

The price you would expect to pay for Tategoi is always high; but patterned fish (especially Go-Sanke) are more expensive, all other factors being equal, than varieties such as Ogon or Soragoi. It is easier to breed good examples of single-coloured Koi, or those of more than one colour which are not regarded by the Japanese as 'patterned' (such as Ochiba Shigure), than it is to breed good Showa or Kohaku.

Hobbyists wishing to obtain true Tategoi should develop a good relationship with a respected Koi dealer who personally visits Japan to buy fish shortly after the October mud pond harvest. That dealer must be fully briefed as to the size and variety of fish sought, and paid in advance (all transactions between breeder and buyer are in cash).

The dealer will then use his own judgement to select a fish to meet his client's requirements, but there is no guarantee that such a Koi will be found – if it is, the asking price may well be over the pre-set limit. The dealer will expect, and deserve, a commission for his trouble. Tategoi are never purchased in bulk, but individually, and negotiations can be protracted. It is far better, if funds permit, for the Koi keeper to accompany the dealer – several companies offer 'package deal' buying trips to Japan with this in mind.

An easier (and cheaper) way to obtain 'Tategoi' is to attend one of the special weekend events organised by some Koi dealers on their own premises, when high-grade fish with potential are offered for sale on a first-come, first-served basis. Often there will be the added incentive of a valuable prize for the fish that shows the most improvement in a year, when the Koi are taken back to the dealer and judged by the Japanese breeder. This is obviously excellent publicity for all parties, and so the quality of the fish is high. But the winning Tategoi are always those which are kept in heated ponds to achieve maximum growth over 12 months.

The third option is to find out from your Koi dealer when his next shipment of show-grade Koi is due in, and be among the first to view them. The fish you will be interested in are those purchased individually in Japan; you must then pay a holding deposit and collect your Koi after they have been quarantined (usually a wait of three or four weeks). For this to happen, your pond must be heated, since the best shipments arrive in November, much too late in the year to subject a new arrival to winter water temperatures. If your pond is without heat, the dealer will board out your Koi for five or six months for a fee.

All the above sounds like an expensive quest with no guarantee of results, but that is part of the fascination of Tategoi. A top-class Koi is truly a fish in a million, and the satisfaction of owning one and seeing it improve still further over the years far outweighs any disappointments and shocks to the bank balance along the way.

UNIQUE KOI

In the sense that no two Koi are ever exactly alike, every fish is unique. But the word is used quite specifically in the hobby to describe the 'one-offs'. These either do not fit into a recognised variety or, while doing so, differ greatly from what one has come to expect of the standards laid down for that variety. Either way, they can still be entered into shows as Kawarimono.

A further subsidiary definition of a 'unique' Koi worth the name is one which has some aesthetic merit. Flock spawnings tend to throw up all manner of strange-looking creatures with undefined pattern, random Doitsu scalation or muddy colours. But these home-breds are merely poor Koi – except, inevitably perhaps, in the eye of their proud owners.

THE KAWARIMONO CLASS

The Kawarimono 'catch-all' class was created to recognise truly unique non-metallic Koi as well as to embrace fish well established in the hobby, such as Chagoi, Benigoi, Kumonryu, Soragoi and Ochiba-Shigure. Four main groups make up this interesting gathering: Karasugoi (black Koi, fully-scaled or Doitsu, in which the percentage and positioning of the white markings determines the sub-varieties); single-coloured Koi, including those with scale reticulation; cross-breds; and

Gin-Rin Matsukawabake: The distribution of black and white patterning changes from summer to winter.

Photo: Keith Allison.

what could be termed, for want of a better definition, 'oddballs'.

Some initially 'unique' Koi later achieve recognition within a variety other than Kawarimono, but, to further confuse the issue, the Japanese and the English do not always agree on their status. For example, until recently Kage Showa were benched Kawarimono in the UK, and still are in Japan. In acknowledgement of the fact that Kage (shadowed) scaling can be confused with still-developing sumi, such Koi are now benched Showa under BKKS judging standards.

It is a similar story with Kindai Showa (fish where the white areas predominate over the reds and the blacks). When they first appeared they looked so different from the traditional variety, in which the three colours are more or less equally distributed, that they were sought out as something very special. Nowadays, Kindai are arguably more popular (and more successful in shows), than their forebears. Demand has created a plentiful supply and few Koi keepers would now regard them as 'unique'. They do, however, blur the sharp divide that once existed between Showa and Sanke, to the extent that what was once the classic beginner's Koi identification problem can now cause fierce debate among the experts, too.

CROSSES

Further unique Koi are recognisable crosses between established varieties. These are often referred to as 'hybrid' Koi but the term is not accurate, as true hybridisation occurs only between fish of different species, and all Koi are *Cyprinus carpio*.

Again, many of today's long-established varieties began life as deliberate crosses; Goshiki are Kohaku x Asagi; indeed all today's Koi carry some Asagi blood, as this is the oldest variety from which all others arose. Cross-bred Koi are destined to remain in

Kawarimono, if only because they occur randomly and infrequently, or are not worth commercial production. Thus we see Showa Shusui, Asagi Bekko, Koromo Sanke and so on. Rarely are the parental attributes shared out equally or immediately identifiable; when they are, the result can be stunning.

KANOKO KOI

Kanoko fish (where the hi appears on individual scales, giving a dappled effect) are a source of contention in the unique Koi stakes. A Kanoko Kohaku, for example, fulfils the criterion of being a non-metallic red and white fish but differs so much from the accepted standard that it cannot realistically compete against conventional Kohaku. Besides, this dappling is often a sign of very unstable hi that will completely disappear, the oddball fish then becoming a Shiro Muji (an all-white Koi).

The difficulty arises when Kanoko scaling appears alongside the normal areas of hi; is the fish then a true Kohaku or a Kawarimono? Given that top prizes for Go-Sanke tend to be won by fish with characteristics that set them apart from the norm, it can be tempting to buy 'borderline' Koi – but their ambiguous status can cause dispute at benching time. Obviously the owner of such a fish would prefer it to be entered into Kokahu, rather than Kawarimono.

'ODDBALL' PROBLEMS

Other oddities cause similar problems. Gotenzakura are Koi with hi markings resembling bunches of grapes and are benched Kawarimono – but how grape-like does the pattern have to be? Kage Utsuri are also placed in Kawarimono, but, as in Showa, the long-term stability of shadowed sumi is uncertain. One only has to see how prizewinning Koi change year on year to see that there are few absolutes.

The best gallery of unique Koi is presented in the book *Modern Nishikigoi* by Takeo Kuroki (ISBN 4-88024-102-4 C2076), first published in 1986. A large section is devoted to these fish, which the author names individually – though, as he points out, the names are not carved in stone but are given merely as a guide to anyone wishing to purchase something vaguely similar and needing to describe it to the dealer.

For example, a black fish in the Karasugoi group is designated 'Tancho Karasu'; the normal belly hi extends up into the body and one patch forms the classic circular head marking. This fish could never be entered in the Tancho variety, however, as this is reserved for normal and Gin Rin-scaled Go-Sanke. It would go, then as now, into Kawarimono.

Unique Koi provide a wonderful opportunity for the hobbyist to grow on and observe the changes in fish that are interesting without being too expensive. Uncertain lineage and bloodlines can go either way, so that uninspiring small Koi can blossom with age or merely grow into uninspiring large Koi. Pattern changes can be even more dramatic than in the more stabilised varieties. In instances of straight crosses, the phenomenon of so-called 'hybrid vigour' may lead to fast-growing fish which are highly resistant to disease.

But in Kawarimono, as in all classy Koi, body shape, finnage, skin quality and deportment are all-important. Clarity of colour, good Kiwa and even scale reticulation (where appropriate) all come into play, too.

5 ISRAELI KOI

By Dean Barratt

In the 1980s the popularity of water gardening, in all its many guises, exploded. The availability and subsequent mass marketing of 'new' products, such as ultra-violet clarifiers, meant that some of the problems related to having a pool or water feature could now be controlled or eliminated. The increasing demand for water gardening products led to a growing number of garden centres opening aquatic sections, which itself prompted further interest, and therefore further growth. In relative terms, the hardware and 'software' became cheaper and a bit of smart thinking resulted in the promotion of the 'non-pond' water feature. These new concepts caught the imagination of the public and media alike and suddenly water gardening was being promoted everywhere, on the TV, in the garden and lifestyle magazines, and at the big gardening shows.

The increased popularity of Koi keeping was the result, in part, of this new trend – but in the late 1980s it was, in many ways, the actions of a couple of Israeli Communal Collective Settlements (Kibbutzim) that really opened Koi keeping up to a mass audience.

THE BACKGROUND

Nowadays less than two per cent of Israelis actually live on Kibbutzim (there are about 250 in existence), but the importance of these communal settlements to the Israeli Jews should not be underestimated. The first Kibbutz was formed in 1909, and from then right through the 1920s and 1930s, hundreds more were established by the hundreds of thousands of Jews who fled Eastern Europe and Russia. Today an individual Kibbutz could provide a home and employment for anything from a couple of hundred to more than a thousand people – all living by the philosophy of giving according to your ability and taking according to your needs. Every worker earns the same small amount of money (by Western terms); with food, clothing, education and health care provided free – for the community by the community.

Kibbutzim aim to be as self-sufficient as possible, and so it was only natural that a number of them started to farm food fish. Nowadays such farming is big business on certain Kibbutzim, with fish such as Tilapia and Striped Bass satisfying not only a domestic, but also an international, market.

However, over-production in the late 1970s and early 1980s resulted in the government introducing a quota system. Diversification was called for – something not alien to the Kibbutzim – as the production of furniture, baby foods, breakfast cereals and plastic fabrication, to name but a few have all flourished alongside the more traditional agricultural work. It was not hard to see, with a knowledge of fish farming, enormous freshwater lagoons, an advantageous climate, and a growing world-wide market, that breeding ornamental fish was an ideal sideways step.

GETTING STARTED

The first Kibbutz to go into ornamental production was Hazorea, a large Kibbutzim located in the Jezrael valley. The marketing name for the venture was Dag Noy, meaning 'ornamental fish'. Two other Kibbutzim also went into ornamental production during this time, Gan Shmuel and Ma'abarot.

With brood stock coming from Japan, the farms produced not only Koi but also Comet Goldfish, Blue Comet Shubunkins and Sarasa Comets. This commercial 'off shoot' quickly became successful. There was a strong demand, especially from England, for the Israeli ornamentals, especially the Goldfish varieties, as retailers and wholesalers now had a plentiful supply of strong, healthy and cheap fish. The quality of the Koi, in terms of variety, colour and body shape, was poor – but time and skill was to remedy this.

The production of strong and healthy fish came from the pool of skilled fish farmers

An example of the enormous food fish lakes at Kfar Ruppin.　　　*Photo: Dean Barratt.*

who had experience of both intensive and extensive fish farming techniques. Modern technology was used where relevant, and the Israelis' mentality of getting things right, and listening and learning from others, also played a part.

Another advantage was the shorter flying times from Israel compared with the Far East, resulting in less shipping stress. The farms were also able to negotiate very favourable air freight rates. This, plus the low labour and land costs in Israel, helped to make the fish very competitively priced.

The climate is also very much in Israel's favour. A comparison of minimum and maximum daytime temperatures for central and northern Israel compared to Akita, just north of Niigata on the west coast of Japan, shows that Japan has a much shorter growing season – about five or six months – compared to Israel, which could be potentially year round. Indeed, between October and March the maximum daytime temperatures in Akita are less than the minimum temperatures in Israel. Average summer temperatures also make most of Israel at least 5 degrees Centigrade (approx 2 degrees Fahrenheit) warmer.

The only drawback to the Israeli Mediterranean climate is lack of rainfall. Whilst average rainfall figures for Akita shows at least 100 mm (4 ins) of rain even in the driest month and more than 200 mm (8 ins) in the wettest, in Israel it is a different story. In Northern Israel the wettest months are January and February with over 100mm (4 ins) of rain for each, but between May and October monthly figures fall below 15 mm ($^1/_2$ in).

The farm most affected by this lack of rainfall is Hazorea (one of the other farms, located farther inland, has very little rainfall, but it has a plentiful supply of water from the River Jordan). At Hazorea, they have to rely on winter rains, allowing water to be drawn

Ma'agan Michael's famous Ghost Koi in the concrete holding pools, which are netted to reduce losses through birds. Photo: Dean Barratt.

from a river (which often dries up in the summer) to fill the massive lagoons on the farm. Poor winter rains can result in a near crisis for the farm and production has been known to be noticeably affected.

MARKET FORCES

In the mid- to late-1980s, Hazorea and the other fish farms had additional concerns. Their Goldfish varieties were almost universally greeted with open arms by the retailers and consumers alike, but it was a slightly different story with the Koi. To 99 per cent of people, a pond Goldfish is a pond Goldfish. This, for the reasons explained elsewhere in this book, is not true of Koi.

Koi keeping is really little different to any hobby or the industry that serves it, and as such three distinct markets exist.

The mass market (like it or not) is for cheap, colourful (aka cheerful) and, almost always, small fish. The majority of such fish are bought by people who would usually class themselves as pond owners rather than Koi keepers. The appeal of Koi lies in the fact that their colours are diverse, they grow big and may even become friendly in the pond.

This market usually has little or no interest or appreciation of variety standards.

The smallest market – in terms of numbers – is what one could variously call the 'top-end', the specialist, serious or professional end of the market. Despite being the least important to the industry in direct financial terms, this market is ultimately why the hobby exists. It sets standards and establishes views and opinions. An analogy is the fashion industry – the average person may sneer and view the cat-walk fashion shows as irrelevant, but they drive the 'High Street' forward with innovation and, more importantly, with aspiration!

The market that really drives the hobby is the 'middle market', within which most Koi keepers (as defined from pond owners) fall. These are the people who start off in the hobby in a small way, but soon get the bug! The typical Koi keeper has an interest and appreciation of variety standards, but is not a slave to them. His pond does not cost the equivalent of a two-bedroomed terraced house, and a typical fish purchase is more likely to pay for a good night out rather than a fortnight's holiday for a family of four.

This is the market that most suppliers of fish and equipment are trying to influence and satisfy. As such, it is a market which itself has much influence on suppliers and people looking to enter or develop in the hobby.

Israel saw that their Koi were satisfying the 'pond owner market', but not the Koi keeper. Indeed, in the mid-1980s not only did "real men not eat quiche" but "real" Koi keepers didn't keep Israeli Koi!

THE GREAT LEAP FORWARD

Improved brood stock and careful spawning and culling began to improve the quality of the Koi's shape, colour and variety. Metallic fish, especially Platinum Ogons, Yamabuki and Hariwake, as well as highly saleable Doitsu fish, were starting to 'make the grade'.

This was enough to start convincing people that Israel could begin to compete with Japan for the hearts and minds of Koi keepers. Still the Israelis realised that more had to be done, both in terms of the quality of their fish and how they were marketed.

In terms of marketing, the great leap forward was made in 1991 when a fourth Kibbutz, located on the coast, decided to join the other three farms and diversify into ornamentals. The farms could have continued to operate independently from each other, but this would have jeopardised the overall strategy. The fourth farm, called Ma'agan Michael 'wished' for its name to be incorporated into that of the marketing groups, and so Mag Noy was born. Mag, in this context, meaning 'great or grand'.

With Hazorea acting as a head office, Mag Noy's aim was to improve the worldwide marketing of the group's fish. The UK was, and still is, its chief market – then accounting for nearly 60 per cent of their business – but a big growth potential was seen in North America and Continental Europe, especially Belgium, Holland and Germany.

This marketing took various forms, such as placing full-page adverts extolling the virtues of Israeli fish in consumer aquatic magazines, as well as producing promotional material for retailers. Mag Noy has also tried to have a strong presence at major Koi shows worldwide. Most importantly, the individual farms and Mag Noy as a whole have made themselves very accessible to their customers – both main importers and retailers. This has allowed them to find out what their customers wanted, what improvements they needed to make, and what business

opportunities could be developed. As a result of this, Hazorea went into producing water lilies as well as other hardy and tropical aquatics, and Mag Noy started acting on behalf of smaller specialised tropical fish producers.

It was listening and working with its customers, especially in England, that led to an action being taken that was to provide the Israelis with their big breakthrough in terms of winning over more and more retailers and, ultimately, Koi keepers.

QUALITY KOI

The general growth of interest in Koi keeping led to an increasing number of people looking for larger Koi, but at more affordable prices. For just as Israeli Koi developed a negative reputation in certain circles, Japanese Koi were perceived by newcomers as expensive and for the serious or specialist hobbyist only.

Larger Koi (between 8 ins and 24 ins) had always been available to retailers by buying whole boxes of farm-selected, standard grade fish, but this would result in receiving what were, at times, some very poor-quality fish. Some very fine, larger Koi could be found with their origins in the holy land, but fish with poor bodies, colour and pattern were all too common. The reasons for this were many, but a major cause was that poor culling/grading was resulting in poor fish being grown on. This was also, in part, due to a shortage of quality fish for growing on.

Some consumers just want large, cheap fish, but, the greater percentage of people want to buy higher grade fish. The person who most helped the Israelis to tackle quality

The quality of this Sanke, selected on a handpicking visit, shows just what Israel is capable of producing.

Photo: Dean Barratt.

control was an Englishman, Colin Wilcox, of what was then called Staffordshire Waterlife. The company had previously dealt with Japan, but when Colin started to experience problems with his Japanese contacts, he started looking elsewhere for fish.

After a period of negotiation, Mag Noy agreed to supply direct. Colin quickly built up a good relationship with Mag Noy, especially with their then marketing director, Oden Cohen, so much so that the Israelis went to Colin when they were looking for new broodstock. In 1987 Colin started to work more and more with the farms, even down to helping with the autumn harvests of their main growing on pools. Colin used this opportunity to hand-select larger fish for his wholesale set-up back in England, and quickly saw that retailers would jump at the chance to select their own fish from the nets.

From then on, certain retailers had the opportunity to go out to Israel and select the best fish available at that time in a variety mix to suit their market. Initially, hand-picking was just seen as a way to sell larger quantities of bigger fish but there was another benefit. English retailers could now show their customers what big, year-by-year improvements the Israelis were making. This would start to improve the reputation of Israeli Koi in general, resulting in a massive market growth for small, standard grade fish. This is immediately illustrated by hard commercial facts. In 1989 the United Kingdom imported £1.9 million worth of ornamental fish from Japan and £1.3 million from Israel. Five years later the value of those imports from Japan had decreased by 15 per cent, whilst those from Israel had more than doubled. This growth in Israeli imports has also been seen in Central Europe, and to a lesser extent in North America, where economies in freight are not so significant and the shorter flying times do not apply.

This success led to an increased polarising of opinions within the industry and the hobby, and with money and vested interests at stake, it was inevitable that negative rumours started to fly. However, it is worth bearing in mind that comparisons between the quality of fish produced in Japan and those produced in Israel are largely extraneous as the fish, in many ways, complement each other.

The very best fish, in show terms, are produced in Japan. But a good proportion of Israeli hand-selected fish are of better quality than a lot of the Japanese fish that are exported. Most hobbyists have to stick to a certain budget, and, for many, the Israeli Koi will offer better value than many of the Japanese fish.

Many aspects of Koi appreciation (some would argue all) are subjective and so, ultimately, if you like the fish you see in front of you – and you are happy to pay the asking price – then that is all that matters.

FERTILISATION TO FLIGHT

Looking more specifically at Koi production, whilst the marketing for the farms comes under the Mag Noy banner, the farms still operate independently in terms of production. Mag Noy can make recommendations to the individual farms but not necessarily make demands. The farms seem to operate on a friendly, competitive basis. There is an exchange of ideas and help is offered if required – but financially each Kibbutz is independent, which makes some competition inevitable.

On each farm, brood stock is held in separate pools. Most of the females are tagged on the caudal fin, or even have electronic glass tags, which can be scanned, injected into the dorsal muscle tissue. This tagging allows for the future assessment of different spawnings, so that what could be classed as a commercially successful spawning could be repeated. This assessment can be

Growing-on pool at Kfar Ruppin.
Photo: Dean Barratt.

made, if necessary, by taking a proportion of the fry and growing them on in special pools with individual spawnings placed in growing cages. The requirement for improving spawings – in terms of a greater proportion of the fish having a commercial value – is becoming more and more important.

This is because not only does Israel have to improve their quality (and quantity of said quality), to meet worldwide demand for year-on-year improvement, but, more specifically, must satisfy the growing sophistication of what has become their a key market – Central Europe. In the late 1980s to mid-90s, the UK received the bulk of the A-grade standard production (UK retailers were not even allowed to purchase the lesser, B-grade fish, probably due to the fear that these fish would damage their growing reputation for quality fish), whilst Central Europe's demands could be met by B-grade fish. These demands have changed, Central Europe now wants its share of higher grade fish and, interestingly, the UK can now purchase B-grade Koi.

Spawning is manipulated by controlling day length and water temperature, as well as with the use of hormones. Pituitary extracts were normally used, but a synthetic hormone is now most widely employed. Whilst some fish are induced to spawn on mats or brushes, most are stripped of eggs by hand, 24-30 hours after the hormone injection, and the eggs mixed with the sperm of a number of males. The fish are usually tranquillised and also injected with antibiotics to greatly reduce the risk of disease/damage which could result from the stress and handling.

The fertilised ova will then go into incubation cones, with iodine used to sterilise the eggs. After two-and-a-half to four days, the eggs hatch and the young fry are then moved to the indoor larval holding vats/tanks. After a further two to three weeks, the young fry are taken to the growing-on pools, which are usually 4,000-10,000 sq metres in surface area. The fish could stay in the pool for only two or three months, or anything up to three years. Individual pools are netted as and when needed, with required fish being kept in holding vats or pools at the hatchery, and those not required being left to grow on.

At one of the larger farms – Ma'agan Michael – in an average year in the mid-1990s approximately 400 million larvae were produced. Only 10-15 per cent of these would be expected to reach 'market size'. A typical survival rate for larvae up to 0.1g in weight is 70 per cent: 35 per cent of these will then be culled or be lost through natural causes before they reach 2 ins in length. Finally, 30 per cent of the balance don't make it to the market or are lost before reaching 5 ins in length.

Where possible, the farms will aim to keep a few thousand of each species of fish in as many different sizes as are available from the growing-on pools within the holding vats at the hatchery. These fish can then go on to the availability list which is sent out of Hazorea. Standard grade Koi in all sizes are ordered by wholesalers/consolidators, by fax or phone, approximately four to seven days before the intended shipping date. Depending on availability, Mag Noy try, as far as possible, to split orders amongst the five farms. (A fifth farm, Kfar Ruppin, joined Mag Noy in 1993.)

Netting 4-5 ins Koi from a growing-on pool at Hazorea.   *Photo: Dean Barratt.*

HAND-PICKING

In the case of hand-picked Koi, retailers and importers have direct visits to the farms arranged between February and, usually, June. Generally, up to three businesses could be on a single trip which lasts three to five days.

The farms prepare for a visit by partially netting growing-on pools which could contain fish from 6-24 ins. The fish are graded out of the nets, with suitable fish being taken to the holding pools within the hatchery complex. The holding vats vary from 2 m to 9 m in diameter, and could be made from concrete, acrylic, fibreglass or stainless steel, or they may be just 'flexi' vats.

Specific sizes – by which a fish is priced – are held in separate vats, and it is from these that customers select individual fish. As competing retailers are often on a single visit, it is the usual practice for a single person from each business to physically go into the vat to select their desired fish by net. Selection is a serious business, as things work on a first come/catch, first served basis. Many hundreds of fish will be in a vat, and the quality and variety can vary enormously.

Customers used to make pre-visits to each farm to assess the quality, variety mix and break-down of sizes available. This no longer occurs, which only adds to the challenge – you could live to rue your selection on the first couple of farms, once you finally get to see what is on the others! Regular buyers can start to get a feel for each farm's individual personality. Trends do occur, in terms of which farms are most likely to have maintained or improved on their quality, but, ultimately, the quality of fish on display could vary from visit to visit on each farm.

Certain farms also tend to be more likely to produce quantities of certain varieties, for example Ma'agan has been known for its excellent Chagoi (the quality of which was only improved when frozen Japanese sperm was obtained from England), Kfar Ruppin for metallics and Gan Shmuel for Kujaku.

After selection each customer's fish are taken to individual holding vats. A couple of

A hand-selecting pool at Hazorea containing fish that have just been brought in from the growing-on pools.   *Photo: Dean Barratt.*

Dean Barratt hand-picking fish.

A selection of 14-inch Koi at Hazorea ready for selection.   *Photo: Dean Barratt.*

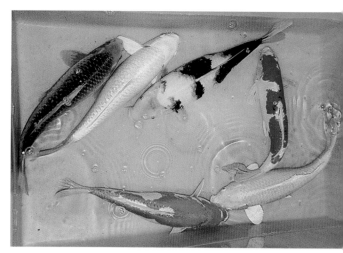

A typical box of hand-selected Koi.

days before shipping the fish are put through any required treatment, and are fasted (three to five days for larger Koi and 24-48 hours for smaller fish). About 12 hours before final packing, the fish are split into box quantities and placed into cages inside cooling vats. Here the water is cooled by approximately 1 degree C (approx 2 degrees F) each hour, down to 10 degrees C (52 F).

The fish are bagged with approximately 3 kg (6 1/2 lbs), of fish to 12 litres (2 1/2 gallons) of water, and the bags filled with oxygen and then boxed ready for their flight, which lasts only five hours from Tel Aviv to London, Heathrow.

FROM THE PLANE TO YOUR POND

So what are the pleasures and pitfalls of buying Israeli fish? Firstly, there are some great-value fish to be had, as from a cost point of view – size for size – the Israeli fish are generally cheaper to the retailer than Japanese fish. This is to be expected as the quality of the average Israeli Koi is inferior to the average Japanese, but better quality fish can also be found for a lot less money. Be aware, though, that the very best Israeli Koi will often be sold at a higher price to offset lesser fish. You may also find that you will see a much larger mix of varieties in a selection of Israeli hand-selected fish, with less of a bias towards Go-Sanke.

Whilst the quality of hand-picked fish will vary considerably within any single variety, and trends may alter, over the past five to ten years the Israelis have been producing very good Ogons (Platinum Ogon, Yamabuki and Hariwake), Shiro Bekko and Shusui. Real improvements have also been seen in recent years with regards to the quality of Kohaku, Sanke, Koromo and Kujaku – especially Doitsu.

With regard to pitfalls, firstly, do not confuse a pool full of larger standard grade fish (also known as pond fillers!) with, what should be, better selected hand-picked Koi. Be aware that the best fish are generally most available in retailers between February and June. Good fish can be found all year, but they do tend to be thinner on the ground after June.

Be careful about being tempted to buy fish in February and March however, as the fish may not be fully rested/quarantined. Plus, if the retailer is holding the fish indoors above 14 degree C (59 F) then it would be better not to add these fish to an outdoor pool until your water temperature stabilises above 11-12 degrees C (54-56 F).

Finally, pay attention to the fish's body shape. Culling and grading is not to the standard that it is in Japan, and, as such, Koi with poor bodies and finnage are commonly seen even in larger sizes.

6 *FROM JAPAN TO YOUR POND*

The Nishikigoi swimming in our ponds have come a very long way in every sense. Each Koi we are privileged to own is a very special survivor, having undergone not only thousands of miles of travel but a painstaking and ongoing selection process during the early stages of its life. Without this attention to quality control on the part of the breeders, the continuing improvement in the overall standard of fish from Japan would not be possible.

SURVIVAL OF FRY
A large female carp in the wild can produce a quarter of a million eggs; cyprinid spawnings have to be this prolific because only a minute percentage of the resulting fry ever reach maturity. There is no parental care, in fact the depletion begins with carp consuming their own spawn. Most of the early survivors then fall victim to predators right down the line – from tiny hydra which snare hatchlings in their tentacles, through to the larvae of aquatic insects and, later, other fishes and land or airborne opportunists.

Koi spawnings result in just as many eggs, and, although natural predation is not such a problem, there are still relatively few fish to show for the Japanese breeder's efforts in any given year – perhaps a few hundred Tategoi with the potential to earn him serious money, and a few thousand more general-grade fish that he can sell in bulk at very low prices.

The rest are sacrificed in a series of culls which ensure that only the Koi with a likelihood of improvement enjoy the intensive care necessary to bring them on to the point where they attract the buyer's Yen.

The All Japan Show: An opportunity to see Koi of the highest quality.

Photo: A. McGill.

BREEDING METHODS IN JAPAN

The mountainous Niigata Prefecture is the home of Nishikigoi, where climate dictates to a very great degree the various stages of fish production. Spring is the time for spawning, summer the time for growing on, and in winter those Koi thought worthy of the trouble come inside. In Southern Japan, where the weather is warmer, Koi can be mass-produced and grown on in concrete ponds. But traditional techniques arguably still result in the finest fish of all.

Mud ponds used to rear fry and grow on promising Koi during subsequent summers were once exclusively the holding reservoirs for rice paddies, but they are now also purpose-dug to the required depth and near to access roads, to make harvesting that much easier. From late October the ponds are left untouched, but in late March/early April they are prepared in readiness for the coming season's activity. First they are drained down, then raked over and limed to destroy parasites. Refilled with stream water, they are then seeded with chicken manure. This is to promote the growth of infusoria, the ideal first food for fry.

Not all breeders spawn their own Koi or own mud ponds; often eggs or newly-hatched fry will be bought in from other Koi farmers in the district and reared in rented water.

The precious parent Koi are spawned in narrow indoor concrete tanks lined with protective nets, at the base of which are placed beds of artificial spawning grass. The ratio is two or three males to one female. The fish are normally allowed to spawn in their own time, though breeders will sometimes hand-strip eggs and milt from Koi when they reach 'critical mass' and mix these under controlled conditions. This is done to compare the resulting fry with those from other pairings.

The practice adopted in some other countries and known as 'hypophysation', where Koi are artificially induced to spawn with injections of carp pituitary extract, is not used in Japan. It saves time, for the fish can be bred virtually to order, but it is thought to promote weak Koi.

Once natural spawning is complete, the exhausted parent Koi are taken out to recuperate in their own mud ponds. The fry take 3-5 days to hatch, and, once they have filled their swimbladders and become free-swimming, they are moved to the already prepared ponds which by now are quite opaque and have a healthy population of food organisms.

CULLING

Three to four weeks later the first cull takes place; this is an intensive operation, often involving the breeder's whole family. The pond is harvested, and deformed fry or those which are not developing true to variety are discarded. Also destroyed are 'Tobi', fish showing an abnormally rapid growth rate, as their impressive dimensions are almost always down to cannibalising their brothers and sisters. Either traditional fine-meshed culling dip nets with bowls the diameter of a dessert spoon or suction pipettes are used to separate out the fry.

The surviving 20 per cent of fry go back into the rearing pond, and a month later their numbers are reduced by half in the second cull. By now the natural food supply will be nearly exhausted and powdered food will be fed, either automatically or by hand. A further cull in August will see only around five per cent of the spawning making it through to the October harvest – but the thinning-out does not stop there. Less than a third of these little Koi, by now around 4 ins long, will be overwintered – the rest will be destroyed or sold.

REARING PROCEDURES

Indoor facilities vary from the large and ultra-sophisticated to simple garage ponds, but in all cases the high stocking rates are made possible only by the Japanese knowledge of what it takes to maintain good water. They are aided by an unlimited top-up supply from springs and mountain streams.

The following spring, those Koi that have not been sold will go outside to spend another summer in a mud pond. With supplementary feeding, high temperatures and the health-giving benefits of the Niigata clay, rapid growth is made (stocking density is kept deliberately low), and, by the end of their second year, the Koi can have reached 15-17 ins in length. The October harvest is a time of both anticipation and trepidation for the breeders, for, until the fish have been netted, there is no way of knowing how the summer has treated them, whether they have developed better or worse than expected, and if they have encountered major parasitic problems such as high infestations of anchor worm.

From the mud ponds, the fish make their way in an oxygenated tank on the back of pick-up trucks, back to the breeder's indoor facility. There, depending on his opinion as to their future potential, they will be checked for external parasites and either be offered for sale or retained inside in readiness for sale the following spring, or perhaps a further year or more in the mud ponds will be considered. Sometimes the decision will hinge on the price offered for these Tategoi.

SELLING THE FISH

Late October sees dealers from the UK and the rest of the world converging on Niigata to purchase the pick of the crop. They may be accompanied by valued customers who have made the journey to Japan with the object of selecting their own special fish, but, unless they have some experience of the Japanese way of doing business, they may go away disappointed. The dealer will usually purchase Koi on their behalf, a safer option.

The very high-grade fish are individually priced, but often a dealer who has built up an understanding with the breeders he visits regularly will be able to negotiate a price for the remaining stock of Koi which, while still good, are not in quite the same league. It is essential to buy fish to match anticipated demand; in the UK, Go-Sanke are favoured among the top collectors, whereas, in the USA, metallic Koi find a more ready market.

In recent years, collectives such as Koi Ichi Ban Japan have grown up to purchase good-grade Koi from a number of top breeders for export to the UK and Europe. Such an arrangement provides a guaranteed market for these mainly smaller Koi, and a centralised holding and packing station expertly prepares them for their long flight. In the destination countries, dealers can order boxes of Koi unseen, but of pre-specified size and grade. This is a good option if, for whatever reason, they cannot travel to Japan to hand-pick their own fish.

EXPORTING KOI

Individual breeders also pack Koi to be forwarded to the shipping agents, who nearly all have premises close to Tokyo's Narita Airport. The fish travel by road, and, as weight is not yet an issue, they are double-bagged in large volumes of water. Meanwhile the shippers have made available water of the correct temperature and condition in readiness for the new arrivals, which are held for up to two weeks. During this time they are starved, so that they do not pollute their transit bags with their own ammonia-laden excreta. They may also be treated for parasites, such as any remaining anchor worm (which, while not a great problem in large-volume mud ponds, can be a headache to get rid of in a hobbyist's set-up).

Koi packed for the air journey travel with the minimum amount of water in their vinyl bags, partly to keep freight charges to a minimum and partly to benefit from the larger volume of oxygen that can then be pumped into the void above them. October/November is the ideal time for them to fly, as water temperatures are lower than in summer and the water in the bag can take up more dissolved oxygen. The additive Elbagin calms the fish and reduces their respiration rate.

After packing, the consignment is picked up by freight forwarders who pay a customs entry charge (which is passed on to the importing dealer). There follows a 12-hour direct flight over the North Pole to Heathrow Airport in the UK, but Customs clearance, value added tax calculations and paperwork at the destination can add hours to the total journey.

For the dealer waiting anxiously to pick up his Koi, this can be a stressful time. While it is possible to load the boxes direct into the transit vehicle, this puts the Koi at some risk

in the event of traffic delays. Some dealers open the boxes at the airport and move the fish into heavily-aerated portable vats which offer stress-free travel conditions.

Back at their premises (and often in the early hours of the morning), the dealers and their staff move the Koi into holding ponds – if the fish are still bagged up, the normal floating procedure is adopted to equalise temperatures inside and out. The new arrivals are usually kept separate from existing stocks, and the water is heated to equate to what the Koi have been used to. No food will be offered until the consignment has had a chance to settle down.

DEALERSHIP PRACTICES

What happens next is down to the dealer. Some highly respected outlets will offer their Koi for sale the very next day, on the basis that they have already been adequately quarantined with the shippers in Japan. Others will hold on to them for two or three weeks, to see if any stress-induced ailments appear in that time, and will medicate if they do.

Whatever the policy, dealer quarantine can never be a guarantee of good health, as some diseases take far longer than a mere few weeks to manifest themselves.

The process of buying Koi and getting them safely home is covered more fully in another chapter, but do not be surprised if your fish seem a little quiet and off-colour for the first few days. They have undergone a traumatic and protracted journey involving travel by road and air, semi-starvation and several changes of water, after which they find themselves in an alien environment. Human jet-lag is nothing by comparison!

A new consignment of Koi always attracts interest. Here, some top-quality Koi are bowled for inspection.

Photo: Nick Fletcher.

7 *WHAT A KOI POND MUST ACCOMPLISH*

When Koi were first imported from Japan into Britain around 1966, it came as something of a culture shock – not least for the fish themselves. It was assumed (wrongly) that because these were carp, and fairly close relatives of the almost indestructible goldfish, they could be successfully kept in the ordinary garden pond. Forward-thinking Koi buyers scaled up the gallonage in line with the potential size of the fish, but for some years thereafter the role of filtration and other parameters essential to life was not fully understood.

Unfortunately, these pioneering Koi found themselves in much the same situation as canaries in a 19th-century coalmine – though, instead of succumbing to noxious airborne gases, they indicated the presence of equally harmful toxic substances in the water by falling sick and dying. This distressing situation resulted in many would-be Koi keepers giving up after the first attempt, dismissing these fish as 'impossible' to maintain. Luckily, the dedicated few were more persistent, and made it their business to find out what Koi needed, not only to survive, but to flourish in the confines of a pond.

REQUIREMENTS OF A KOI POOL

At the time, flexible pool liners were being marketed in the aquatic press with the beguiling promise "Build your pond in a weekend!". A little optimistic, perhaps, but essentially such projects entailed digging a contoured hole with shallow marginal shelves to accommodate the obligatory plants, and incorporating a deeper 'fish refuge' (usually no more than a couple of feet down). Once the liner was installed, the pond would be filled direct from the tap, the pool edged with any stonework to hand, and plants and fish introduced together. The height of sophistication was to add a fountain and/or waterfall for ornamental purposes.

Goldfish would survive and thrive in such a pond, especially if the water was circulated, as this assisted the establishment of a 'natural balance'. Nobody seemed quite sure what this balance was, or how it was achieved. Few wondered why fish sometimes died on hot summer nights, or why the water periodically turned green – and, in any case, inexpensive goldfish could always be replaced.

This type of pond is still being built today, and there is nothing inherently wrong with the concept – except that it is totally unsuited to Koi. A purpose-built Koi pond not only makes due allowance for the eventual size of its occupants, but permits the owner to exercise full control over every aspect of what is, in essence, a scaled-up outdoor fish tank with built-in life-support system.

There are several routes to achieving this

objective but, as a general yardstick, the more time and thought invested at the planning stage into a Koi pond project, the less labour-intensive daily maintenance need be. Just one inexpensive example – automatic topping-up can be accomplished by means of a domestic ballcock or float valve installed in the filter, allowing evaporation losses to be made up, or new water to be trickled in through a purifier.

The following criteria will help you decide on the Koi pond that is best for you, taking into account the space you have available, what you can afford to spend on the project, and whether you intend keeping just a few fish for pleasure or becoming seriously involved. A word of warning here – Koi keeping can quickly become obsessive, and what you consider the last word in sophistication may still look very unambitious when you visit the ponds of dedicated enthusiasts.

POND DIMENSIONS

Back garden fishponds typically hold a few hundred gallons, whereas Koi pond capacity is usually measured in the thousands. It is difficult to stipulate a minimum size, but a pond 10ft x 10ft x 5ft deep would hold 3,120 gallons if filled to the lip, not including

The Koi pond must make allowances for the eventual size of its occupants.

Photo: Dave Bevan.

the filter. Anything less in terms of surface area would not really give the Koi a chance to get up speed – indeed, if you really could not accommodate more than 100 sq ft it would be better to build a rectangular pond 16ft x 6ft, or an irregular shape with one long dimension.

A depth of 5ft is the bare minimum to consider, and even that would be considered a shallow pond by some. Old reasoning was that plenty of water over the fishes' backs enabled them to seek out the warm bottom layer in the winter, but this was based on the false premise that a thermocline (temperature gradient) operated in small bodies of water. It does not, especially as today's ponds are filtered 24 hours a day, 12 months of the year, and the preferred draw-off point(s) into the filter is the bottom drain(s).

What deep ponds do is enable Koi to exercise all their fins and muscles in both horizontal and vertical planes, and this encourages good body shape. Koi deprived of regular work-outs, just like their owners, will pack on weight at the expense of grace and elegance, and come to resemble rugby balls.

Deep ponds, paradoxically, make for tamer Koi. If fish can retreat several feet down when a predator or an unknown human approaches – they do recognise the hand that feeds them – they will feel more secure than if they have to dash frantically around seeking non-existent cover.

The final argument for sensible depth is tied in with getting the maximum gallonage from a given surface area. The more water a pond holds, the less susceptible it is to sudden changes in temperature, and water parameters will be more stable, too.

That said, it is better to have a small Koi pond properly filtered and easily managed than a swimming pool-sized construction with inadequate facilities to constantly remove solid and dissolved waste products

into the filter. The larger the pond, the more difficult it is to avoid so-called 'dead spots'; doing so will be expensive in terms of more powerful pumps, additional bottom drains and sub-surface water returns, not to mention scaled-up filtration to cope with the waste generated. So remember, big ponds need more ancillary equipment – can you afford it?

RELATIONSHIP BETWEEN POND AND FILTER SIZE
This is one of the most contentious issues in modern Koi keeping, not least because the hobby has grown to a point where manufacturers can profitably mass-produce filtration equipment. Today there is a bewildering choice, all brands claiming advantages over their rivals. Broadly speaking, the market is polarised between the 'big is beautiful' approach and those companies promoting ultra-compact filter units which can be installed with the minimum of effort.

The old rule of thumb was that the surface area of a filter should be a minimum of one-third that of the pond, and preferably half; anything larger was seen as being proportionally more efficient. This was in the days when a typical pond filter was merely an enlarged version of the aquarium undergravel concept, in which water is pulled through a gravel bed acting both mechanically and biologically. Such in-pond filters had to be large if early blockage was not to occur, so their size was some compensation for their inefficiency. While they worked, they worked well – but, from the moment the pump was switched on, the countdown to disaster began. Sometimes this was due to pump failure, but more often it was a slower process involving progressive blockage of the media, to a point where water tracked through narrow channels while the rest of the gravel stagnated.

The early gravity-fed external filters, too, relied upon gravel or flint chippings alone to perform both mechanical and biological functions, and the inherent defects mentioned earlier applied equally to these, except that the pump was more accessible.

Relating filter efficiency to size still holds good in some respects, but it is by no means the whole picture. If we take as an example a chambered gravity-fed filter 10ft x 3ft wide serving a pond 10ft square, that would more or less fulfil the traditional minimum size requirement. But it is a mistake to look only at one dimension, while ignoring how that filter operates. What we should be considering are universal criteria for efficient filtration, and whether they are being met. Is the filter designed to remove the maximum amount of suspended solids before the biological stages – in other words, is the settlement facility adequate? How deep are the chambers? Is there an adequate void beneath each, and is there a facility to drain them to waste? Is the media right for the job it is expected to perform? If the answer to any of these is 'no', then your filter can be as large as you please and still not perform as it should.

Filtration is all about water quality, and the parameters to aim for are as follows.

Ammonia/nitrite – nil
- pH – a stable reading between 7.3 and 8.5 (opinions vary as to ideal readings, but water more acidic or alkaline than within this band will not facilitate maximum growth, while in water with a pH consistently below 6.5 or above 9.0, long-term survival is unlikely).
- Dissolved oxygen content – a minimum of 5-8 ppm. To be sure of achieving this, particularly at higher temperatures, aim for a mean reading as high as possible.
- Nitrate/phosphate – as low as possible.
- Metals and other contaminants from mains water – ideally zero.

These parameters are all to do with the water chemistry, but water clarity is also important, for two reasons: it enables the Koi keeper to derive maximum enjoyment from the fish, and it shows that no particulate waste is getting through the filter and being recirculated. The other obstacle to water clarity, a 'green water' bloom of single-celled algae, is easily rectified with an ultra-violet clarifier/steriliser.

The amount of space in any filtration system devoted to the biological stages can be relatively small, providing that the media is dealing with water from which most solids have already been removed. That means efficient mechanical stages. The space taken up by this important process has been greatly reduced with the advent of vortex settlement. One vortex chamber will perform the same task as a passive settlement chamber many times its size.

POND HEATING
The aim of many Koi keepers is to achieve the maximum growth potential in their fish, and this can be done only if water temperature is maintained above 55 deg F all year round, enabling them to be fed.

But there is another, more important reason to heat the pond. Doing so levels out the rapid temperature fluctuations that would otherwise occur, particularly in the spring. Koi are not true coldwater fish, and in Japan they never experience chilling. In summer, out in the mineral-rich mud ponds, they can happily cope with water in the high 80s F. When the weather begins to cool prior to the short, sharp Japanese winter, they are brought indoors where their holding ponds are not allowed to fall much below 70 deg F. Coming to an unheated hobbyist's pond is a shock to their system, particularly over the first winter. Koi lying on their sides on the pond floor are not 'hibernating' but making a valiant attempt to conserve dwindling energy.

If they get through this ordeal successfully, they will still be in a weakened state and vulnerable to pathogens which can begin to attack at temperatures where the Koi's immune system is not able to offer them any resistance.

Even in the British summer there can be a significant variance between daytime and night-time temperatures. A thermostatically controlled heating system, turned down, will economically even out the peaks and troughs and promote happy Koi.

If pond heating is such a desirable commodity, why is it not more commonplace? It boils down to two things – affordability, and the perceived difficulty of installation. The expense can be broken down into initial installation and ongoing running costs. As we shall see, a gas boiler/heat exchanger system is pricey to put in, but subsequent bills are lower than those incurred with a simple electric heater, though the latter is easier and cheaper to install.

To derive maximum economy and efficiency, heat should be combined with some form of pond covering. In its simplest form, this can be sheets of bubble-wrap floating on the surface, though this is not attractive to the eye and can be blown away in winter gales. Better is a pitched, framed timber structure firmly anchored down and 'glazed' with heavy-duty polythene or rigid polycarbonate sheeting. On large ponds this should be constructed in several sections, so that it can be removed in stages when the weather starts to warm up.

The best covering of all can be incorporated into ponds which already have a pergola built over them. In summer, the roof is covered in plastic-mesh greenhouse shading which inhibits blanketweed growth and protects Koi from sunburn. In winter, it is a relatively simple matter to wall in this open structure and cover the roof with polycarbonate sheet (offcuts can usually be obtained cheaply from double-glazing companies). The pond is now effectively within its own greenhouse, offering a space-heating option instead of – or in addition to – a gas boiler or electric immersion heater. Not only will the Koi remain active, but their owner can sit inside the structure, protected from the elements, and extend his enjoyment to twelve months a year.

Gas central heating for ponds does not necessarily require a separate dedicated boiler – depending on the distance from the pond to the house and the capacity of the boiler, it can be run from the existing domestic system. All modifications should be done by a qualified gas installer, never attempted by the hobbyist. In essence, hot water pumped from the boiler is conveyed through insulated pipework to a stainless steel heat-exchanger, usually mounted in a dry chamber. The unit has inlet and outlet ports for the pond water, which passes through the outer jacket, absorbing heat from the water coming from the boiler. The finned internal design of the hot water exchanger offers a high surface area for maximum heat transfer, and contact time is maximised by a restrictor. Water now circulates back to the boiler and is brought back to temperature ready for the next pass through the exchanger.

Typically, a thermal sensor in the pond runs back to a digital thermostat which can be pre-set to the required temperature and is accurate to within one degree.

Electric pond heaters (not to be confused with the small floating models designed to keep a small area of a garden pond ice-free) consist of an element contained within a stainless steel chamber through which water is pumped. The digital stat is mounted on top of the unit, which means it cannot monitor the whole pond, only the water passing through; this makes electric heating less controllable. These heaters are rated in kilowatts, and, as a rule of thumb, 1KW is required for every 1,000 gallons.

To keep down costs, some Koi keepers run an electric heater only during the night, on off-peak electricity. This is really defeating the object of the exercise, which is to iron out temperature fluctuations, but if the choice is between this option and no heating at all then it is worth considering. Good insulation (a cover) will prevent the temperature dropping back too fast on a winter's day.

In pond heating there should be no grey areas – either the water is brought to a temperature where the Koi can feed uninterruptedly, or it is allowed to fall below 50 deg F, so that the Koi slow down and cease feeding. Some hobbyists, even those with heating, still like to give their fish a natural 'winter' of a couple of months' duration, reckoning that this extends the lifespan of the Koi and allows for more natural development. It is dangerous to hold the water temperature around 50 deg F – if the fish are not being fed, they will still be expending energy as they swim around, while, if food is offered, their metabolism will be only marginally able to cope with digestion.

WATER PURIFIERS

Any 'serious' modern Koi pond should incorporate some form of purifier through which all mains water (for top-ups and water changes) first has to pass. It is a fallacy that because water is fit for human consumption – debatable! – it will necessarily be suitable for fish. Or, for that matter, suitable for a healthy growth of filter bacteria, which can be wiped out by unscreened water changes.

The commonest additives to mains tap-water are chlorine and the more persistent chloramine, both of which are toxic. But it does not end there. Old iron mains pipework can lead to metal contamination; the chemical aluminium sulphate, used to 'polish' water at the treatment works, has been known to wipe out ponds; and lead, cadmium, copper and zinc have all been identified in mains water. Even at supposedly 'safe' trace concentrations, metals can debilitate fish, inhibit their growth and lay them open to attack by pathogens.

The level of contaminants in mains water varies geographically and seasonally; at times of highest demand, chlorine and chloramine levels are at their highest, while pyrethrin is commonly used in summer to kill crustaceans (freshwater shrimps). Although prior warnings are sometimes issued by the water company, these cannot be guaranteed.

The main function of the basic purifier, which contains granules of activated carbon, is to remove chlorine. Most models will incorporate a mechanical filter prior to the main module, after which additional cartridges remove other contaminants. But beware of what you are buying – some, far from taking out metals, actually put them into the pond. Also be sceptical of claims about the life of the cartridges – this should not relate to pond gallonage alone, but to the concentration of contaminants. For example, in a 'clean' area, a pre-filter cartridge will last for months, while in areas where the iron mains pipework is old and flaking the same cartridge can block in days. The cost of regular replacement can be high, but consider how the fish would feel if all that material were not intercepted at source!

Flow-rate through a typical purifier is not high, and so for convenience top-up water should be controlled by a simple cistern ballcock that will shut off the mains supply when the required level is reached (this device will also automatically compensate for evaporation loss in hot weather). In a gravity-fed filter with a vortex settler it is best to site the inflow so as to feed into a subsequent passive settlement chamber, as otherwise the vortex action will be interfered with.

What A Koi Pond Must Accomplish

To comply with water company bylaws, the tap feeding the purifier from the mains should be of a type that prevents back-syphoning and possible contamination of the drinking water supply. All modern outside taps should comply, but it is worth checking to avoid a possible fine.

POND SHAPE

The most efficient shape to achieve good water circulation is a circular pond with vertical walls, and a floor tapering to a central take-off point. This acts as its own primary settlement chamber, and, as long as the surfaces are smooth and the return water from the filter is fed in tangentially, solids will slowly spin down to the bottom drain.

The use of an 'airdome' type of bottom drain-cover helps this process along, as the rising bubbles set up currents conducive to drawing particles along the pond floor to the drain and thence to the filter.

Oval ponds are almost as good as circular ones in promoting mechanical cleanliness; it is square or rectangular designs that can hit problems, as nothing slows water quicker than meeting a wall head-on. To overcome this, such ponds should incorporate 'faired' corners, so that instead of there being a harsh right angle where any two walls meet, the junction is rounded off. There are aspects of filtration where it is a positive advantage to slow water velocity, and these are dealt with elsewhere in the book.

The fussier the pond shape, the less likely it is to offer acceptable water circulation. A good example of what not to emulate is seen in some pre-formed goldfish ponds with tortuous contours. Complex shapes can be properly filtered, but only by installing more equipment than a comparably-sized, conventionally shaped pond would need – and, of course, volume is sacrificed to appearance. Apparently harsh contours can easily be disguised or softened later on, at the landscaping stage, by means of imaginatively placed rockwork or overhanging plants. If your pond is 'formal' (i.e. of a shape which makes no pretence to emulate Nature), clean lines are a virtue, and a bonus is that much better use of available space can be made for adjacent filtration.

Finally, while a pond's prime function is to give a good year-round home to Koi, it should also be designed to appeal to the eye. After all, it is going to be a very prominent feature of your garden for years to come! A common fault is to spend the full budget on the basic structure, leaving little or nothing saved for the finishing touches. Hence exposed blockwork is left unrendered so that the pond resembles a half-buried outbuilding, or perhaps the rockery/waterfall is made, not of the appropriate stone, but of spoil from the excavation peppered with random chunks of brick and concrete. It is amazing that even accomplished amateur pond-builders can let this happen in their eagerness to complete the project.

Removal of spoil should be costed into your plans from the start. I have seen gardens ruined as the owners attempted to distribute barren subsoil around the flowerbeds, or disguise the waste material as a totally inappropriate raised feature which they would otherwise never have contemplated.

Other projects are ruined by unburied electric cables (illegal as well as unsightly), poorly thought-out pipe runs, or filter housings that do not come up to the standard of finish of the main pond. The difference between an accomplished-looking pond and one which is merely a large filtered outdoor holding tank is down not so much to budgetary considerations as to patience and care taken over the finishing touches.

8 *FILTRATION*

Koi keeping is still a 'young' hobby in world terms. Looking back over the 30 or so years since Nishikigoi were first exported from Japan in numbers, it is amazing the progress that has been made in respect of understanding them and responding to their needs. The learning curve has not been smooth, however – and nowhere is this more apparent than in the field of filtration.

We began at base with the hopeful notion that Koi could be kept alive with no filtration at all – a misconception based on our earlier experiences with goldfish, and vague theories that a heavily-planted pond with perhaps a fountain and/or cascade to circulate the water would somehow achieve a natural balance. Koi placed in such ponds quickly died. This was a painful and expensive experience, fostering the notion that they were 'impossible' to keep.

THE UNDERGRAVEL AGE

Phase two was the recognition that some form of filtration was necessary to combat 'dirty' water. At this time (the early 1970s) there was little information forthcoming from the Japanese, and so we turned to the aquarium hobby for inspiration. The most popular filter then – still in universal use today – was the air-driven undergravel. A simple concept, this relies on a gravel

substrate supported on a perforated grid covering the tank base. Connected to this grid is an airlift tube down which is fed an airstone powered by a diaphragm airpump. As the bubbles rise in the tube before exiting back into the aquarium they entrain with them water, which has to be drawn down through the gravel bed. Today's undergravels accomplish the same thing more effectively by replacing the airlift with a powerhead attached to the top of the tube. This device is basically a small water pump, often with an aeration device on the return port.

Early Koi keepers thought that a scaled-up version of the pump-driven undergravel filter would serve their needs, and to a degree it did. Typically, a raised section of the pond representing a third or more of the surface area would be walled off below water level to accommodate a bed of pea gravel 9-12 inches deep. Beneath this gravel lay a drilled grid of domestic waste pipe which acted as the pond equivalent of the aquarium undergravel plate. Attached to the central meeting point of this pipe network, a submersible sump pump drew 'dirty' water down through the filter medium and returned 'clean' water to the pond via a waterfall or venturi.

Pond undergravels certainly delivered the promise of clear water, for dirt particles would be taken out of suspension and down into the gravel bed. Their real benefit,

Filtration

though, had nothing to do with water clarity but shifted into the realm of biological filtration, which is explained fully elsewhere in this chapter. It was enough for early Koi keepers that their home-made filters kept fish alive. But just as most of us are happy enough to start our cars with only a hazy concept of the principles of the internal combustion engine, so not much thought was given to why undergravels performed the way they did.

If these filters apparently worked so well, why are they no longer popular? The main reason is that sooner or later they clog up with solids and need cleaning. Washing a few handfuls of aquarium gravel is a minor chore, but in ponds we are talking tons of the stuff and backbreaking hours, or even days, to clean it. During this time the filter is inoperative, water quality deteriorates, and the cleaning process itself destroys most of the beneficial bacteria that have built up in the gravel bed. Other drawbacks are:

1) If the pump fails, it is very difficult to access and replace.
2) As dirt accumulates in the gravel, water circulation through it takes the line of least resistance – large areas of the medium then stagnate.
3) Ironically, as progressive blockage takes place, the filter becomes a more efficient solids-remover – and the Koi keeper is lulled into a false sense of security because the water remains clear, even though it is not being rid of its full complement of toxins.
4) Koi, being great diggers, can root around in the gravel bed and disturb sediment.

Commercial versions of the undergravel filter for ponds are still available, but it is significant that these are sold with the option of a maintenance contract so that, when they block, someone else gets to do the dirty work!

THE FIRST GRAVITY-FED FILTER

The next breakthrough for the hobby was the development of the external, chambered gravity-fed filter. Early versions were so limited in what they could accomplish that their performance compared only superficially with that of today's sophisticated systems. This is why they are now a part of Koi keeping history – but it must be remembered that when they first appeared they were at the cutting edge of current knowledge, and everything that has emerged since is based on refinements of these prototypes.

A glass fibre bayed gravity-fed filter with a lid and exit pipework to drain each chamber from its hopper-shaped base. Photo: Nick Fletcher.

All gravity-fed filters rely on the fact that water always finds its own level. To illustrate the principle, imagine a filled aquarium with a central partition that has one small hole drilled through it. If a cup of water is baled out from one side the level there will obviously fall, but will quickly equalise with the other side of the partition as water flows through the hole from the side that has not been baled. If a small pump is now sited to draw water from one compartment and return it to the other, there will be a constant flow through the partition and, providing the pump is not so powerful as to outstrip water transference through the hole, levels will remain constant.

If we now imagine that one side of the tank is the pond and the other the filter, we see how the gravity-fed principle operates. Instead of the simple hole through the partition, there is connecting pipework of a diameter compatible with the pump's flow rate.

The first gravity-fed filters were really only an attempt to utilise the undergravel principle in a more accessible way. The medium – gravel – was the same, and was expected to perform mechanical and biological functions simultaneously. As we now know, biofilters work effectively only if solids are removed before the water reaches these chambers.

There are two flow patterns employed in chambered filters to this day – upflow and downflow. The directional change is effected by transfer ports which determine whether water exits the top or the bottom of each chamber on its journey to the next, and hence the route it takes through the media. The early bayed filter units would have a perforated but rigid support grid suspended a few inches above the floor of each chamber to take the considerable weight of the gravel. In upflow mode, water flows into the base of the chamber, up through the medium and exits to the next stage. This tends to settle out larger solids in the void, but unless there is a way of draining this space beneath the grid it quickly fills with silt.

Downflow mode is self-explanatory – water enters high in the chamber and flows down through the medium. With gravel, this soon leads to compaction and all the problems associated with restricted flow pattern.

EARLY SETTLEMENT

It was soon realised that the solids loading on a biological filter could be reduced by turning over the first chamber to settlement – a principle well known to sewage engineers. Initial reluctance to do so stemmed from a feeling that an 'empty' chamber was somehow a waste of space, whereas in fact settlement is probably the most important filtration stage of all.

There are two types of settlement, termed 'active' and 'passive'. The definitions indicate the complexity of the process, passive settlement being the simpler but the less efficient. How does the process work? If water is being pulled from the pond into the filter through a 4-inch diameter pipe and suddenly enters an empty chamber, its flow velocity is immediately reduced dramatically. This, in itself, is enough to encourage larger, denser particles to fall to the chamber base, and, as the water exits to the next stage via a transfer port (i.e. at surface level), this dirt is trapped and can later be removed, either by vacuuming or by opening a drain-cock to waste.

The best passive settlement chambers were (and still are) large and deep, with steeply benched bases. If a U-bend is fitted to the pipe in the floor of the chamber so that the flow is directed back against the far wall, efficiency is greatly improved.

In the early 1980s, filter brushes came into general use among the world's Koi keepers and for a while they were viewed as the complete alternative to gravel. Unfortunately,

Filtration

Vortex chambers on firm, level standing. Note slide valves to isolate feed from pond, and on drainage pipework.

Photo: Nick Fletcher.

like gravel, they were initially expected to perform mechanically and biologically in the same chamber. And, although it took longer for them to block, they still allowed unwanted solids to penetrate deep into a filtration system.

However, incorporating just two or three rows of closely-enmeshed brushes into a passive settlement chamber at the point where water exits to the next stage is a useful way of trapping finer suspended solids and particles of blanketweed, which have neutral buoyancy.

Active settlement can be defined as solids-removal by dynamic means, where flow patterns are engineered to remove the dirt more efficiently. An ordinary passive chamber can be converted to active mode merely by incorporating a series of baffles which force the water to take a longer route through it, with several directional changes along the way.

But even this technique has been superseded by the arrival of vortex settlement chambers – after early incredulity, these are now an essential requirement for all modern Koi pond installations. A gravity-fed vortex is basically a vertical-sided cylindrical module, tapering into a cone for its lower third to a solids collection hopper. Pond water is drawn in low down and tangentially – in other words, the entry pipe is angled so as to impart a slow spin to the water. Two forces now come into play to separate out solids – centrifugal and centripetal.

The larger particles are spun centrifugally to come into contact with the smooth inside surface of the cylinder. The interface of water with the vortex wall is known as the 'boundary layer', down which the solids slowly spiral to the hopper collection/drain point. Meanwhile, the finer solids are drawn by centripetal force into a slowly spinning central column of water and gradually gravitate to the same hopper. Largely solids-free water then exits to the next chamber from a point high up the wall. Early vortex designs had an exit pipe coming into the module, ending with an upward-facing U-bend just below surface level. But any unnecessary obstructions to the spiralling motion of the water reduce efficiency, and now vortexes tend to have an exit point that does not intrude into the chamber.

If one vortex is efficient, two fed in parallel are more than doubly so, and such a layout eliminates virtually all solids prior to the biological stages. Alternatively, a traditional 'box' settlement chamber can precede a vortex to reduce the loading of heavier solids.

NEW MEDIA, NEW THINKING

In the mid-1980s, a material known as Japanese matting began to be used by Koi keepers as a purely biological filter medium. The genuine article (there are many cheaper imitations) is a blue polyester material in sheets 3cm (approx. 1 in) thick, but for pond application it is formed into cartridges. The medium has several ideal properties: it is virtually everlasting, it provides a huge surface area for nitrifying bacteria, it is light yet holds its shape well in cartridge form, and it is easy to clean.

Modern filter media are light and efficient. Here are reticulated foam and matting cartridges and net bags of plastic biomedia for biological water treatment. Photo: Nick Fletcher.

Given good pre-settlement, such cartridges are suited to all biological chambers of traditional bayed gravity filters, but they also suggest a means of simplifying the whole filtration process while improving settlement at every stage. A cartridge can rest on a shallow ledge around the wall of a vortex chamber with no other means of support, doing away with the need for the grid associated with heavier media. So it is now possible to connect a series of vortexes together with 'S'-shaped pipework. The first is left free of media, while in the top of subsequent chambers a circular matting cartridge is fitted to intercept upflowing water. Every chamber after the primary vortex now has a dual settlement/biological role, and each has its own drain to waste.

PUMP-FED FILTRATION IN PONDS

The basic difference between gravity and pump-fed filter systems is that in the former the pump is pulling water through the filter, while in the latter it is delivering it to the filter direct from the pond – the first, rather than the last, stage.

Koi purists tend to decry pump-fed filtration on several counts:

1) The submersible pump within the pond shreds larger solids into fine particles which are difficult to settle out.
2) As water returns to the pond by gravity, it is not possible to incorporate a venturi aeration device.
3) The pump, with its cable and delivery hose, is an unsightly presence in the pond.
4) The delivery pipework is rarely more than $1^{1}/_{2}$ ins in diameter, and the resulting high entry velocity into the filter is not conducive to good settlement.
5) The filters are perceived as being too small to cope with the large amounts of solids generated within a Koi pond.

However, the majority of pondkeepers with

Koi still use pump-fed external filters – they are easy to install on ponds that would otherwise have no filtration at all, they do not require connection with a bottom drain or midwater inlet and, because they are at ground level, no excavation is needed to install them.

Filters of this type became popular for general garden-pond use around 16 years ago, with the adoption of open-cell foam as the main medium. In their simplest original form (still in production by several companies), they consist of a header tank derivative into which water is pumped via a spraybar over three sheets of progressively finer-grade foam, then through an open-void plastic biological medium before return to the pond. Upflow versions minus the spraybar soon followed – the foam being prevented from rising in the chamber by one or more trays of gravel weighting it down. These filters can be buried partially in-ground, level with the exit pipe.

The first sheet of foam in contact with the dirty water traps most of the solids and is periodically removed for rinsing. The other sheets act both mechanically and biologically. As the foam progressively blocks, the tiny channels through it narrow to give a better degree of mechanical filtration, but this property is lost at the next clean. Partly for this reason, and partly to minimise the loss of too many filter bacteria, it is recommended that the foam sheets be washed in rotation – and not too vigorously – in pondwater.

It was not long before foam cartridges mounted on perforated manifolds were introduced to pump-fed external filters as a refinement on the sheet material. In these, water is first pumped through rows of removeable brushes, to strain out large particles, then passes by gravity through the cartridges into a separate chamber beneath containing the open-void plastic biomedia. As the only connection between the two

A pump-fed biofilter with foam cartridges, brushes and plastic media, is one alternative to gravity-fed filtration.   Photo: Nick Fletcher.

chambers is via the manifolds, every drop of water has to be drawn through the cartridges en route back to the pond. Cleaning consists of a) periodically rinsing the brushes and b) gentle washing of the cartridges in rotation.

A gravity-fed version of this type of filter, aimed primarily at Koi ponds, is still very popular for smaller systems.

In order for pumped filtration to work properly, the pump must be of the solids-handling type and situated at the deepest part of the pond. Koi droppings can be 8-10mm in diameter, and ordinary submersible fountain pumps with their fine strainers to prevent impeller blockage would also stop solids entering the filter.

For years, many small-scale Koi keepers who did not mind a fairly intensive maintenance regime used the largest possible external box filters on their ponds with some success. The pump would not draw in solids from a wide area around it, and so regular manual or powered vacuuming would be necessary to augment this rather basic filtration. Then manufacturers developed modular filters – using brushes, foam cartridges and biomedia, but configuring the inner structure to give integral and drainable settlement. Predictably, the filter body changed from being box-shaped to resembling the by-now familiar vortex chamber, and gravity-fed as well as pump-fed options emerged.

The breakthrough came with the development of the pumped vortex – this meant that these very compact filters could benefit from prior solids-removal. The main objection to pumping into a vortex – excessive water velocity – was solved by stepping up the narrow-bore pump delivery hose to a wide-bore pipe before entry into the chamber.

TRICKLE FILTRATION

Nitrifying bacteria are aerobic – they function in the presence of oxygen, which is not always at ideal concentrations in a fully submerged filter bed. However, if instead of the medium being underwater it is kept constantly damp by a stream of water passing over and through it, the air/water interface provides abundant oxygen, and the bacteria flourish. Trickle filtration makes use of this principle, and as an add-on to a more conventional filter it enables higher fish stocking levels than would otherwise be possible.

To see where the idea originates, look no farther than the local sewage farm, and the circular beds of clinker over which a rotating spraybar delivers liquid effluent.

Many Koi keepers make their own trickle towers from cylinders of plastic or fibreglass, built into which are perforated media support trays. Commercial modules are available, too. Both must be the final stage of filtration, and

both must be pump-fed with solids-free water. For this reason they are really only suited to gravity-fed systems, and another possible drawback is that they must be sited close to the pond.

The bacteria are in such an ideal environment that their population turnover is huge, and trickle filters can quickly accumulate 'floc', waste material comprising of billions of sloughed dead microbes. If these find their way back into the pond they can interfere with water clarity, so the best trickle filters are designed in such a way that floc collects in a drainable hopper at the base of the unit.

BOTTOM DRAINS

Bottom drains are nowadays the favoured means of conveying pond water constantly to a gravity filter, but not so long ago they served a completely different purpose. The first BDs were merely purge drains,

The builder of this small pond has left an 'escape step' which will be dug out last. Note the flat roof bottom drain, an economy measure that may lead to maintenance problems at a later stage.
Photo: Nick Fletcher.

Filtration

Standard 10-inch bottom drain.

Photo: Nick Fletcher.

Airdome bottom drain.

Photo: Nick Fletcher.

connected to 'O' ring standpipes in discharge chambers plumbed into the domestic sewage system. These drains were 'pulled', once or twice a day, to rid the pond of ammonia-laden water that had collected on the bottom. It was left to a midwater inlet through the pond wall to feed the filter, so reducing the mechanical burden placed upon it. Occasionally the bottom drain would be valved to give the option of intermittent filter feed, but that was as far as it went. Before efficient settlement arrived, this arrangement was probably a good compromise; the downside was that the 'heavy' water laden with nitrogenous waste stayed around in the pond for hours before being flushed away.

The midwater inlet had to be fitted with a grille to stop smaller fish vanishing into the filter, and the mesh needed frequent cleaning if the filter was not to be starved of flow. Very few solids found their way into the sump of the bottom drain until standpipe pulling time, when the domed cover of the BD would draw them in from all around its perimeter.

We probably have the advent of water

metering to thank for putting an end to the 'pull and purge' way of going about things, which threw away far more water than current filtration systems. All that happens now is that the bottom drain connects directly to the filter via wide-bore (usually four-inch) pipework and operates constantly to feed the first, settlement, stage.

Two basic types of bottom drain are available, for installation into either liner or concrete ponds. In the former there is an additional flange which makes a watertight seal, sandwiching the liner where the circular hole is cut to access the drain pipework. Common to both types is a base sump with rim installed flush to the pond floor, a solvent-weld pipe-fitting and a circular domed cover which push-fits into the sump to leave an adjustable perimeter gap. The narrower this gap is, the greater the 'pulling power' of the drain – but the greater, too, the likelihood of blockage. As you can imagine, clearing blanketweed from this assembly is a major headache, so some manufacturers now produce a hinged dome cover which can be flipped up to allow access to the sump.

A variation on the standard bottom drain is one incorporating an airdome. This has several benefits: it aerates the pond water without interfering too much with the viewing of Koi, and the current that is set up by the rising stream of bubbles draws in bottom debris which might otherwise be outside the drain's catchment area. The dome is a flat rubberised membrane with minute perforations, and, when air is pumped beneath it under pressure, it takes on a convex shape and each perforation expands enough to release fine bubbles. The original design necessitated an airline being run through the drain pipework and out to the pump, but later models have got around this problem with an external connection.

The number of bottom drains in a pond is dependent on the area of its base, the normal rule of thumb being to site them six feet apart (measured from the centre of the dome). Each drain must have its own separate pipework – if attempts are made to connect them in series, only one will pull water properly and the other will be wasted.

It used to be thought that, in order to be effective, the base of the pond around each bottom drain had to be 'dished', to enable solids to roll down into the catchment area. In practice this concept works only if the incline is 60 degrees or more. Commercial bayed filter chambers are sloped this steeply towards the base so that solids to be discharged to waste will collect where they are meant to, in the hopper. Dished pond floors would perhaps be more viable if Koi droppings were not sausage-shaped.

As long as the pond is rendered smoothly, the movement of Koi, especially large ones, will constantly stir up bottom sediment. If the flow dynamics encourage no dead spots, all debris will sooner or later come within the pulling catchment of one or other drain and be transferred to the settlement chamber.

VEGETABLE FILTERS

All photosynthesising plants containing chlorophyll, from simple single-celled algae upwards, require additional nutrients. These are absorbed from their immediate environment, and aquatic or semi-aquatic plants are typically greedy consumers of two by-products of biological filtration: nitrates and phosphates. These same substances are essential for algal growth – so if higher plant life is introduced into a Koi pond it will compete with the nuisance algae that cause green water or proliferate as blanketweed.

The problem is that Koi, given the opportunity, are avid plant browsers. So it is essential that a vegetable filter is installed somewhere in the system where the fishes cannot snack on the tender leaves. The simplest solution in bayed external filters used to be to push cuttings of watercress into the Canterbury spar bed of one of the biological chambers. Here it would quickly root and spread, and if kept regularly trimmed so as not to flower and seed it would absorb quantities of nitrates.

Handy tip: Thread plastic biomedia on string. It makes removal of the 'necklace' much easier than taking out individual pieces.

Photo: Nick Fletcher.

Disadvantages were that the roots bound into the gravel and compacted it – the chamber also had to be lidless for light to reach the plants, and it was rare for such a bed to be large enough to make a significant impact.

A better solution is to have a vegetable filter installed between the other filtration stages and the point where water returns to the pond. A gravel substrate is there purely for the plants to root into, and plays no part in biological filtration. A laminar flow of nitrate- and phosphate-laden water passes the plants – whose leaves, if closely enough knit, will act in the same way as baffles in a settlement chamber, intercepting any fine suspended particles which the filter proper may have missed.

As a vegetable filter like this is often the Koi keeper's only concession to plants, it can be designed as an ornamental subsidiary pool with a floor contoured to accept marginal reeds and rushes around the perimeter and deeper-rooted aquatics towards the pool's centre. Obviously vegetable filtration in temperate climates is viable only during the warmer months, but that happens to be when the nitrate loading is at its greatest.

Another way of stripping nitrates is to plant watercress in a stream return to the pond. To increase the time during which water is in contact with the plants, concrete baffles can be built into the structure to create a meander – these baffles will also help prevent the plants being uprooted and washed into the pond.

The bigger a vegetable filter, the more effective it will be – some Koi keepers build them with a surface area equal to that of the pond itself.

SAND PRESSURE FILTERS

These are sometimes used as the final stage of a gravity system to 'polish' the water of fine particles. Water is pumped into a pressurised container and through a fine sand medium –

these filters were designed for swimming pool use. However, unless regularly back-washed through a multi-port valve, they can clog. If a system is properly designed there should really be no need for sand filters, although some Koi keepers substitute a sintered glass medium for the original contents; nitrifying bacteria will establish on this, while in the tiny 'blind' pores nitrates will be reduced to free nitrogen.

ULTRA-VIOLET UNITS

Ultra-violet treatment of ponds is an important tool in Koi keeping, one that has been borrowed and adapted from the aquarium hobby to serve a rather different purpose in larger bodies of water.

Aquarium UVs are known as 'sterilisers', their function being to expose pathogenic bacteria and protozoans to a fatal dose of ultra-violet light. This is done by recirculating the tank's contents several times an hour through a contact chamber surrounding a silica quartz tube that houses the UV lamp. The tube prevents direct contact between the water and the light source but still allows the UV rays to pass through it – with ordinary glass this does not happen.

Sterilising efficiency is dependent on the contact time between the water and the lamp, lamp wattage, dimensions of the contact chamber (determining how close the pathogens pass by the UV radiation) and the recirculation rate. Pathogens are killed as they pass the light source, so an aquarium UV will reduce, though rarely eliminate, populations of harmful bacteria.

This is not the prime function of today's pond UVs, which are installed to eradicate 'green water' – the algal bloom caused when a nutrient-laden pond is exposed to warmth and light. Individual algal cells are tiny enough to pass through most filter media and recirculate, but what the UV lamp does is to interfere with their internal structure so

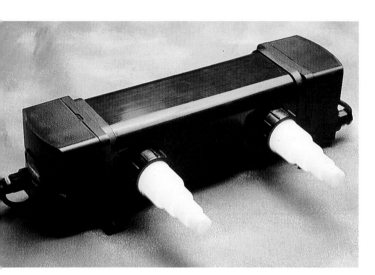

A compact UVC (ultra-violet clarifier) with reducing hosetails to take a variety of pipework or hose diameters. Its sole function is to promote clumping of single-celled greenwater algae, which are then mechanically removed by filtration.

Photo: Nick Fletcher.

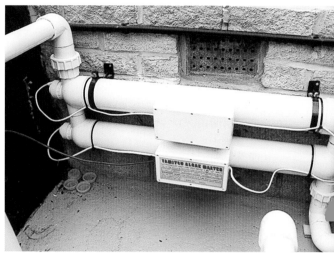

A powerful UV unit mounted in the dry pumping chamber of a well-thought-out pond. Note ventilating air brick.

Photo: Nick Fletcher.

that the cells flocculate, or clump together. These clumps can then be intercepted by the mechanical filter media, resulting in a noticeable improvement in water clarity within days. UV treatment is far preferable to algicidal chemicals, which inevitably have some effect on higher plants, if only to retard their growth.

There was some initial resistance to the first commercially available pond UVs because it was felt they might harm filter bacteria. This assumption was based on the false premise that nitrifiers were motile, rather than sessile. But *Nitrosomonas* and *Nitrobacter* colonise filter media, or the pond walls, and stay put, where the UV has no effect on them. Add to this the relatively slow recirculation rate of pond – as opposed to aquarium – filters (once every couple of hours being the norm), and it can be seen that such fears were groundless.

Modern pond UVs do not have to be very powerful to clear green water. In a Koi pond

of reasonable depth, where the water is not exposed to direct sunlight all day, 10 watts per 1,000 gallons will do the job. Yet the myth persists that higher wattages will kill pathogens, and so large banks of UV are still to be seen on quite modestly-sized systems. It is debatable whether these justify the higher running costs involved, not only through power consumption but from regular lamp replacement. At relatively slow pond turnover rate, only a tiny percentage of the total water volume is in contact with the lamp at any one time, and only the organisms passing the lamp will be knocked out.

In quarantine facilities the situation is rather different. Here, a smaller body of water is being recirculated more frequently and a UV will act as it would on an aquarium, killing significant numbers of pathogens on each pass through the unit.

In pump-fed filter systems the UV must be the first piece of equipment after the pump, so that treatment precedes filtration. In gravity-fed systems, filtered water is pumped through the UV prior to returning to the pond. In working situations it makes little difference to the unit's efficiency whether the UV is handling filtered or unfiltered water, providing that which passes the quartz tube is not so turbid as to interfere with light penetration.

A UV may not need to be run all year, in which case the lamp(s) can simply be switched off and water left to flow through the chamber. Inoperative UVs should be removed if not continuously pump-fed, however, or ice may form within, expand, and crack the quartz or even the outer casing.

FILTER PUMPS

Ordinary submersible pond pumps are no use for feeding pumped filters, as they cannot pass solids through the impeller. The only option used to be upright 'sump pumps'. But while these handled dirt effectively they were not designed for continuous running, so the motor had a limited lifespan. They also tended towards high power consumption. The modern crop of submersibles, with or without float switches, are a very mixed bunch in terms of cost, performance and reliability. Check the period of the guarantee, and exactly what it covers; whether the quoted performance is at zero head and, if so, how quickly it drops off when water has to be pumped to any height. And note the power rating. By law, this has to be displayed on the pump by the manufacturer. Otherwise you could buy an apparently cheap powerhouse which costs a fortune to run.

Submersibles fall into two main categories, direct and induction (magnetic) drive. In the former, the drive shaft and its impeller run from the pump chamber to the motor through waterproof seals which may eventually fail. Magnetic drive pumps may seem the more attractive option for that reason alone, as there is no shaft, the two

Submersible solids-handling pumps are the only option for non-gravity-fed filter systems.

Photo: Nick Fletcher.

components of the pump, motor and impeller, being in entirely separate compartments. But they tend to be relatively expensive, and are not as effective as direct drive models at pumping water to a head.

Some submersibles will actually double as external pumps if a non-return valve is fitted between the remote in-pond strainer and the connecting suction hose. But this is not an application recommended for Koi ponds.

Low-voltage submersible pumps that step down the mains supply to 12 or 24 volts through a transformer are fine for ordinary garden pond use, where they give great peace of mind. Their usefulness in Koi ponds is restricted to very small or quarantine systems, and then only in the final wet chamber of a gravity filter, where solids-handling is not an issue.

Gravity-fed filters are usually powered by an external swimming pool-type pump, housed (ideally below water level) in a dry

Plenty of elbow room here. Note ball valves which can isolate all pipework to surface pump, which serves filter, UV and surface skimmer.

Photo: Nick Fletcher.

but ventilated chamber. These same pumps can be the power unit for vacuuming kits. As with submersibles, a low purchase price can blind the user to ongoing operating costs, so perhaps the best buy is one of those designed specifically for Koi pond use. You pay more initially, but the difference becomes apparent on receipt of the first electricity bill.

The other external pump worth a mention is the central heating circulator. This is inexpensive on all counts, usually offers three speed settings, and can give years of trouble-free service – this despite virtually every guarantee exclusion clause being violated in a typical outdoor pond situation. Cast-iron-bodied CHCs must never be used if salt and other chemicals that react with it are introduced to the pond water, otherwise there is a real danger of metal contamination. Pump bodies of non-corroding phosphor bronze raise the price of CHCs, and a cheaper option might be to fit a readily available conversion kit in place of the standard cast-iron impeller housing. To give of their best, central heating circulators must handle only clean water – even slight impeller congestion will knock output right back. Isolating valves should be fitted either side of the pump to make it easily removable for maintenance, but even so it can be a tedious business dismantling and reassembling the pump body with Allen keys to access the impeller.

AERATION

Warm humid nights, combined with low atmospheric pressure, can cause the oxygen levels in pondwater to fall to the point where the Koi's gills cannot extract enough of the life-giving gas, and the fish suffocate – usually the largest dying first.

Koi require an absolute minimum of 3-5 milligrams per litre of oxygen, easy enough to maintain except that the dissolved oxygen (DO) content of fresh water is very much temperature-dependent. Saturation point can vary from over 12mg/litre at 5C (41F) to a mere 7.5mg/litre at 30 C (86F). Unfortunately, supply is in inverse ratio to demand – the warmer the water, the more oxygen the fishes will need. Their requirement falls with the approach of winter, by which time oxygen is once more plentiful.

Aerobic filter bacteria are the other major consumers of oxygen and need a constant supply to carry out the nitrification process. Insufficient DO can lead directly to fish deaths and, more insidiously, adversely affect water quality. The way to overcome the deficiency is by means of aeration.

Bubbling air into the pond and filter is not the complete answer, as gas transfer from coarse bubbles is minimal. With ordinary airstones the stream of bubbles breaking on the surface creates turbulence, and this alone improves the air-water interface. Fine bubbles take the longest to rise through the water and

Filtration

improve gaseous exchange. The most efficient aeration device is the Japanese 'Micala', which shears an air-water mix into bubbles only a few microns in diameter and discharges them horizontally, increasing their dwell time in the pond.

Waterfalls, besides being decorative, are useful tools in oxygenating a Koi pond. A thin sheet of water exposed to the air will absorb oxygen from it, and a splash return will give added turbulence. Fountains are almost as good, but they are not a common feature of Koi ponds as they interfere with the viewing of the fishes.

This 'natural' aeration should be supplemented by other means of supplying oxygen to pond and filter. This is done either by entraining air in the return from a gravity-fed system, via a venturi, or by directing a generated source of air through various diffusing devices. For this, we need a reliable pump.

The Hi-Blow, with output measured in litres per minute, was for years the first choice for all but the smallest pond. Strangely, this pump has never been specified as suitable for pond use by the manufacturers, and diaphragm replacements can be costly. Other pond-dedicated pumps are now available, including a type that does away with the traditional diaphragm in favour of an electrically-powered 'engine'.

All airpumps must be sited indoors, or in a ventilated, weatherproof chamber where the heat they generate can disperse. Instead of running individual airlines from the supplied manifold it will extend the life of diaphragm pumps and improve their output if a 'ring main' is built from plastic piping. This reduces back pressure by creating a reservoir of air from which airlines can be bled off – silicone tubing is more expensive than ordinary PVC but remains flexible at low temperatures and does not degrade in sunlight.

The simplest diffuser of all is the ball airstone, which generates fairly coarse bubbles. Diffusers of limewood give a finer stream, but block more quickly. Do not place airstones too deep in the pond or they will stir up sediment. If more than one is running off the same ring main, the usual scenario, you may have to experiment with the lengths of airline in the water to maximise performance; air takes the easiest route, and a mere couple of inches could make the difference between a healthy crop of bubbles and nothing at all.

Airstones in the filter generate oxygen for the bacteria and create the turbulence that ensures inflowing water reaches all areas of the media, with no dead spots. In multi-chambered filters something approaching 60 per cent of the nitrification is said to occur in

Hi-Blow airpumps are still the most popular aeration tool in most Koi ponds.

Photo: Nick Fletcher.

the first biological bay, 30 per cent in the second and only 10 per cent in the third. One or more airstones in each chamber (with the exception of settlement) will ensure an adequate oxygen supply to all population levels of bacteria. If Japanese matting is the biological medium, airstones are simply dropped down through the cartridges; with denser media they rest on top. They should not be placed in transfer ports, where an airlift effect could impede flow. The ports should be kept media-free for the same reason.

One stage up from airstones are weighted diffusers. In these, air is forced through a material resembling horticultural porous pipe, guaranteed non-toxic to fishes. Ring diffusers, in diameters to suit all applications, require less pressure than airstones to work effectively. But they do need regular cleaning, as otherwise the fine pores will eventually block with debris. The same applies to rod diffusers, which can be laid across a filter bay to intercept the throughflow with a curtain of bubbles.

Airdomes have already been mentioned in the context of bottom drains, but free-standing weighted domes are also available to give finely diffused aeration in ponds and filters. It is advisable to tie a cord to these if they are to be used at any depth – the only other means of attachment is the airline itself, which can easily pull free.

Fixed spraybars have limited application in Koi pond filtration, as their use is largely confined to external single-chamber pump-fed filters. But rotating on a bearing to feed a trickle tower – the last stage of a system – spraybars restore oxygen to water that would otherwise be depleted of it through the action of the bacteria in the biological chambers.

Venturi devices perform the same service at the point where water is being pumped directly back into the pond from a gravity-fed system. They are inexpensive to buy or make, working on the principle that if a pipe with water travelling through it is restricted at some point, a pressure drop will occur. If the pipe is teed off to above water level just before this restriction, air is drawn down, entrains with the water and exits as a stream of bubbles.

A deep-water venturi is preferable to one operating just sub-surface. Not only do the bubbles have maximum contact time, but the considerable current generated can be directed to circulate water in the pond itself and eliminate dead spots. Working this way, the venturi supplements other sub-surface returns which together create currents that encourage the pond to act as its own giant primary settlement chamber and direct solids to the bottom drain(s).

Home-made venturis of standard plumbing components can generate considerable back-pressure on the pump and delivery pipework, but sophisticated commercial improvements to the basic design now overcome this problem to a large degree.

On gravity-fed systems the venturi operates off the filter pump, usually after UV treatment. In pump-fed systems a separate, dedicated submersible pump with its own venturi attachment is the option, but this entails dirty bottom water being moved around the pond. It is still a useful option to call on in emergencies where, for example, inexpert medication or a sudden algal bloom has brought about a crash in dissolved oxygen levels.

HOME-MADE FILTER SYSTEMS

A Koi pond and its filter should be seen as a single entity, the two main elements of which work in harmony to provide our fishes with the best possible living conditions. Whether we buy a commercial filter or make our own, we still have to make provision at planning stage for bottom drains and pipework,

Transfer ports being cast in reinforced cement, using simple framework formers.
Photo: Nick Fletcher.

Bayed blockwork filter chamber under construction. Transfer ports are cast in concrete with Rein fibre reinforcement.

Photo: Nick Fletcher.

A pond project viewed from the part-finished filter housing. The RSJ will support a bridge.   Photo: Nick Fletcher.

A gas-fired stainless steel heat exchanger. The lagged pipework carries water to the outer jacket.
Photo: Nick Fletcher.

skimmers, venturis, sub-surface returns, pump and discharge chambers, and work out how to best incorporate them in the overall scheme. As with all major construction projects, a little forethought will save a lot of heartache later on – it is best to have a clear picture of the final objective in your mind from the outset, then draw up your plans, cost them out and finally ascertain that they can be executed. All this should be done before the site is touched. Modifications and afterthoughts are never fully satisfactory, and invariably involve more trouble and expense than getting everything right first time.

If you discount the cost of your own labour (and know what you are doing), there is no question that building your own filter can work out much cheaper than purchasing a system 'off the shelf'. More importantly, you can dictate its size, configuration and performance in a way not always possible with commercial units. So rather than looking on a home-built project as merely a way of saving money, it can be seen as a means of utilising the funds you have to best effect.

A shop-bought filter, especially if gravity-fed, involves considerable work to install. Bricklaying, concreting and plumbing skills are brought to bear, so it is not as though the do-it-yourself filter builder is likely to lack the expertise necessary to go a few steps further and tackle the whole project from scratch. In that sense, all filtration systems are home-built. It is just that some Koi keepers use mainly bought components, others improvise wherever possible, and still more come to a compromise.

Let us look at how a typical home-built bayed filter system comes together. The first component is settlement, and the first choice for that is a vortex. You may feel that commercial plastic or glassfibre modules cannot be matched by a do-it-yourself alternative, as it is hard to reproduce the

smooth inner surface down which solids spiral. Or you may go ahead and construct your own from bricks laid on end, rendered and fibreglassed. This is one of the smaller cost savings you will make, as vortex modules are now mass-produced with supporting skirt and the necessary delivery and discharge pipework connections included.

If you opt for commercial biological chambers, the next stage involves an excavation with block walls and a level concrete floor, to act as a firm supportive base. Although it is possible to back-fill around filter modules, most Koi keepers prefer to retain access to the discharge pipework, so the modules are left free-standing and the housing chamber is roofed over with removable covers, perhaps decking or slabs. Enough space should be left around all filter components so that they can be reached for servicing.

However, having gone to the trouble of constructing a concrete shell anyway, the do-it-yourself enthusiast can easily convert it into a multi-chamber filter by forming it into compartments separated by weirs or transfer ports. Each chamber should incorporate a generous void beneath the media, the support grid resting on a framework of hardwood or engineering bricks. If possible, each chamber floor should be steeply benched to a discharge pipe to waste. Transfer ports can be cast from a cement mix containing Rein fibres, or else stainless steel rebates can be screwed into the side walls of each chamber to take sheets of twin-wall polycarbonate or other rigid, non-toxic plastic.

The chamber walls should be rendered smooth with the same Rein mix and then either fibreglassed or painted with G4 (the clear version is cheaper than the black).

The final dry compartment can contain an external pump, UV, possibly a stainless steel heat-exchanger, and ball-valves to purge the

Filtration

filter modules and bottom drain to waste into the nearest sewage inspection chamber. It is better and more hygienic to have this arrangement than merely to run discharge pipework into the chamber and site the valves there.

Home-made pumped filtration systems appear much simpler and cheaper to construct, but they are rarely fully successful. Typically, they are based around header tanks connected together with pipework, which does not allow the even transfer of water between chambers possible with full-width ports. The pipework must be of a diameter wide enough to prevent flow starvation, so you need at least 6 x 1.5-inch pipes to equate to one 4-inch pipe. Large free-standing header tanks can easily bow outwards when full of water, despite some inner reinforcement, which can interfere with flow and lead to dead spots.

The main objection to such systems, however, is that they are prone to solids overload because settlement is not easy when the water is being pumped directly into the first chamber. This can be overcome by having two settlement modules – the first of the passive type, feeding into a vortex which then serves the biological stages.

'Dwell time' is important in calculating the size of any home-built system. This is defined as the residence period of water in contact with the media, and 20 minutes should be seen as the minimum if the nitrifying bacteria are to work effectively. If, for example, the pump is turning over 2000 gallons per hour and the biological chambers together hold 500 gallons, then it will take only 15 minutes for that volume of water to pass completely through them. To be fully effective, the chambers should have a capacity of at least 666 gallons; alternatively, pump flow rate can be stepped down to 1500 gph, but only if the total volume of pond and filter does not exceed 3000 gallons. In that way it is still possible to maintain a twice-hourly total turnover.

9 POND MATERIALS

Liner ponds attract a very poor press in serious Koi keeping circles. Yet, properly installed, they can be a valid option, particularly if funds are limited. The prejudice against liners may stem from recollections of ordinary small ornamental garden ponds which were nothing more than shallow bowl-shaped depressions with a waterproof PVC membrane dropped in. Many of us started our pondkeeping careers at this modest level, only to find that such ponds were totally inadequate for Koi. However, the fault lay not so much with the material as with the way it was used and the small scale of the operation.

Butyl rubber (EPDM) was originally developed for large-scale industrial applications, and current uses include lining drinking water reservoirs, flat-roofing, and containment of toxic materials on landfill sites. So it is serious stuff! The material is inert, resistant to chemical attack, flexible and long-lasting, the better grades carrying a 50-year guarantee.

However, Butyl can be punctured in a variety of ways. The commonest cause of leaky liner ponds is insufficient care taken to cushion the membrane against sharp objects in the excavation. No problem is apparent when the liner is laid in dry, but the minute water is introduced it compresses the rubber against stones, roots or builder's rubble, with inevitable results.

This problem is easily overcome by protecting the excavation with an underlay. Non-woven polymer sheeting is made for the purpose, but other materials can be used too: fine sand mixed almost dry with a little cement powder so that it will lay up against vertical surfaces, coarse bubble wrap, carpet remnants, even layers of old newspaper (though these will rot away in time). Polythene sheeting, which should never be used as a main liner, gives considerable protection against sharp objects but is an awkward material to work with, being very slippery and difficult to fold and pleat. Expanded polystyrene in sheet form, as sold to insulate shed walls, is an excellent underlay with heat-retaining properties and plenty of 'give'.

The roots of certain plants can penetrate Butyl. Reeds and rushes have sharp rhizomes, so they should never be grown in or beside a liner pond. They insinuate themselves into folds and pleats, but the punctures they make are initially almost self-sealing – the problem arises when the reeds die down or are pulled out. Tree roots can be invasive too, especially willow, but then siting a pond close to overhanging foliage is never a good idea, irrespective of the construction materials chosen.

The third source of punctures is direct damage by humans, animals or birds; any clawed animal falling into the water and panicking, especially a dog, can shred a liner. A stab from a heron's beak is always a possibility, while garden tools or any sharp or heavy object accidentally dropped into the pond can damage the Butyl. Finally, if your pond is close to a public thoroughfare, vandalism may occur – a liner is a tempting target.

Butyl repair kits for small punctures work well, providing the patch is applied over a clean, dry and roughened surface – but locating leaks is not always easy. If one occurs near top water level, the pond owner should wait until the level stabilises and then drain down another foot or so to give himself room to explore round the perimeter.

Another drawback to Butyl is its tendency, over a long period, to become hard and brittle when exposed to sunlight. UV degradation should not be a problem if, as should be the case, the liner is properly concealed. In a modest ground-level pond with a rock or walled surround, the liner can be brought back behind the edging so that none of it is visible above water level. In double-skinned walls, the Butyl can be sandwiched between the bricks or blocks which are then capped with coping stones.

The major disadvantage of Butyl is that it does not provide such a uniformly smooth surface as glassfibre or rendered blockwork. Its slightly rough texture accumulates calcium deposits in hard water areas and these, in turn, provide anchorage for blanketweed. The need, in most pond designs, to fold and pleat the liner into the hole means there will be dead spots which attract dirt, or even flaps behind which Koi can disappear.

The answer, for formally shaped ponds, is a box-welded liner. Several companies offer this option, which provides a tailor-made rubber shell vulcanised together to mould accurately to the contours of the excavation. Box-welding is not cheap, but the end result is very neat. Alternatively, you could consider

purchasing large circular irrigation tanks. These are made of galvanised steel with a box-welded liner that drops inside and secures over the perimeter lip. These make ideal quarantine ponds, but with a bit of creative disguise a main system can be designed around them, too.

Butyl's very flexibility can be a drawback if the ground in which the pond is dug is prone to subsidence. If the contours of the excavation shift, the membrane adjusts to them, but this, in turn, means that stress will be placed on vulnerable points, such as where pipework passes through the liner. In extreme instances the Butyl will tear. An associated problem is where groundwater seeps in between the liner and the hole. A rising water table can even cause the liner floor to 'balloon'.

If you decide on a Butyl-lined pond it is best to ignore the traditional advice to stretch the liner over the excavation and allow it to be pulled into shape as water is introduced. For Koi ponds the method is to lay the liner in dry, pleating and folding as neatly as possible, and make the necessary pipework/bottom drain connections at this stage. Bottom drains for Butyl have flanges which clamp either side of the liner and are screwed down over a bed of mastic, while for pipes, tank connectors work in much the same way, sandwiching the liner either side of an adhesive cushion of flexible waterproof material.

Final pleating and pulling out of creases can be done from within the pond as it is filled, a job for which bare feet are advised.

For best results and greater permanence it is advisable to use Butyl in conjunction with other pond-building materials, and a common combination is a blockwork shell with a liner dropped in. The rubber membrane replaces the various renderings or glassfibring procedures necessary to give a smooth, non-toxic coating to the walls, and is chosen for its relative cheapness and ease of installation. Butyl can currently be obtained for around 50p per square foot (about £6 per square metre). This compares against a minimum of £20 per square metre for fibreglassing.

If, at any stage, the pond builder wishes to upgrade his system it is relatively easy to drain down the pond and remove the liner, leaving the superstructure intact. But never try to use a second-hand liner in a new excavation – it is likely to crack.

PRE-FORMED PONDS

One can be easily beguiled by the apparently huge glassfibre garden pools stacked around the sites of aquatic centres, particularly if they are labelled as suitable for Koi. They seem the almost 'instant' answer to the impatient pond builder, and their glossy interior finish suggests they will aid water circulation and be easy to clean and keep free of clinging blanketweed.

However, the majority of such ponds, besides being very expensive, are simply not deep enough to support Koi, very few holding even 1,000 gallons. To be fair, the regular, formal shapes are less wasteful of potential volume than the elaborate designs which are supposed to be more 'natural' (in reality few ponds occurring in nature are either kidney shaped or resemble miniature versions of Lake Windermere).

Installing a pre-formed pond is a far more skilled and exacting operation than using a liner. First, the shell is laid on site and canes or stakes are pushed vertically into the ground around the lip to act as a digging template. The aim is a contoured hole several inches greater in all dimensions than the pond itself – but if the terrain is difficult, this can be impossible to achieve.

The hole has to be lined with cushioning material such as sharp sand before the pond shell is laid in. Usually there has to be further

spoil removal at some points and replacement at others, and the perimeter gap has to be back-filled with more sand washed in with a hose. The pond must end up flush with the hole, level, and fully supported all across the base.

Pre-formed ponds can still be useful to Koi keepers, either as header pools or portable quarantine facilities. If they are to be incorporated halfway up a waterfall or rockery feature they must rest on infallible foundations, as they will be carrying a great weight of water. RSJs concreted into place and decked over with treated timber would not be over the top. Installing any necessary connecting pipework will involve glassing it into place, as these ponds are never supplied with bottom drain fittings, overflows and and like.

BLOCKWORK PONDS

In Chapter Twelve (Pond Building), Terry Hill describes a professionally built pond centred around a steel-reinforced, rendered blockwork shell finished off with fibreglass. In his example, the rendering is applied to give a smooth key to the GRP, rather than making much of a structural contribution.

However, there is a product variously known as Rein or Fibromix which greatly adds to the strength and flexibility of the render. Over this can be applied either fibreglass or G4 – the latter acting both as a sealant and as a finishing top-coat. The end result is not quite as smooth as glass, but much cheaper and far less messy to apply. Two coats of clear and one of coloured G4 are normally brushed or rolled on to the blockwork, taking care not to let the initial coats dry out fully before applying subsequent ones. If you are making your own filter chambers from blockwork, the reinforced render/clear G4 treatment will waterproof and strengthen them. By bolting together formers from pieces of batten over marine ply, you can even cast your own filter transfer ports from cement to which Fibromix has been added.

Fibromix looks like chopped glassfibre mat, but is a softer, plasticised material. Incorporated into the normal mix of one part masonry cement to five of sand, it enables the rendering to be laid up, even vertically, without 'slumping', providing not too much water is added. Half-inch thick is the norm, but in square or rectangular ponds extra coats can be used to round off or 'fair' the corners, to aid water circulation.

Hand-mixing even small quantities of cement is a crippling task, and it is much better to either hire a petrol mixer or purchase your own, cheaper, electric machine. If this is carefully cleaned between batches its cost can be partially recouped by selling it at the end of the project.

The Fibromix must be teased out and introduced gradually into the dry mix of sand and cement – if it is added all at once it will clump together. Some pond builders add a squirt or two of washing-up liquid to the mix, which seems to distribute the fibres more evenly and give a smoother, more plastic rendering material.

However carefully your Fibromix rendering has been trowelled on and smoothed with a plasterer's float, fibres will still stand proud. Once the render is dry, these need to be melted off with a blowtorch – otherwise, when the G4 is applied, sharp points that can injure fish will result.

BLOCKS, CONCRETE AND MORTAR
The standard-size concrete block, solid or holed to take reinforcing rods, is 18 x 9 x 9 ins (450 x 225 mm). For ponds rendered with Fibromix, dense concrete plain-wall blocks laid in stretcher bond are a good choice. Buy the type with halving joints, as cutting these with hammer and bolster chisel is made easier.

Always order more blocks than your estimate suggests will be necessary, as invariably there will be some wastage resulting from inexpert cutting. As most of the blockwork will be below ground level, choose a mortar of 1 part Portland cement to 3 parts of sand. Sulphate-resisting cement is advisable if ground water is present, as otherwise the chemicals in the soil will react with the mortar and cause it to crumble. Avoid rapid-hardening Portland cement unless your pond is being built in winter, when frost is likely – this type cures fast and gives out more heat than the standard product.

Concrete – which is simply cement, aggregate and sand – will be needed for the initial ring beam of the pond and later for the floor. The amount required for the beam can probably be mixed on site, the ratio by volume being 1:2.5:4 (1 part Portland cement to 2.5 of sand to 4 of coarse aggregate). Buying bags of dry-mix concrete is an expensive exercise unless only a small amount is needed, for example to secure pergola posts in the ground.

For the pond floor, a load or part-load of ready-mixed concrete is the only solution, both from a cost and an efficiency standpoint. You can stipulate whether or not the mix is to include waterproofing powder. Estimate how much you need, and, if the smallest load is still more than that, it may be that neighbours will be willing to take up the surplus for their own path/patio projects.

Check that the delivery vehicle can reach your property, and that your work has progressed to the stage where the concrete can be worked straightaway. Often it can be chuted straight into the hole, but first ensure that the ends of pipework and bottom drains are securely plugged and capped with polythene bags.

GLASSFIBRE

If there is one job a pond builder should leave to the professionals, this has to be it. A pond smoothly rendered with Fibromix-reinforced cement and than glassed over is an incredibly strong structure, but poorly applied GRP is dangerous to fish because toxic styrenes can leach out of incompletely cured resin.

Several professional glassfibring companies specialise in Koi ponds and will guarantee their work. At least one company also makes GRP filter systems. The traditional pond specification consists of two layers of mat laid up with resin and finished off with a gelcoat containing a wax additive, which is essential to a full cure. However, a single layer of GRP mat is advocated by some quite respectable companies and, providing the surface on to which it is laid is smooth, it is hard to argue against the money-saving logic.

Gelcoat comes in many colours, but the only two suitable for Koi ponds are black or British racing green. Pale shades look tacky when algae forms on the GRP, and the Koi do not show to their best advantage against a washed-out background.

Successful fibreglassing is highly weather-dependent, as it is best to complete a pond within a day to get full structural integrity. You may therefore have to wait some weeks for the contractor to arrive, as every spell of wet weather will push his schedule farther back.

Once the GRP has fully cured (2-3 weeks in a typical British summer), the pond should be thoroughly steam-cleaned, then filled and emptied before the water for the fish is introduced through a meter and purifier.

POND EDGING

The finished appearance of a Koi pond can be enhanced or ruined by the choice of edging materials and the way they are incorporated into the structure. Formal ponds, where no attempt is made to imitate Nature, are rarely a problem. If part-raised, the walls need to be capped off with some form of coping – this can be of natural or reconstituted slabs, varnished planks or even tiles. These should all shed water readily, and preferably be angled so that the minimum of run-off enters the pond.

All mortar joints should be given two or three coats of clear G4 to prevent lime contamination, and if there is any doubt about the inertness of the coping slabs these should be coated too.

The same precautions apply to ground-level ponds. Perimeter slabs should be sloped slightly away from the water to run rainfall on to the garden, and, if the pond is on a lawned site, it is a good idea to have a 'mowing strip' all round, at least 12 ins wide. This can be a shallow perimeter trench, treated with weedkiller before black polythene is laid in and topped off with gravel. The lawn should be slightly proud of this strip, and separated from it with metal edging hammered into the ground to give a clear demarcation line.

Informal 'rock' ponds are much more difficult to carry off convincingly, and provision has to be made at planning stage for a reinforced concrete shelf to carry the considerable weight of the rockwork or any cobbled beach features.

If possible, use local stone. This will be cheapest because of lower transport costs from the quarry. For example, in Wales slabs of slate are readily available but, if these had to be carried across the country, the cost would be prohibitive. Whichever rock is chosen, first take advice on its suitability. Run-off from some limestones will raise the pH, while other sedimentary rocks can split and flake after a hard frost. Ore-bearing rocks may be attractively coloured but can bring about metal contamination. In general, dense igneous rocks such as granite are the safest to use. The best effects come from large, water-worn pieces rather than those blasted out of a cliff face.

As a general rule, large rocks are more imposing and convincing than smaller ones and every pond should have several 'feature' stones. If possible, visit the quarry and choose these individual pieces, rather than relying on some being included in the load. They will probably be more expensive weight for weight, but the investment is worthwhile.

In natural rock formations the strata are angled in one direction and this fact must be mimicked around the pond. If you want to include plants in the perimeter rockwork, slope the rocks upwards and use the pockets formed at their base.

Pond rockwork can be interspersed with other features found in a traditional Japanese garden. Aim for an asymmetrical effect – for example, if a line of bamboo poles is incorporated, vary their height to give the impression of age and informality. Timber 'piers' emerging from the water, or cobbled beaches, are interesting variants, although cobbles can soon grow a slimy coating of green algae in the shallows, where sunlight and warmth combine to give ideal growing conditions.

All the above are structurally incorporated into the whole, as opposed to ornaments such as stone lanterns, which can be added any time. It goes without saying that all rockwork, including that for waterfalls, should be firmly bedded in (cemented into place if necessary) so that it cannot move underfoot or run the risk of toppling into the pond when weight is brought to bear upon it.

PIPEWORK, VALVES AND FITTINGS

A typical Koi pond will require a host of pipe runs, some relatively accessible but others integrated into the structure and impossible to get at once the system is complete – the classic example being the pipe taking water from bottom drain(s) to filter.

It is tempting to cut costs and use domestic drainage pipework, either push-fit or solvent weld. But this is only intended to act as a conduit for waste water – for most of the time it remains empty. BSP pressure pipe, on the other hand, is made to hold as well as to conduct water and is far more durable. It is also far more expensive, but this drawback should be weighed against the potentially disastrous consequences of a burst pipe or a sprung joint.

Several items of equipment exert back pressure on their associated pipework, notably venturis and sand filters. Push-fit joints can easily pop out, and the rubber seals will eventually perish.

Solvent weld joints, properly made, are immensely strong and permanent. The surfaces to mate together should first be cleaned with methylated spirit, then wiped dry and roughened with coarse glasspaper. The cement is then brushed on to the union and the pipes assembled with a twisting motion.

The bond is almost instantaneous, so, if pipes are not properly aligned, there is no room for manoeuvre. For this reason, assembly should always be made 'dry' as a dummy run, and aligning marks should be scratched on to both pipes before they are brought together.

Once the joint has set, a fillet of cement is run around the external union for added strength.

The wider the bore of the pipe, the more flow it can handle and the less friction loss will occur. The majority of bottom-drain pipework is of 4-inch diameter minimum, so that water being pulled to settlement enters the chamber relatively calmly. But in systems pumping less than 2,500 gph this can actually lead to material settling out in the pipe, rather than being moved up to the filter. Progressive blockage then results. On small systems, 3-inch bottom drain pipework may be adequate, but anything less and the water will move too fast into the filter.

Pipework runs should be kept as short as possible, and incorporate the minimum number of directional changes. Where these are unavoidable, 'sweep' bends offer less flow resistance than than 90 degree elbows.

Rigid pumping pipework is dictated by the fittings on the pumps themselves, though most submersible and external pumps feature reducing hosetails which give some choice in the matter. The widest bore pipe possible should be selected, and the rest of the hosetail sawn off flush at the appropriate diameter.

Valves at key points in pipe runs make maintenance of the system much simpler. Every filter chamber, for example, should be drainable to waste. Some vortex settlers incorporate a valve in the base sump which can be operated remotely via a stainless steel extension rod. Ideally, entire filtration systems should be capable of being isolated module by module from the pond.

Four-inch valves are expensive items, slide valves being cheaper than ball valves but more prone to failure. One should always be plumbed into the feed pipe to the settlement vortex. This pipe can then be teed into the vortex's discharge pipe to waste via another, smaller-diameter valve. This arrangement allows the bottom-drain pipework to be purged of sediment build-up.

Pipework is the arterial network of the Koi pond, conducting away waste matter and bringing in purified water and life-giving oxygen. In a typical installation there will be dozens of solvent-weld joints to make; each one should be tackled as though the whole system depended on it, because, in most instances, it will!

10 POND BUILDING

By Terry Hill

As a professional builder, I am often asked if there is a 'best' way to construct and filter a Koi pond. I can only speak from personal experience, as almost everyone has their own idea of what is right – and who am I to argue? However, you get nothing for nothing in this world, and the more thought and effort you put into your 'dream' pond, the more you will reap the benefits.

What are the criteria to aim for? Certainly a pond that looks nice and ties in pleasingly with its surroundings. It should be easy to maintain – so an extra 4-inch slide valve is worth the money if it later saves you hours of work. But first and foremost, you should be looking to create an environment in which your precious fish will thrive and grow.

On that basis, I believe that a pond of concrete block construction, rendered and fibreglassed, is the best long-term investment in enjoyment you can make. Not that other methods do not have their own merits. Take liners: if cost plays a big part they have their place, or perhaps the aim is to build a starter or a temporary pond. But liner ponds also have their drawbacks.

Accurate fitting of the Butyl is extremely important, especially around drains and pipework, where splitting is possible without correct sealing. Creases are a big problem, as these can harbour harmful bacteria. Remember, any creases must all lie flat in the direction of the intended flow. As a tip, try coarse bubblewrap as an underlay.

The sealer known as G4 is a super product,

A 2,000 gallon liner pond under construction.

Photo: Terry Hill.

but it is just that – it is not at all structural. The basic construction stages of my best pond, which I will discuss later, will still have to be carried out prior to application of G4. If your pond shell is not structurally sound, then there is not a sealer in the world that will hold in water if, for instance, the 'shell' moves and cracks. So, where do we start?

PREPARATION

Draw a rough plan of the garden showing the house, any large trees, shrubs and outbuildings. Remember to mark east and west, and plot an approximate line that the sun takes, since ponds in full sun are harder to keep clear of the dreaded blanketweed. Try to plot the position of drains, gas and electricity cables.

At this stage, do not worry about pond size or shape, just get an idea of the siting options. Once you have asked yourself some basic questions, and with the knowledge you have gained from the above, most ponds will virtually design themselves! The questions are:

1) Formal or informal?
2) In-ground or out of ground?
3) Waterfall or not?
4) Where to position the filter?

Most people's ideal pond would be sited near to the house, for easy viewing night or day; close to drainage for ease of maintenance; not in full sunlight all day; convenient for services such as gas (if heated) or electricity; and would incorporate a moving water feature – a rockery/waterfall.

If your criteria are similar to mine, you probably do not have many options left.

SHAPE AND DIMENSIONS

The next stage is to position the pond and filters in your sketch – try various shapes and sizes. This is the fun bit – play with the alternatives, and imagine looking out of the window on to your imaginary waterfall.

We will assume, for the purpose of this exercise, that the space we are left with is 20 x 12 ft. Incidentally, it is unlikely that we will require planning consent from the local authority but it is best to be on the safe side, so check your local building codes .

An area 20 x 12 ft, less the structural walls (say 12 ins all round), leaves us with 18 x 10 ft – less, say, about a quarter of the space for the filters (4 ft 6 ins x 10 ft). That leaves us with a pond 13 ft 6 ins x 10 ft wide. My ideal depth is around 5 ft 6 ins to 6 ft deep, so let us go for the full 6 ft.

The gallonage of such a pond is calculated using the following formula: 13 ft 6 ins (length) x 10 ft (width) x 6 ft (depth) x 6.23

THE IMAGINARY GARDEN

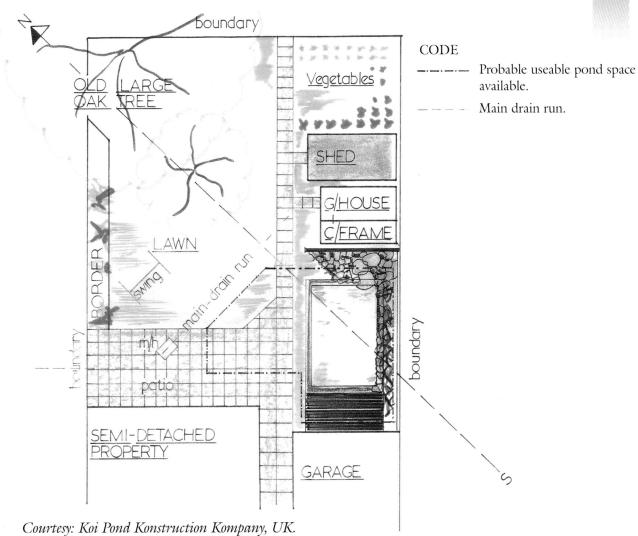

CODE

—··—··—··— Probable useable pond space available.

— — — — Main drain run.

Courtesy: Koi Pond Konstruction Kompany, UK.

Ready for the fibreglass.

Photo: Terry Hill.

(galls per cubic foot) = a nice-sized pond of 5,046.3 gallons. Multiply by 7.48 instead of 6.23 to give the capacity in US gallons (6,058.8 gallons).

A pleasing shape is a straight back and oval front with filters one end and waterfall the other – part out-of-ground for child safety, with somewhere to sit and view the fish.

I have put the filters, for ease of electrics and heating if required, next to the garage, although this way the drainage and waterfall returns will be longer. The filters could just as easily have been at the other end, behind the rockery.

COST

We now know we are planning a pond of about 5,000 gallons, and are confident that we can get it, with filtration, into the space allocated. Money obviously plays a big part, and it is now that we start to work out how much the project will cost.

Some companies offer a design, consultancy or part-build service, or they can carry out work on the complete pond. They will come to the site, contribute ideas, provide sketches and prepare a full specification of works, including drawings.

You could, for instance, have your pond designed, dig your own hole, have the structure built, carry out your own plumbing and electrics, employ a fibreglass contractor and have the landscaping finished by experts at a much reduced price (but not guaranteed).

What follows is not intended to show you the only way to build a pond, but it puts into practice the tried and tested construction methods I have used myself over many years. You will have your own ideas, I am sure, especially about filtration; but build your pond like this and it will not let you down. Do it once – do it right!

DOWN TO BUSINESS

Set out the desired shape of your pond. Mark it out with pegs – I use 1.5 ins x 1 inch roofing battens cut to about 12-15 ins long with a point. Space these about 2 ft apart.

Digging out the pond.

Photo: Terry Hill.

TYPICAL SECTION OF POND IN GROUND

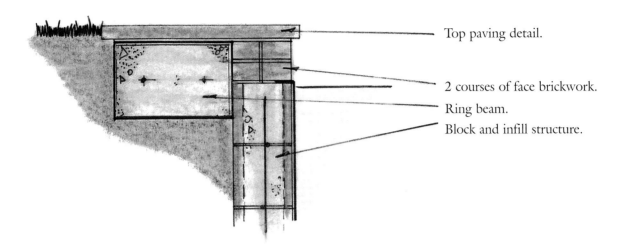

Top paving detail.

2 courses of face brickwork.

Ring beam.

Block and infill structure.

Courtesy: Koi Pond Konstruction Kompany, UK.

Measure outside this ring about 12 ins and put in another set of pegs as before. This is the template for the vital concrete collar.

Now the hard work begins. Dig out approximately 15-18 ins deep between the pegs. It is important that this is done accurately, with nice vertical sides and a level bottom (remember, the better the sides, especially the inner, the better the concrete ring will be, once the pond is dug). Now fill the trench with concrete 4:2:1 mix, this being 4 parts aggregate, 2 parts sharp sand and 1 of cement.

Most ballast you can purchase is already specified to the above mix, so do not worry – just use 6 parts ballast to 1 part cement. Mix this fairly free-flow (quite runny) and pour it into the trench, levelling as you go. The more accurate the level, the easier it will be to measure down to your main dig. Keep the concrete about 6 ins down from your lawn level, so you can reinstate the grass or paving at a later date. The ring is now complete. Its purpose is five-fold:

1) It will retain the sides during your dig – very important if you are on particularly wet clay, for instance.

2) You will be able to accurately measure down for your base levels. If your concrete is level, this will be your main datum point. Every level and measurement can be taken from this point, i.e. pipework, drains, concrete, brickwork, water features, filter and water levels.

3) On to this ring will be built your outer decorative brickwork or patio.

4) This being a structural ring, it will help your side walls to withstand the water pressure. For added support, insert two 10mm reinforcement rods, wired together in a continuous ring.

5) The concrete ring or collar will help keep the site clean, with no fall-ins.

Remember, the better this ring is, the easier everything else will be!

My basic philosophy for a pond is to keep it simple and uncomplicated. Build it structurally sound, have a good big gravity-fed filtration system which is easy to maintain, get the flow rate through the filter right, add air and a UV clarifier, and you are on the road to successful Koi keeping.

A vortex filter.

Photo: Terry Hill.

DIGGING

How you dig is your choice, and obviously access is important. Lucky pond builders can get a mechanical digger in to do the job, and these can be hired with a driver. This is the quickest way, and most ponds will be dug in a day. To get the muck away, a specially equipped lorry is the most effective (one load equates to approximately 1,000 gallons of finished pond volume). If you choose 6 ft skips, you will probably get only 3 cubic yards into each one.

If you cannot get a full-sized machine on to the site, you can hire a smaller mini-excavator. Some will pass through a single door but, be warned, they are not the easiest machines to get to grips with and can be extremely dangerous in inexperienced hands. By the time you have got used to the controls and paid for the hire, it might have been cheaper

to have paid a driver, or called in a couple of good labourers to hand-dig.

TIP: If you encounter heavy clay, use a clean spade and have a bucket of water handy. Dip the spade into this after every spadeful.

Let us assume you want a 2 ft wall around the pond, and that the water level will be 6 ins down from this. That means your water level is 18 ins above ground. Now let us assume a finished depth of 6 ft, less 18 ins above ground. That is 4 ft 6 ins, plus depth of concrete and render/screed (say 12 ins). This gives you a hole 5 ft 6 ins deep to dig.

So the depth of the hole is the depth of water minus water above ground level (which could be zero if the pond is entirely in-ground), plus the depth of flooring concrete.

Bottom out the hole as level and flat as possible, then tunnel under the ring beam and start to dig the trench to take pipework to the filter bay, the digging of which can also be started now. The depth of both trench and bay depends on which filters are being used.

It is now that you *MUST* transfer a water level 'datum' peg across to the filter bay. From this you can work out the bay's depth. Make it a permanent mark, perhaps a couple of nails in the fence or wall, as this will be extremely important.

The filter manufacturer will tell you the depth from water level in the filter to the underside of the filter legs. Let us say 42 ins, for example. The depth of dig for the filter bay below our water level datum is this 42 ins plus the thickness of the concrete base (6 ins) making 48 ins in all.

I prefer the vortex type of filter in which all the contained water is slowly set spinning – in the first chamber for non-biological removal of solids and in subsequent chambers, with Japanese matting, for biological removal of ammonia and nitrite. Vortexes give minimal flow restriction

Laying bottom drains.

Photo: Terry Hill.

These drains have lift-off fibreglass lids.

Photo: Terry Hill.

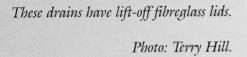

The mesh is wired over and under the pipework.

Photo: Terry Hill.

through the system, do not clog up like some filters, and are easy to maintain.

The trench from pond to filter bay should be 48 ins deep too, to eliminate too many vertical pipe bends. This will assist flow rate to and from the filter.

If you are lucky, you will not hit ground water during your dig. But suppose that 2 ft down you encounter the water table (the term used for the natural water level underground). This varies from area to area but, in principle, if you live in a valley, you will find water and if you live on a hill you will not. This is an oversimplification, but it will do as a rough guide.

Do not panic – simply dig a sump pit about 3 ft square, 2 ft deeper than the main pond and about 6 ft away from it, with an adjoining trench. You now have to keep a pump running. Either hire a sump pump which handles solids or buy a decent heavy-duty submersible (you can use this later for maintenance). Remember to shore up the sides of this sump pit during digging, for safety's sake.

Now any water from your main dig will run into your sump and will be pumped away. As a belt and braces approach you could, in serious ground-water cases, put a small drainage system into this sump from the pond and cover it with builders' Visqueen (damp-proof membrane) prior to concreting. Four-inch plastic slotted land drain from your local builders' merchants is ideal for this, and fairly inexpensive.

DRAINS

So now we have a hole – what do we do with it? Buy bottom drains. The number depends on pond size, and for this 5,000-gallon exercise I have opted for two. Lay these in position centrally in the width, split the pond into four along the length, and place drains on points 1 and 3 for an even pull.

If, for instance, the pond had been 15,000 gallons and 30 ft long, I would have gone for four bottom drains numbered 1, 2, 3, and 4 and four returns also numbered 1, 2, 3 and 4. I would have had two filters for back-up safety.

Drains 1 and 3 would go to filter 1, returning via returns 2 and 4; and drains 2 and 4 would go to filter 2, returning via returns 1 and 3. Drains should be set dead level on a pad of concrete and weighted down internally, or plugged and filled with water. Remember to thicken up your base around pipework and have a shallow trench beneath it.

I like the fibreglass lift-up lid type of drain. Maintenance (for example blanketweed removal) is simple, and, being made of fibreglass, the drain is perfect for joining to the final pond lining.

NOTE: All pipework within this pond will be high-pressure pipe, solvent-welded. I know from bitter experience that domestic waste pipe, under movement or extreme heat/cold, can fracture. High-pressure pipe can withstand impact (just in case you drop something) and one main advantage is that you have got slightly more time with the solvent cement adhesive during joining.

Try to avoid too many joints by using the longest lengths of pipe possible. Glue 4-in pipe to the drains and position in the direction of the filter trench. To avoid too many bends, dig out the end of this trench to the full depth of the pond dig. Just to accommodate these two pipes, put an elbow on each and a short length of pipe to be cut at a later stage. This will take the filter trench pipework. Do not connect these pipes together. The number of drains determines the number of 4-in pipes to the filter area. Use plenty of solvent cement (do not scrimp). Once this has cured, test the pipework for leaks, using either compressed air or water, as it is impossible to rectify a

Tamp the concrete roughly.

Photo: Terry Hill.

Dummy run for rod positioning.

Photo: Terry Hill.

problem once the concrete has been poured. No other pipework is required at this stage, so we move on to reinforcement and base.

This is belt and braces time. Some ground will not require all these precautions, but it is better to be safe than sorry. Follow this design and you will not go far wrong.

Cover the whole of the pond base with reinforcing mesh – BS 4483 6 mm bar – cutting neatly to shape with bolt-cutters or a mini-grinder. Cut and bend 8-ft lengths of 16mm reinforcing rods to a right angle and wire these around the perimeter of the base reinforcement at approximately 9-in centres – these will be sticking out when the base is complete, ready to receive the hollow-block walling structure.

Cut the mesh either side of the 4-in pipework and wire it over and under. Put spacers under the mesh and take time to wire the whole lot together to form a complete mesh raft (spacers are available from any steel stockholder, or use quarter-bat bricks). Now position 8 lengths of 16 mm reinforcing rods on top, lapped at the ends and approximately 12 ins apart over the whole raft, and wire them in.

If you encountered water during your dig, this whole operation can be done over 1200-gauge builders' polythene to keep the mud down and to help the concrete cure. Remember, the mesh and pipework should end up central within the concrete thickness, and the base should be a minimum of 9 ins thick.

CONCRETING

Now comes the good bit – concreting. Depending on access and size of the pond, ready-mixed concrete is probably the best bet. Readymix is rarely used in the US, so ask your builder or local merchant if they can recommend a suitable alternative. Readymix is not as expensive as you might think; it is instant and, with a couple of labourers on wheelbarrows and another two in the hole, the job is all over in an hour or two, and cleared up. Remember the mix – 4:2:1 – and include waterproofer and frostproofer during the winter months. In very hot weather, sprinkle from time to time to avoid the concrete drying out too quickly and cracking. If necessary, cover it for a few days with wet sacking.

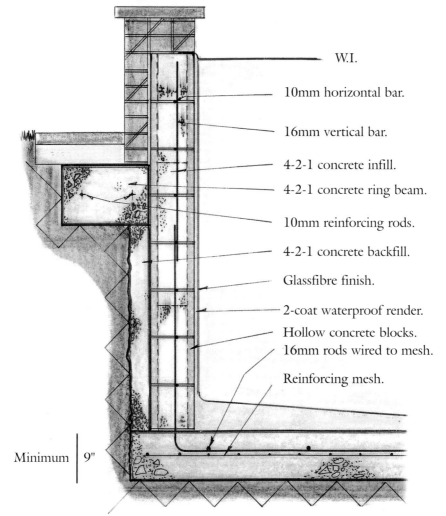

W.I.

10mm horizontal bar.

16mm vertical bar.

4-2-1 concrete infill.

4-2-1 concrete ring beam.

10mm reinforcing rods.

4-2-1 concrete backfill.

Glassfibre finish.

2-coat waterproof render.

Hollow concrete blocks.

16mm rods wired to mesh.

Reinforcing mesh.

Minimum | 9"

Typical section through raised pond.   *Courtesy: Koi Pond Konstruction Kompany, UK.*

4-inch configuration from bottom drain.

Photo: Terry Hill.

Tamp the concrete roughly – do not be too fussy, but try to get it fairly level. The final levels and falls will be obtained in the floor screed, described later. While you have the Readymix delivery, it is wise to concrete the base of the filter bay.

Depending on the size of the pond and filter and the ground conditions, blockwork specifications will vary. We will take probably the worst scenario, clay. Clay moves dramatically from summer to winter, so we need our shell to be able to take up this movement.

We use 9 x 9 x 18ins hollow concrete blocks – they are heavy and a bit awkward, but there is nothing better. Pass them over the 16mm bars and you should end up with two bars per block. At each horizontal joint, wire in a continuous 16mm rod (see details). After you have laid four courses, i.e. 30 ins high, stop work. Next day you will have to

Pond Building

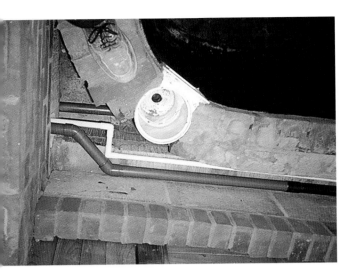

All pipework is neatly behind the pond wall

Photo: Terry Hill.

A surface skimmer (powered) set into the pond wall and showing strainer basket.

Photo: Nick Fletcher.

fill in all the hollow pots with concrete (mixed up, as earlier, fairly wet) and pour it down into the blockwork, punching down with a piece of batten and gently tapping the blocks as it goes down. This will help release any trapped air, which will rise to the surface.

Do not fill the top block right up, but stop 3-4 ins down, as this will be your bond when you carry out pot filling on the next four courses.

Where your blockwork goes round bends (as in an informal kidney-shaped pond), cut, bend and insert upturned hoops from block to block for added strength.

The wall now has to be back-filled. You should allow about 4 ins at the base for back-filling behind blockwork, but do not start until the blockwork has gone solid – say, two to three days. Never underestimate the weight and power of wet concrete. Back-fill too soon, and it will push the wall over. Be patient, and build and fill approximately four courses every two to three days, doing something else in the meantime. You could be getting on with the filter bay – same principle, but 6-in concrete base, with mesh, and 10 mm bars at 12-in centres.

Depending on the size of the filter base – in our case about 12 ft x 4 ft 6 ins – use 18 x 9 x 4-in concrete blocks laid in the normal fashion, but back-fill as before, and remember – finish and point this blockwork to a nice standard. There is nothing worse than showing off your pond, opening up your filter lids and having visitors see a load of rough blockwork.

PIPEWORK, HEATING AND LIGHTING

As blockwork goes up in the pond, we must think about pipework and what must be built into the side walls. If you intend to heat your pond, build in one length of 2-in pipe about 2-3 ft down from water level, at an angle of at least 45 degrees to the face of the wall and in the direction of the intended flow (this will end up as the heating return if you require one).

You may like underwater lights. The low voltage swimming-pool type is best, and these can be built straight into the side wall no more than 18 ins below the surface. Any deeper and it is difficult to change the bulb without swimming. Position the light in the front wall of the pond or the side from which

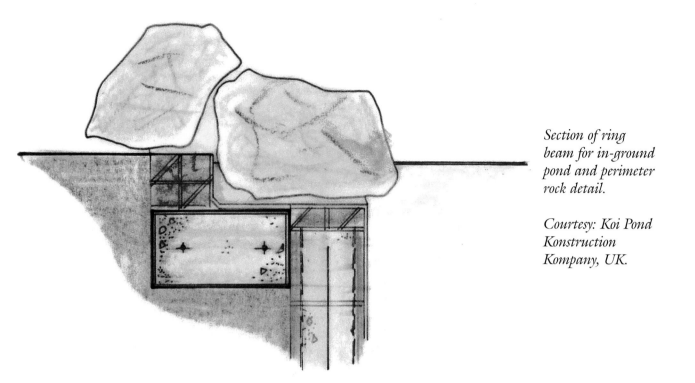

Section of ring beam for in-ground pond and perimeter rock detail.

Courtesy: Koi Pond Konstruction Kompany, UK.

you view, so as to illuminate the far side.

All return pipework should be built in now – consider a couple of deep-water returns as well as surface returns. Position them, again at 45 degrees to the face of the wall, in such a way that they push the water in one direction around the pond. Site the surface returns, especially if fitted with venturis, to the rear of the pond. This will leave the water nearest to you relatively undisturbed for viewing and feeding your Koi.

This pond requires one surface skimmer. As autumn leaves are a problem, try to position your power skimmer in any otherwise slack area where it will pull water towards it. Such an area could be at the end of a kidney shape. I use traditional swimming-pool skimmers with the weir set so that the water level is one-third the way up it.

If the pond is heated, the skimmer is the ideal feed point. Skimmed water does not have to be filtered, as a skimmer is there purely for surface debris removal through its own strainer, which has to be regularly cleaned. The skimmer is totally independent of the filter system, typically being run through a quarter HP external pump. These external pumps also make a great pond vacuum when teamed with an extra couple of valves and a pipe to the main drain. Pond

vacuuming is made easy with a standard pool brush and flexible hose. Simply shut off the feed to the return, open up the valve to waste and fit the hose into the skimmer with the plate supplied.

Return the water back to the pond via a heat exchanger or electric heater through the 2-in pipework specified earlier. The heat exchanger is the gas option of heating – think of it as the hot-water cylinder on your domestic central heating system, the difference being that it is normally in stainless steel (not copper).

You have a small gas boiler, a programmer, pump and thermostat, normally controlled by a probe within the filter. The whole system can be programmed to come on and off on a timed basis, or operate through the thermostat if left on constantly. Alternatively, the stainless steel heat exchanger could be heated by your domestic central heating system if the boiler is big enough to take the extra load. If you heat the pond only during the night you need not worry, as this is when the boiler is generally not performing its other duties.

Simply tee off from your existing pipework through the heat exchanger and add an extra motorised valve to the system, which is controlled by a probe and thermostat. This

The secondary wall for rocks in water.

Photo: Terry Hill.

RSJs in position as bridge supports.

Photo: Terry Hill.

arrangement can be improved even more with the addition of an extra programmer giving timed pool heating for, say, four hours a night and four during the day.

Remember, in the UK your plumber must be Corgi- (Council for Registered Gas Installers) registered and ACOPS-certified to carry out any gas work.

The electric option is more expensive to run but easier and cheaper to install. Heaters range from 1 to 9 kilowatts, 6 kw being enough to heat approximately 6,000 gallons. The unit is plumbed into your return pipework and wired in permanently to the electricity supply via a local isolating switch and RCD protecting device, for safety. It could, of course, be run on off-peak electricity if this is available.

We are getting close to the top of the pond now, so we need to think about anything else that needs to be built in and that will not be seen when the work is completed – this includes return and skimmer pipework, underwater lighting cables, and any other cabling for spotlights or perhaps a pergola, to be built at a later date.

The dangers of water and electricity cannot be overstressed. Always use a qualified electrician and ask to see his credentials.

Have a separate fuse board run out to a convenient space. On our specimen pond, the garage is an ideal site. Have, say, four different breakers in the board, all RCD-protected so that, if you have a problem, you should be able to isolate it by a process of elimination.

When the internal blockwork reaches the structural ring, just below ground level, start to leave brick butterfly ties sticking out. These will enable your outside facework/stone to be built on, giving, in effect, $13^1/_2$ ins of wall structure above ground for added strength. Complete the final back-fill up to concrete ring level and flatten it off smooth, ready to receive the final face work.

Incidentally, you may be asking why I did not build the internal blockwork up from a bottom structural ring instead of a solid base. I personally do not like this method. It is virtually impossible to link the side wall reinforcement to the base mesh, and the fact that the base is separate from the walls leads to unequal movement, which is not ideal. The aim is to end up with a complete metal cage within the structure.

This particular 5,000-gallon pond is to have part-submerged informal rocks and poles to the back and around the left-hand end. We must stop the internal blockwork 6 ins down from water level to any area having such features.

Build a secondary wall up to full height plus 2 ins, approximately 12 ins back on to our structural ring and infill with concrete – this is our feature ledge, later to be rendered and fibreglassed.

It is much the same for a pebble beach detail. Simply stop the internal blockwork, form a new base and back-retaining wall and you have the platform for any number of details. If, however, your water comes to approximately ground level you will have to accommodate these features in the original ring beam. Simply move out the ring beam to the shape you want the shelf to be in the finished pond.

COATING THE WALLS
The structure is moving on nicely, and it is time to do the rendering and apply the base screed. The walls should have two coats – first coat 1.5 parts soft sand, 1.5 parts washed sharp sand and 1 part cement (with frost and waterproofing added, depending on the weather). Apply this as flat as possible, ruled off as needed and 'scratched' up to take the second coat of the same 3:1 mix, finished off with a steel trowel to seal off the surface

Call in a professional for the fibreglassing.

Photo: Terry Hill.

Header pond supported on steelwork for cave effect.

Photo: Terry Hill.

and provide a good key for the final fibreglassing. Remember – the better the rendering, the better the pond glass finish. Take your time, make it good, and do not cut corners. The overall finish makes it all worthwhile.

Now for the floor screed, which is a 3:1 mix of sharp sand and cement mixed fairly dry and with waterproofer added. This contours the base and forms a gentle slope to each drain, so the thickness will vary from around 4 ins at the junction of walls and floor down to around 1 inch as it nears the drains. Form a gentle fillet around each drain and polish off with a steel float. As you work round the perimeter, form a nice big, soft, rounded fillet – this gives added strength and helps the fibreglassing contractor.

Incidentally, if you encounter a water problem at this stage, keep the sump pump running – we really need the blockwork and rendering totally dry for fibreglassing, or it may part company with the rest of the structure.

FIBREGLASSING

The pond is now ready for fibreglassing and, although you can attempt this yourself, it is not something I would recommend. To obtain a good finish requires specialist skills, materials are expensive, and mixing is very important. Call in a professional, who will finish a pond of this size in a couple of days and give you a written guarantee. Some heat will be required in the winter to aid the curing process, which normally takes three to four days. You may even have to tent over the pond to carry out this work in bad weather, if you are to enjoy fairly dry conditions.

FINISHING OFF

You can now bring up the final two courses of internal and external face work. Infill any gap between and fit capping stones of your choice, insert the junction box for any underwater light, make good around it and point in. Lay all your rockwork on the ledge, bedded in to sharp sand and Portland cement in a 3:1 ratio, and dab this with a clean paintbrush for a natural looking finish.

When this is dry, apply three coats of G4 clear sealer. This will act as a waterproofing agent and stop lime from leaching from the cement into the pond. For this detail, choose rocks that are naturally weather-washed and quite smooth to the touch, and try to avoid sharp edges at or below water level, as these could damage fish.

Bamboo poles can now be fitted – join these together at the back (see detail) and bed them into the brickwork as for the rock detail.

As soon as all the above is complete, fill the pond for the first time to equalise internal and external water pressures, but remember, do not turn off your sump pump until you have filled the pond for the final time through a water meter, to ascertain the exact gallonage of the system.

You may wish at this stage to sink a 12-in diameter polypropylene pipe into the sump pit. Perforate the bottom 18 ins with a jigsaw and surround this with good clean hardcore. Lay a small length of PVC land drain in the trench to the pond, cover all with polythene and back-fill with soil. Cut the pipe off at ground level and cover it with a slab. Now, every time you want to drain your pond, you just drop your sump pump down the pipe and run it for a few hours, purely to equalise water pressure. Make sure all wires and junction boxes are in place at this stage.

Depending on the rockery and watercourse details you choose, you will probably have to build retaining walls as a backing to get the required height. These could be of brick, blocks or even rockery stones. For a more pleasing look, build on a concrete foundation as before.

LEFT: Forming the rockery.

Photo: Terry Hill.

RIGHT: Rocks set on bottom. (step detail).

Photo: Terry Hill.

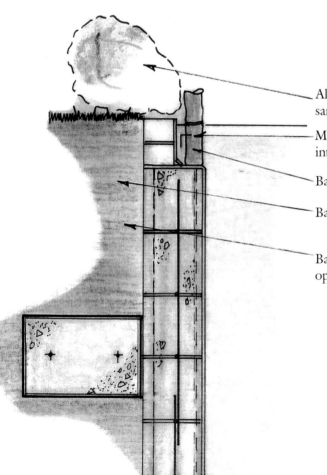

Alternative rock detail set in
sand and cement.

Metal peg into pole and built
into sand and cement bed.

Bamboo or timber poles.

Backfill and lawn option.

Backfill concrete and paved
option.

*Alternative section for
bamboo poles in water.*

*Courtesy: Koi Pond
Konstruction Kompany,
UK.*

LEFT: The finished waterfall with hidden cave behind.

Photo: Terry Hill.

RIGHT: The header pond.

Photo: Terry Hill.

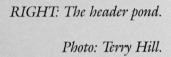

LEFT: The finished rockery.

Photo: Terry Hill.

ALTERNATIVE SECTION FOR ROCKS IN WATER DETAIL

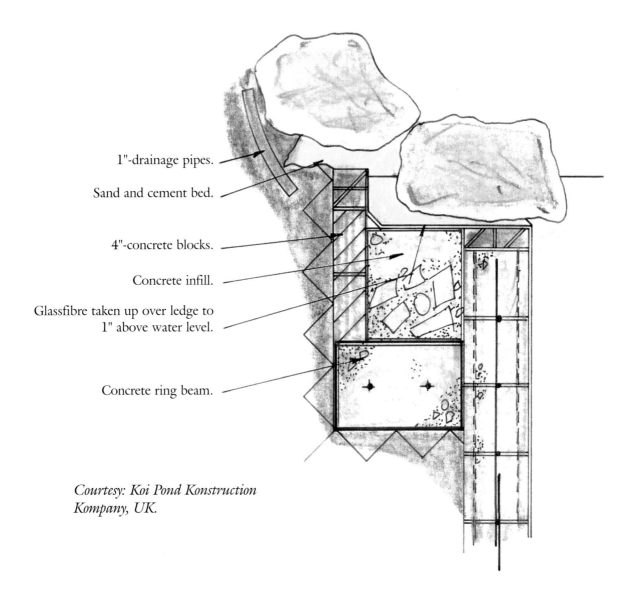

1"-drainage pipes.

Sand and cement bed.

4"-concrete blocks.

Concrete infill.

Glassfibre taken up over ledge to
1" above water level.

Concrete ring beam.

*Courtesy: Koi Pond Konstruction
Kompany, UK.*

Start the rockery off roughly to get some height, using blocks, sand and cement. Cover all this with a Butyl liner, to ensure no water is lost due to leakage through the rockery. Now you have to employ your artistic talents, choosing slabs and stones carefully. If necessary, hand-pick these from your local stone merchant and try to hold a mental picture of the finished structure as you go. Generally, one nice large flat stone overlapping the pond wall 2-3 ins above water level gets you started. Bed this on and back-fill with sand and cement mix as previously specified. Try to form planting pockets as you go. Bed and position your rockery stones either side of the watercourse, pull the liner up behind and back-fill with earth.

Carry on to the next level with another flat stone, overlapping as before, and perhaps at an angle to the lower watercourse. Continue this way to the top and form a small header pool in the liner. This will hold water and prevent splashing. Finish the rest of the rockery, bedding each stone into good quality topsoil.

Water Purifiers: Without one of these, every Koi keeper lives on a knife-edge of uncertainty regarding the quality of the mains supply.

Photo: Nick Fletcher.

Large filter system nearing completion.

Photo: Terry Hill.

An 18,000 gallon pond designed by Terry Hill.

Photo: Terry Hill.

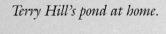

Terry Hill's pond at home.

Photo: Nick Fletcher.

Carefully trim off the excess liner just above the rock detail, as this will prevent earth washing down into the pond in wet weather. The flaps will soon be disguised by overhanging plants. Render over any liner that is showing, stippling with a brush as before, point in all gaps and then seal the complete watercourse with three coats of clear G4 sealer. To avoid too much water washing down into the pond, position 1-in drainage tubes at 6-in centres behind the lowest rocks.

If you have not already done so, complete all pipe runs across to the filter area. This should have been done earlier, as most would have been built into the filter area structure. Surround all 4-in pipes with pea shingle (to allow movement) and reinstate ground levels. Terminate the 4-in pipes with two 4-in slide valves. Add an extra one to the vortex and one to the main drain and you have the perfect set-up for maintenance and for balancing filter flow.

I recommend that you obtain a water report from your local authority – you probably will not understand it, so have it checked by a water purification company who will then recommend the correct mains purifier to rid your tapwater of pollutants such as metals.

Empty and refill the pond at least twice, cleaning the sides and bottom as you go, flushing all pipework and filters through to waste. Finally, fill the pond through a purifier and a water meter. You need to know the exact gallonage of the pond and the filters separately, especially if problems arise and you need to medicate. Other than filtration, which is covered elsewhere, your pond is now complete.

Of course, within reason, it could have been any shape, size or depth, but the example I have chosen gives you an insight into the professional construction methods I use. With 35 years experience in the building trade I am confident that this is the very best method of pond construction, and one that will earn its keep in terms of trouble-free Koi keeping.

It goes without saying that I cannot accept any responsibility for anything that may go wrong if you attempt pond building yourself; my final advice would be, if you are in any doubt about any aspect of your abilities, call in a professional.

11

PLANTS

By Barry James

Wild carp, bred for food and later developed as ornamental fish, were orginally kept in simple earth ponds. Because of the fishes' habit of rooting around the bottom in search of food, these ponds became turbid with suspended matter, and algae turned them olive green in summer.

One such pool in Essex, England, gave me my introduction to carp. It was built in the Middle Ages to supply fresh fish for a local monastery. To me it was an eternal source of mystery – sometimes an angler pulled a struggling monster up from the deep, in the certain knowledge that bigger ones still awaited capture.

As Koi developed (at man's hand) from the ancestral carp, it was quite natural that

The stunning beauty of a large, ornamental pond. *Photo: Barry James.*

the Japanese should want to include them in their traditional gardens, which had always laid a heavy emphasis on water. In this chapter, we consider both Oriental and Western gardens and look for ideas which can be adapted to make an appropriate and effective setting for a Koi pond.

Over the centuries, Europeans have favoured many gardening styles. Classical water gardens based on geometric patterns were built by the Italians, who developed ideas borrowed from the Greeks, who, in turn, had looked to the Persians for inspiration. When artesian water was available, it became possible to utilise the pressure to build impressive fountains and waterspouts.

In England, domestic water gardening came into vogue in the mid-19th century, following the construction of the internationally famous water features at Chatsworth House in Derbyshire, home of the Duke of Devonshire. The Victorians, with their fascination for exotic plants, sent out collectors to all parts of the globe. Seeds and plants were bought back to Kew and other famous institutions. Exploiting these novelties, they created what may be described as the archetypal English water garden. A number of styles became fashionable – some were formal, normally simple rectangular pools set in paving and housing large groups of water lilies, marginal plants and focal points such as statuary and fountains. Others were informal, with areas linked to the pool incorporating rockeries, bog gardens, streams, waterfalls and herbaceous borders with moisture-loving plants.

JAPANESE GARDENS

The distinctive Japanese style of gardening, refined over many centuries, was based on gardens from the T'ang Dynasty of China. The Japanese adapted the structural concepts

to empathise with their ancient religion of Shinto. Their inspiration was drawn from the unique natural features of Japan – mountains, lakes and waterfalls were represented in miniature – and symbolism played a large part in these creations. Zen Buddhism added its own special influence, resulting in the gardens we see today.

Some features of these gardens are purely aesthetic, but others are very practical in their application, bearing in mind the time they were created. The most spectacular examples were the preserve of the rich and powerful, as they required huge labour forces to create them. But, gradually, the ideas were adopted by ordinary citizens in their own gardens, albeit on a more modest scale.

In the wet but mild climate of the British Isles, the focal point of our gardens has traditionally been the lawn. However, in many parts of Japan, grass grows poorly due to the severity of the winters. Gravel was adopted early on as a suitable surface underfoot to prevent mud sticking to sandals and spoiling the hems of kimonos and robes. Stepping stones and simple pathways were developed by 16th-century tea ceremony masters to facilitate the approaches to their tea houses, but, equally, they delighted the eye and impressed the guests.

SAND GARDENS

The material used in sand gardens is what we in the West would call gravel. This can be derived from many types of rock, but granite is favoured in Japan for its durability and availability. The particle size (3-5 mm) is the same as that used for aquarium decoration or as an ingredient of poultry food.

Light-coloured gravels are favoured for use in dark areas, the darker shades being reserved for open spots where reflected glare could otherwise be a problem.

When a new garden is being created, the

Plants

ground is first cleared of weeds, then levelled and tamped down. Either a thin layer of concrete or some plastic sheeting is laid on the surface to prevent further weed growth. The sheeting is perforated at intervals to allow for drainage, and gravel is laid on top to a depth of 5-6 cms (2-2.5 ins).

Boundaries of the gravelled area should be edged with kerbing, to prevent weeds and grass spreading in from other parts of the garden. In the vicinity of the sand garden, it is advisable to plant evergreen trees, rather than deciduous species, as otherwise fallen leaves will spoil the effect in autumn.

Sand gardens are raked on a regular, often daily, basis, as the sand is intended to represent water. With special wooden rakes, intricate patterns can be created to simulate waves and ripples. A variant is the 'dry stream', where rounded slates and cobbles substitute for water.

STEPPING STONES AND PATHWAYS

Stepping stones are used both on land and also to enable the stroller to cross bodies of shallow water. They often meander, the garden owner thereby subtly leading guests through areas of the garden which offer appealing vistas or prized artefacts. The flat-top stones can either be cut or left in their original state.

The uneven side is let into the ground so that the flat side is level with or slightly proud of the surrounding area. Moulded paving stones – either square, rectangular or round – are used today, often with Japanese characters inscribed on them bearing messages such as 'The Seven Steps to Heaven'.

BRIDGES

Bridges, piers or walkways which cross water can be constructed of natural stone, concrete

Stepping stones make an attractive feature.
Photo: Dave Bevan.

Bridges can be made of stone, wood or concrete.
Photo: Barry James.

or wood. They are very much inspired by the owner's imagination, although many acceptable traditional designs are available. Some are elaborately carved and painted creations of wood, but in some instances a plain stone slab may be just as effective. Bridges must always be in keeping with their surroundings, and in scale with the rest of the garden. They can look quite effective painted in the traditional Japanese colours of black and pillar-box red. All stains and paints should, of course, be non-toxic to fish.

POND EDGING

The margins of Koi ponds are generally disguised with massive rock formations, but the owner still needs access to carry out basic maintenance or to feed or simply view the fish. This necessitates the use of either smaller rocks or pebbles around at least a part of the perimeter. Turf can make an effective edging, but then there is the problem of grass cuttings flying into the water. Wooden posts are often used to stabilise the shoreline of natural pools and can make an effective feature beside a Koi pond. The fashion is to vary the height of the posts to give the impression of a water-worn old pier or landing stage.

WATERFALLS AND STREAMS

Artificial streams and waterfalls, or modified natural watercourses, are a satisfying addition to any Japanese garden. Modern materials like Butyl rubber sheeting enable a waterproof membrane to underlay the bed of the watercourse, and the water is easily circulated by means of external or submersible pumps. If possible, waterfalls should be grand affairs reflecting the majesty of Nature – small, plastic, pre-formed cascades are not in keeping with the Japanese garden, and if the builder cannot afford a larger feature it is better to leave it out altogether.

A natural watercourse can be modified to create a waterfall.   Photo: Nick Fletcher.

LANTERNS

Authentic Japanese lanterns are invariably carved from granite, but, in the West, concrete mouldings or reconstituted stone mixed with resin are more popular, as these can be mass produced at a fraction of the cost of the originals.

Lanterns containing candles or electric lamps are used to illuminate paths and bridges, and to cast pools or shafts of light over focal points in the garden. There are numerous lantern designs, most with specialist applications which seem extremely esoteric to the Western observer. Snow-viewing lanterns (Yukimi-gata) are the most popular, and are often used near water to enhance the appearance of the pond in winter. Do-it-yourself lanterns can be made from natural rocks siliconed together, or even carved from Thermalite building blocks which are then treated with a sealing compound.

STONE TOWERS, BUDDHAS, SIGNPOSTS AND TSUKUBAI

All the above add to the uniqueness of Japanese gardens, but their use should never be overdone – they are intended to be focal

Lanterns can be used to illuminate the Koi pond.　　　*A pillar lantern.*　　　　　*Photo: Barry James.*

Oki Gata lantern.　　　*Photo: Barry James.*　　　*Snow lantern.*　　　　*Photo: Barry James.*

points rather than items in a museum. The tea ceremony has great significance to the Japanese, and associated with it are small granite water basins known as tsukubai. These, complete with wooden ladles, were situated at the entrance to tea houses and were provided for guests to wash their hands before entering.

GAZEBOS AND SUMMERHOUSES

To fit comfortably into a Japanese garden, these must be of authentic design and permanent structure (not the flimsy aluminium-framed, nylon-covered type bought from garden centres). They look at their best when situated on an island in the pool and linked to the bank by a bridge or stepping stones.

SHISHI ODOSHI

These devices were originally employed by farmers to scare away wild deer from the rice crop. They are made of bamboo on a pivot – water is piped into one end and, when the

Tsukubai with wooden ladles.
Photo: Barry James.

balance is upset, the cane tips as it empties and strikes a rock placed beneath with a loud clacking sound.

GARDEN BOUNDARIES AND FENCES

Depending on the wealth of the individual, Japanese gardens were bounded and divided up by stone walls, held together either by mortar or mud or else of dry construction. They were topped with a roof of pantiles to keep the rain from penetrating the fabric of the wall. Gates were normally of wood or metal construction and could be quite massive.

Where security is not a factor, bamboo fences are the approved method of demarcating boundaries in a Japanese garden. Bamboo in the Far East is a popular building material as it is strong, flexible, durable – and cheap. Wooden posts and wattle screens have their place, as do branches of willow, beech and conifer, closely woven into animal-proof fences. The various components are held together with strong twine or leather thongs.

In the West, bamboo poles are expensive

Buddha ornament.   *Photo: Barry James.*

and substitutes are often used. Polished hardwood posts with imitation nodal joints chiselled out on a lathe can be almost as effective as the real thing.

STONE GROUPINGS

Japanese gardens are essentially informal, and regular geometric shapes rarely come into play, as the garden is intended to represent Nature on a small scale. Large rocks of an interesting shape are placed in strategic positions such as in sand gardens, but always in odd numbers. Asymmetrical groupings can represent islands in the sea or volcanoes rising from a plain. Such stones should be carefully selected – in past times gardeners roamed the mountains looking for suitable pieces, which were then transported to the garden at enormous cost.

PLANTS FOR JAPANESE GARDENS

Even in large gardens, every tree, shrub or herbaceous plant should be carefully selected and positioned if the effect is to reflect the traditional style.

Japanese gardens are monochrome – flowers seldom come into play, except those produced by evergreen shrubs such as azaleas, or by flowering cherries, which have special significance. Cherries are carefully positioned so that, out of the blooming season, they are unobtrusive. Acers (Japanese maples), on the other hand, are prized for the subtlety of their autumn foliage and are given prominence. Coniferous trees such as pines, clipped and trained, are used as focal points, but most other large trees are planted simply as backdrops.

Boxes and azaleas are carefully pruned and clipped into rounded and oval shapes to represent hills and distant mountains, a form of topiary, though the exotic animal-inspired and geometric forms popular in English gardens have no place in their Japanese counterpart.

Bonsai are a nice touch, especially in smaller gardens where they decorate terraces. Koi keepers often use them on the decking of filters or site them on the larger rocks bordering their ponds. Alternatively, individual trees can be displayed on concrete plinths with a backdrop of slatted bamboo, where they look most authentic.

Bamboos are actually giant grasses, and very decorative. The larger species growing up to 5 metres (16 ft) tall are not hardy in Britain, but are commonly used in the milder districts of Japan. However, there is plenty of choice among plants from 50 cms to 3 metres (20 ins to 10 ft) in height. Once established, bamboos are fast-growing, spreading rapidly by means of runners. These must be pruned back if the plants are to be controlled. *Trachycarpus* palms are bone-hardy and will impart a tropical touch to the garden, as will *Fatsia japonica* – a hybrid shrub with large, glossy, palmate leaves.

Under deciduous trees, Japanese gardeners often use small groupings of shrubs and herbaceous plants such as hosta, lily-of-the-valley, rodgersia, ferns, camellia, rhododendron and mahonia.

Mosses will grow well in moist, shady areas. Some of the numerous species will establish themselves on the ground, while others colonise only rocks and tree stumps. They are very popular in Japanese gardens, but succeed only in the wetter regions of the British Isles – even then, they will need regular spraying to prevent their turning brown. This is no bad thing, however, as stones and cobbles can be wetted at the same time – this enhances the fresh appeal of the garden, and is done as a courtesy before visitors arrive to view it.

TREE PRUNING AND SHAPING

The designs on pottery, ceramics and other expressions of Japanese art have a slightly

It is important to take the longterm view when planning a planting programme.

Photo: Barry James.

Koi keeping and cultivating Bonsai often complement each other as hobbies.

Photo: Nick Fletcher.

Bamboo can grow as tall as 16 ft (5 metres) in height.

Photo: Barry James.

Royal Ferns make a good backcloth.

Photo: Barry James.

mystical quality, enhanced by the unique shapes of the pines and other trees they often depict.

These shapes are inspired by a Japanese love of trees exposed in the wild to strong winds and all the forces of Nature, and are reproduced artificially by careful shaping and pruning in true Bonsai and in larger trees trained along the same lines. Pruning has a practical, as well as an aesthetic, benefit as it ventilates the tree, permitting the access of sunlight to the leaves and preventing die-back of the lower branches. The tree is therefore strengthened and made more resistant to disease, or damage by the elements.

PLANTING THE KOI POND

The Japanese do not normally place aquatic plants in their Koi ponds, barring the odd clump of **Iris laevigata**. Equally, dealers and Koi writers place full emphasis on the fish and equipment, and seldom consider the planting aspects. However, a certain presence of plant life does have its advantages.

Trees and plants can be of great benefit to the Koi pond. The roots of this Taxodium *have an aerating effect.* Photo: Barry James.

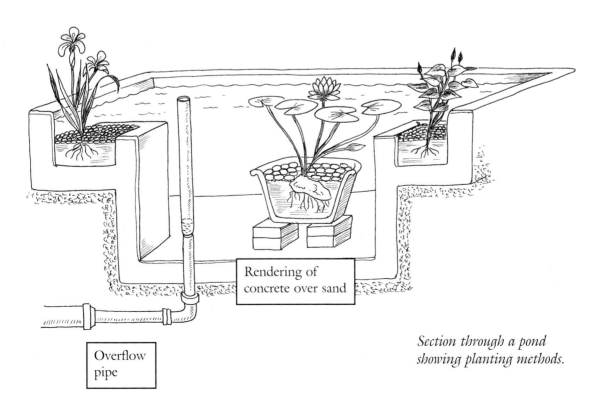

Rendering of concrete over sand

Overflow pipe

Section through a pond showing planting methods.

Iris laevigata: A traditional aquatic plant.

Photo: Barry James.

Nuphar japonicum: *A hardy plant with strong rootstocks.* *Photo: Barry James.*

Apart from the aesthetic element of colour and the softening effect of vegetation on often harsh pond outlines, plants do help condition the water by acting as living filters. In removing build-ups of nitrate and phosphate salts, they lessen the burden on man-made filter systems.

Koi have the potential to grow very large. They are bottom feeders, using their barbels to locate food on and in the mud bottom. In so doing, they stir it up, creating clouds of fine sediment which settles on the leaves of plants, clogging up the stomata and blocking out the light. Only the strongest plants survive this treatment, and then only those whose leaves either float on the surface or emerge clear of it.

When young, Koi do little harm to submerged vegetation. As they grow larger, though, they begin to have a deleterious effect. In the course of feeding they uproot plants, and devastation can be rapid and total. Only the tougher deep marginals, such as **waterlilies**, survive this treatment.

The key to successful planting is to take steps to prevent Koi from being able to root around. Waterlily containers must be heavy and stable if they are not to be tipped over. Large plastic or concrete enclosures should be used. If possible, build them of concrete breeze blocks to dimensions of 24 x 24 x 9 ins deep. Render the blockwork to seal in the free lime with a compound such as G4 or Pool Glaze.

MARGINAL PLANT ENCLOSURE

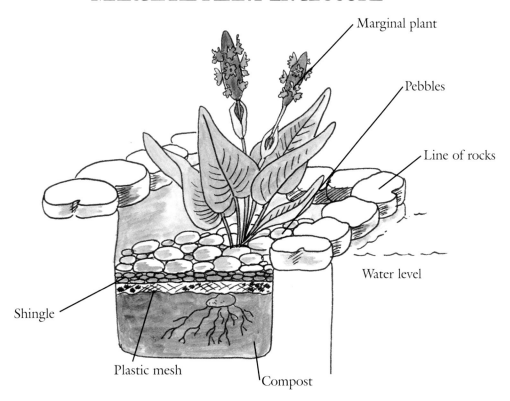

Marginal plant

Pebbles

Line of rocks

Water level

Shingle

Plastic mesh

Compost

WATER LILY AND DEEP MARGINAL ENCLOSURE

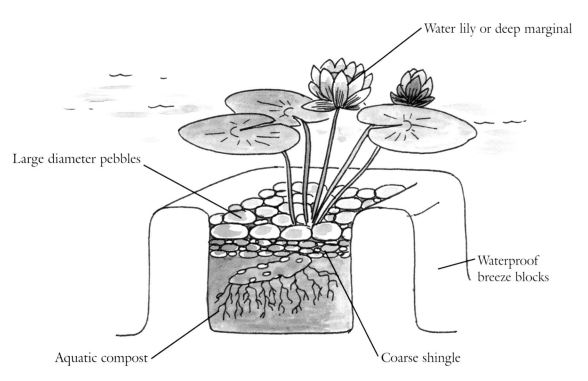

Water lily or deep marginal

Large diameter pebbles

Waterproof breeze blocks

Aquatic compost

Coarse shingle

Fill the containers to within 3 ins of the top with peat-free aquatic compost and plant them up. Over the compost, spread a layer of half-inch gravel, topped up with a further covering of fist-sized pebbles and rocks. Only medium to vigorous plant varieties should be considered, as dwarf or delicate cultivars will not be able to cope with the attentions of large Koi.

Nuphar species (**Spatterdocks**) survive well in rivers and streams, and therefore have strong rootstocks. They are also adaptable to turbid water conditions. Treat them as though they were waterlilies – although their flowers are not as spectacular, their hardiness more than compensates for this.

Aponogeton distachyum is a robust deep marginal growing from a tuberous rootstock. The glossy oval leaves can reach 6-8 ins long and 2 ins wide, and are olive green, often covered in purple blotches. The heavily scented white flowers are freely produced throughout the year, sometimes even in winter. This species has a resting period which, in some instances, can occur in midsummer.

Conventional planting crates are far too unstable in Koi ponds. The illustration shows a design which can be built of breeze blocks or, for a more decorative effect, natural stones. These should be cemented firmly in position, as root growth will exert considerable pressure and may eventually push the containing wall from the pool ledges. Cover the compost – which can contain peat for marginal plants – with a layer of plastic mesh. This will become bound in with the root mass and help stabilise the plants. The surface can be dressed with shingle and pebbles in the same way as for waterlily planters.

Annual floating plants such as **Water Hyacinth** are sometimes used for spawning, on account of their dense, hairy roots. For long-term decoration, however, and to provide shade, the **Water Soldier** is the only floater robust enough to withstand the rigour of life in a Koi pond, and then only when well-established.

AQUATIC PLANT CATALOGUE

WATERLILIES: medium varieties (suitable for depths from 12-24 ins). Spread when established, 4 square feet.

WHITE
Nymphaea 'Wilfred Gonnere:' Often known as 'Snowball' on account of its pure white globular double flowers.
Nymphaea 'Albatross': Very large snow-white blooms with golden-yellow anthers. Rich purple leaves when young, maturing to olive green.
Marliacea albida: Characterised by fragrant, freely produced snow-white flowers borne just above the surface.
Nymphaea odorata: A fragrant species from North America. Fast-growing, but the pure white flowers are not produced in large numbers. Pale green foliage.
Nymphaea tuberosa: Another fast-growing species with pure white cup-shaped blooms that are very sweetly scented.

PINK
'Mme .Wild red Gonnere': Large, double pink flowers and green foliage. Flowers continuously throughout the summer.
Marliacea carnea: Fast-growing with basically white flowers tinged with rose-pink on the outer petals and sepals.
Marliacea rosea: Deep rose-coloured, very fragrant flowers which do not achieve full intensity until the plant is well established.
'Masaniello': Fast growing with soft pink blooms up to 5 ins in diameter.
'Mrs Richmond': Immense globular deep pink flowers. Green foliage.
Nymphaea odorata 'Helen Fowler': Blooms up

Plants

'Mrs Richmond'.

'Moorei'.   Photo: Barry James.

to 9 ins in diameter of a perfect deep-rose shade. Probably the finest of the Odorata group.

'René Gerard': Freely available variety with huge deep rose-coloured flowers flecked and striped with crimson. Free-flowering.

'Rose Arey': A unique variety with stellate flowers standing well clear of the water. A uniform shade of rose-pink with yellow anthers, and fragrant.

RED

'Attraction': Glowing garnet-red flowers 7-8 ins across. Free-flowering and a fast grower.

'Escarboucle': Probably the finest waterlily in existence. Huge scarlet blooms the size of dinner plates are produced prolifically throughout the summer.

'James Brydon': Reliable variety bearing cup-shaped flowers of a rich carmine red. One of the few varieties to succeed under light shade.

'Neptune': Deep rose-crimson with orange stamens. Flowers reminiscent of tropical forms, standing proud of the water.

'William Falconer': The darkest of red blooms. On maturity the foliage changes from red to green with prominent red veins.

YELLOW

'Colonel Welch': Canary-yellow blooms standing well clear of the water. Foliage tends to be over-abundant, and the variety is sometimes reluctant to bloom.

Marliacea chromatella: Reliable yellow waterlily with olive green leaves, blotched and spotted with purple.

'Moorei': A superior form of M. *chromatella* with more intense colours.

Odorata sulphurea grandiflora: Deep sulphur-yellow flowers standing well clear of the water. As with all yellow waterlilies, the leaves are heavily blotched – with chocolate in this instance. The variety is a hybrid between *odorata* and *mexicana*, a species from Florida and Mexico.

'Sunrise': An American variety, and the best of the yellows. Individual flowers are large, fragrant and of a beautiful golden colour, contrasting well with the flecked green foliage. Undersides of the leaves are red.

WATERLILIES: vigorous varieties (depth 30-36 ins, spread 8-10 square feet).

WHITE

Nymphaea alba: Native to Great Britain, this species can grow in up to 10ft of water. Pure

129

white flowers 3-4 ins across, green leaves.
'Richardsonii': Vigorous grower of the
Tuberosa group producing giant, globular,
pure white blooms with green sepals.

PINK
'Collosea': Gigantic free-flowering variety
with flesh-coloured petals. Blooms over a
long period.
'Goliath': Tulip-shaped flowers with long
petals, white but suffused with pink.
Conspicuous white stamens and orange-red
petaloids render this an outstandingly
beautiful variety.
'Lusitania': Seldom seen, but outstanding.
Deep rose with brilliant mahogany stamens.
Young foliage is purple, changing to green
with age.
Tuberosa rosea: Capable of quickly colonising
large areas. Light green foliage sets off soft
pink flowers – very fragrant.

RED
'Charles de Meurville': Huge wine-coloured
blooms up to 10 ins in diameter. This variety
needs plenty of room.
'Rembrandt': Dark red flowers with purplish-
green foliage.

'Sirius': Deep-red flowers with a slight streak
of white on the outer petals.
'Picciola': Expensive and rare, Picciola is an
exceptionally strong grower, bearing
abundant amaranth-crimson blooms up to
10 ins in diameter.

YELLOW
'Texas Dawn': A newer American variety of
exceptional merit. Superb mid-yellow
flowers with subtle peach blush at the base
of the petals. Flowers throughout the
Summer.
'Joey Tomocik': Another large waterlily with
deep yellow flowers.

NB: Most of the yellow varieties in the
'medium' category will adapt to deeper water
if progressively lowered to their final site.

THE ROCK GARDEN
The digging of a garden pond results in a
huge pile of soil which often has to be
disposed of expensively in skips. If the pond
is of an informal design, however, some or
all of this spoil can be used as the basis of a
rock garden and/or waterfall.

A rock garden should not be just a pile of

*Alpines and dwarf shrubs are the
natural vegetation used in creating a
rock garden.*

Photo: Barry James.

soil with a scattering of rocks sprinkled over it. Preparation is all-important at every stage, as mistakes are difficult to rectify later without expending a great deal of time, effort and money. First, let us consider the choice of materials.

There are many types of rock, which are broadly classed as either sedimentary (limestone, sandstone), metamorphic (slate, gneiss) or igneous (granite). As they occur in their natural state, all rock formations are either 'bedded' (laid down in strata) or 'massive' (forming great outcrops).

Look at the rocks local to your area – chances are that your soil incorporates their weathered down particles, and using local stone will therefore give the most natural effect. But for rock gardens and walls (not to mention pond bordering, which should match up), the stone must resist weathering. Search out your local quarryman and take his advice. Stratified or water-worn pieces of rock are best, and to get the most suitable rocks you may have to visit the quarry yourself and pick them out individually. A few large, imposing pieces are always preferable to a scattering of small ones.

When the rock is delivered, make sure that it is unloaded as close to the site as possible, to minimise the task of moving it. A sack truck, low trolley or rollers will be of great help, but there is no substitute for manpower.

When the pond has been excavated, make sure that the topsoil is put to one side, as the subsoil will form the basic mound. Topsoil should be weed-killed (taking great care to avoid contamination of the pond if the rockery is a later project), and then given a generous addition of humus. This can comprise peat, leafmould or well-rotted manure, plus grit such as sharp sand, fine stone chippings or gravel. This should be thoroughly mixed before being placed on top of the subsoil. As a guide, the mix should be 8 parts of topsoil to 4 parts of humus and 3 of grit – measured by volume, not weight. At this stage waterfalls can be built – I prefer to work with Butyl rubber as a waterproof membrane, topped with concrete and rocks to give a natural effect. The concrete must be sealed, and delivery pipes and conduited electric cables installed and disguised at this stage, taking care not to crush them.

Some attempt at an overall design should be made to ensure that the feature blends in with the landscape. In some smaller town gardens, however, a rock garden with a cascade, because of its size, shape and movement, has to be accepted as a major feature.

Building on a slope naturally lends itself to systems of outcrops, each composed of a number of closely-abutting rocks. It cannot be stressed too strongly that all rocks must be bedded at the same angle and in the same direction, to mimic the natural stratification. Single rocks, simply stuck into the ground, will look like the result of a volcanic eruption and will not be easy on the eye. It is also important that rocks are securely placed and slope in the right direction, in other words, back into the mound. This ensures stability and gives good drainage while providing protective pockets for rock plants. Most importantly, take your time and view each rock placing with a critical eye. You will soon get a feeling for the task, but it may be that a particular rock needs to be turned several times before the most satisfactory face is exposed to view. The result should resemble a natural outcrop.

Alpine enthusiasts will be selective in their choice of plants. However, for the beginner, the old favourites are best. Try to choose plants that are interesting all year round, so that even when the pond looks lifeless there is still some vibrancy in the surrounding planting. Many rock plants are evergreen and, because they originate in harsh climates, will flower at different times throughout the year.

Plants for the rock garden can be chosen from dwarf shrubs, herbaceous perenials, bulbs and varieties with tuberous roots. With the right planning, the planting will be tiered, the water plants in the pond giving way to the moisture-loving species and then to the alpines as you move up the slope. Among the most suitable plants are summer and winter-flowering heathers, dwarf conifers, the smaller herbs and potentilla species. Among low-growing, spreading plants the aubretias, saxifrages, alyssums, sedums and smaller varieties of campanula will make a fine show, the smaller bulbs and tuberous plants like narcissus, crocus, anemone and iris giving colour when the rest of the garden is looking somewhat drab. With these plants forming the basis of the display, you can always add other interesting specimens for variety.

PLANTS FOR SHADE OR HALF-SHADE
Anemone nemorosa; Epimedium; Omphalodes; Shortia; Astilbe; Gaultheria; Cappadocica; Thalictrum; Cassiope; Hepatica; Primula; Trillium; Cyclamen; Meconopsis; Saxifraga; Trollius; Dodecatheon; Mimulus.

PLANTS FOR A LIME-FREE SOIL
Andromeda; Calluna; Gentiana; Rhodorohypoxis; Androsace carnea; Epigaea; Lewisia; Shortia; Arcterica; Erica (most); Lithospermum; Trifolium alpinum; Cassiope; Gaultheria; Rhododendron; Viola pedata.

LIME-TOLERATING PLANTS
Achillea; Cyclamen; Gentiana dinarica; Primula auricula; Acanthusus; Cypripedium; Gypsophila; Primula marginate; Aethionema; Dianthus; Hepatica; Saxifraga (most); Aubretia; Dryas; Helleboras; Carlina; Gentiana clusii; Leontopodium.

ROCK PLANTS FOR FULL SUN
Achillea; Cystus; Hypericum; Phlox; Aethionema; Dianthus; Helichrysum; Potentilla; Alyssum; Draba; Helianthemum; Saponaria ocymoides; Arenaria; Dryas octopetala; Iberis; Sedum; Armeria; Erysimum; Linum; Sempervivum; Aubretia; Gypsophila; Oenothera; Thymus; Campanula; Hebe; Penstemon; Zauschneria.

THE BOG GARDEN
There is a great deal of confusion over the term 'bog garden'. A bog is a wet area of land, with the ground permanently or seasonally under water.

Primula pulverenta: Thrives in half-shade.

Aubretia will grow in full sun and will tolerate lime in the soil.   *Photo: Barry James.*

Plants

This pond has an adjoining bog garden.
Photo: Dave Bevan.

Bogs on high ground tend to be formed over impermeable igneous rocks such as granite. The peat which accumulates is from the remains of sphagnum moss, anaerobically decomposed and highly acidic, and so many aquatic plants from such regions do not adapt well to alkaline soils.

Lowland bogs are generally created on a clay subsoil. Here the remains of water plants decay to form sedge peat, which is normally alkaline in reaction. Plants from this habitat do better when transplanted to our artificial bog gardens, as do all aquatic marginals.

A true bog garden is created in almost the same way as a liner garden pond, but is shallower (maximum 12 ins), and filled to a depth of 9 ins with compost. This gives a mean depth of water of 3 ins, but, by contouring the soil, this can be varied. If the surface area is large enough, consider installing stepping stones to enable you to gain access to remove weeds or cut back rampantly growing plants.

Compost for a bog garden should have as its base a good friable loam. To this should be added a generous addition of coarse sand, peat, leafmould and, if available, some well-rotted manure or mushroom compost.

THE MOIST GARDEN

The area adjacent to natural bodies of water is slightly higher than the water itself and seldom waterlogged, but always damp – since it absorbs moisture from the soil beneath by capillary action. Plants which grow in such a habitat are quite specialised, and cannot stand boggy or excessively dry conditions. What many pondkeepers understand as a 'bog garden' should more properly be termed a 'moist garden', and this is constructed as above, except that the liner is punctured with a fork at 1-foot intervals to give better drainage.

A watch must be kept to ensure that the area does not dry out; alternatively a slow drip-watering system can be installed. A useful site for a moist garden is adjacent to the overflow pipe built into a raised pond.

MOISTURE-LOVING PLANT CATALOGUE

Acanthus mollis (Bear's Breeches): Spectacular plant for the waterside. Large glossy leaves, mauve flower spikes. Well-drained soil only. Height 3 ft.
Acanthus spinosus: Dark green, deeply divided leaves, mauve flower spikes. Well-drained soil only. Height 3 ft.
Aruncus dioicus (Goat's Beard): Broad fern-like leaves, long cream plumes. Height 6 ft.
Astilbe x Ardensii: Mixed hybrids of these

PLANTS FOR THE WATER GARDEN

Photos: Barry James.

White Astilbe.

Caltha palustris.

Hosta sieboldiana 'Elegans'.

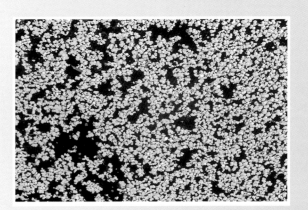

Lemna major.

Primula floridae.

Calla palustris (Bog Arum).

Lysichiton americanus.

Scropularia auriculata var.

Pontederia cordata.

Arum lily.

Cortaderia argentea – pampas grass.

Houttynia cordata var.

Azolla caroliniana (Fairy moss).

Ceratophyllum submersum.

Eichornia (Water hyacinth).

Miscanthus zebrinus.

Rodgersia.

Golden bamboo.

Ferns.

Phormium Tewax.

popular waterside plants. Height 2 ft.

Gunnera manicata: Giant rhubarb-like leaves. Height 8 ft. For larger gardens only – may need winter frost protection (cover tubers with the dead leaves).

Eremurus bungei (Foxtail Lily): Ruiter hybrids bear huge stems of small lily-like flowers in various colours. Well-drained soil only.

Filapendula ulmaria 'Aurea': Heads of white blooms resembling those of meadowsweet. Golden leaves. Height 12 ins.

Geum chiloense 'Lady Stratheden': Pure yellow flowers. The cultivar 'Mrs Bradshaw' has flaming brick-red flowers.

Helxine soleirolli: Creeping carpeting perennial, ideal for disguising the pool edge.

Hosta spp. (Plantain Lily): Hardy perennials with attractive foliage and lily-like blooms. Foliage height 6-9 ins, flower spikes 20 ins. Assorted varieties with green, coloured or variegated leaves, all prone to slug damage.

Ligularia dentata: Imposing and very attractive leaves. Liable to attack by slugs and snails.

Ligula 'Desdemona': Rich dark brown leaves, orange flowers. Height 2 ft.

Ligula 'Gregynog Gold': Handsome heart-shaped leaves, vivid orange flowers.

Lobelia vederense: Intense purple flowers. Height 20 ins.

Lysimachia punctata: Spires of brassy yellow flowers. Height 18 ins.

Macleaya cordata: Large, rounded, lobed leaves. Plumes of buff-coloured tiny flowers. Well-drained soil only.

Malva moschata (Musk Mallow): Large pink flowers. Height 18 ins.

Monada didyama 'Panorama Mixed': Assorted red, pink and white flowers on erect stems.

Pulmonaria sacharata 'Sissinghurst White': Matted leaves with white flowers. Well-drained soil only. Good ground cover for pool surrounds.

Peltiphylum peltatum: Huge umbrella-like leaves on tall stems. Flowers deep pink in early Spring. Height 4 ft.

Rodgersia aesculifolia: Bronze-tinted chestnut-like leaves.

Rheum palmatum: Huge curly leaves with talls spires of crimson or white flowers.

Sisyrinchium striatum: Grey-green iris-like leaves, with stems of numerous pale yellow blooms.

S. striatum 'Variegatum': Cream-striped leaves. Height 18 ins.

Tradescantia andersoniana: Hardy perennial with upright stems, ideal for moist soil. Mixed hybrids in deep blue, pale blue, white and deep red.

Trollius europeus 'Golden Queen': Lovely golden globose flowers.

BOG PRIMULAS
Mostly from China and Tibet, these colourful plants can easily be grown in moist, peaty soil.

Primula 'Candelabra Hybrids' mixed: An assortment of beesiana, bulleyana, chionantha etc. Mixed colours.

Primula denticulata (Drumstick Primulas): Numerous hybrids with globose heads including 'Alba' (white), mauve and red.

Primula florindae: Large plants reaching 2 ft with yellow flowers.

Primula sikkemsis: Another large yellow-flowering variety reaching 18 ins.

Primula veris: The cowslip, ideal for naturalising.

HARDY FERNS
Asplenium cristatum: A variety of the Hartstongue Fern. Leathery, oblong fronds, dark green with very wavy edges. Height 10 ins.

Dryopteris felix-mas (Male Fern): Very finely-toothed fronds. Height 3-5 ft.

Polystichum aculeatum (Hard Shield Fern):

Leathery texture, upright growth.
Athyrum felix-femina (Lady Fern): Lacy, fresh and light green.
Matteuccia struthiopteris (Ostrich Feather Fern): Tall, vase-shaped fronds.
Onoclea sensibilis (Sensitive Fern): Creeping habit, will even invade the water.

GRASSES AND BAMBOOS
Miscanthus sinensis (Hardy Sugar Cane): Tall grass to 6 ft, blue-grey leaves.
Miscanthus zebrina stricta: Upright species with yellow crosswise bars on blue-green foliage.
Carex morrowi 'Evergold': Golden grass reaching 8 ins. Likes a damp position.
Cortaderia argentea (Pampas Grass): Tall silvery plumes to 4 ft.
Cordateria 'Gold Band': A spectacular pampas grass with golden striped leaves.
Phalaris picta: A noble grass striped in green and white. Height 2 ft-plus.
Arundinaria: The most popular bamboo genus. All prefer moisture at the roots and protection from strong winds.
Arundinaria auricoma: Golden variegated leaves on erect, purplish stems. Good tub plant, 3-6 ft.
Arundinaria fortunei 'Variegata': Low, dense thickets of erect zig-zag canes, with dark green, white-striped leaves. A good dwarf bamboo. To 3 ft.
Arundinaria japonica: Common bamboo. Tall grower; makes a dense thicket, 6-8 ft.
Arundinaria simonii: Vigorous and erect. Tall olive-green canes. Ultimate height 6-8 ft.

PLANTS FOR STREAMS AND WATERFALLS
The aquatic flora of streams and waterfalls face quite different growing challenges from those posed by ponds and lakes. The plants have evolved mechanisms to cope with the pressures of living in the dynamic conditions created by fast-flowing water.

Water mosses such as those belonging to the genus *Fontinalis* contain species which grow in either stagnant or flowing water. Riverine types attach themselves firmly to the rocks with special root-like organs. In stillwater species their tendency is to grow in loose, spreading masses where the attachment organs are very weak or absent altogether.

Plants from fast-flowing water normally grow poorly or perish when transferred to ponds, although they can thrive in watercourse returns, providing the current is strong enough. In absorbing nitrates/phosphates through their roots, they perform a useful role.

WATER GARDENING IN WARM CLIMATES

Although carp are endemic to the temperate climatic zones of Europe and Asia, they adapt very well to other regions. Singapore, lying near to the equator, is one of the major exporting countries, yet its climate is tropical, with average temperatures of around 30 degrees Celsius. The water varies greatly in its characteristics, often being highly acidic, yet these fish adapt very well to these alien conditions. Koi keepers in warmer climates are very fortunate as the fish grow faster under these conditions and do not have to survive the traumatic conditions of winter.

Aquatic plants are found in greater variety in the sub-tropical regions, often possessing more spectacular foliage and larger, more showy flowers than their northern cousins. It is often possible to grow these beauties alongside plants from cooler areas.

Countries bordering the Mediterranean, climate zones nine and ten in the USA, South Africa and Australia are all examples

PLANTS FOR WARMER CLIMATES
Photos: Barry James.

Water poppy.

Tropical lily (hybrid).

St Louis Gold (Tropical Waterlily).

Missouri tropical lily.

Yellow lotus.

Cyperus papyrus.

of areas where a much larger range of plants can be grown and where the danger of frost is so low that these more delicate plants can remain outside all year.

TROPICAL WATER LILIES

Tropical water lilies do everything on a grander scale than their hardy cousins. They grow larger and taller and have a wider range of colours. Their flowering period is extended over a longer period, even continuing throughout the whole year in truly tropical conditions. Half the species bloom during daylight hours, the other at night. The scent is often more intense in the night bloomers.

Most propagate by seed and runners, but a few produce viviparous plantlets on the leaves. In many species, the flowers and leaves grow above the surface of the water. Tubers are not the thick woody tubers of the hardies, but instead resemble nuts and small sweet potatoes (yams). When planted, it is possible to remove the small shoots given out by the tuber as propagating stock. The tuber will then produce new growth.

Tropicals are treated in the same way as hardies except that they must be started in shallow water. Later, when larger, they can be moved into deeper water.

The minimum temperature for survival in winter is 65 degrees Fahrenheit. However, 80-90 is needed for active growth. Until this temperature is reached in early summer, comparatively little growth and flowering occurs. If winter temperatures are too low, it is best to lift and overwinter ripe tuber indoors. In many areas, it is common practice to treat tropical varieties as annuals. However, with the increasing cost of plants, overwintering is preferable where possible.

RECOMMENDED VARIETIES OF TROPICAL WATER LILIES

Below is a list of just half a dozen varieties.

Readers are advised to consult a specialist work for a more comprehensive list.

DAY FLOWERING HYBRIDS
Evelyn Randig (L) Brilliant magenta flowers.
Tina (S/M) Deep-blue flowers with a purplish tinge at the base.
St Louis Gold (S) Golden-yellow flowers.

NIGHT FLOWERING HYBRIDS
Sir Galahad (L) Pure white.
Maroon Beauty (L) Maroon red.

LOTUS (NELUMBO)
Lotus are some of the most ancient and revered flowering plants in the world. They grow from two to eight feet in height with parasol-like leaves up to 2 1/2 feet in diameter. Leaf colour is usually bluish-green and gently frilled on the edges. The huge and showy blooms are like giant full-blown roses and are up to 12 inches in diameter. They are borne high above the foliage on stout stems.

Lotus grow from strong running tubers, and it is in this form that they are usually sold. Lotus need sub-tropical temperatures during the growing season. They will survive in very cold areas provided the tubers can retreat into the mud below the influence of frost.

LOTUS VARIETIES
Nelumbo Debbie Gibson. Large cream scented flowers, Height 5 feet 6 inches.
Nelumbo Mrs Perry Slocum. A very large grower with apricot-tinted blooms.
Nelumbo Shiroman. Lovely double-white flowers.
Nelumbo Momo Botan. Dwarf Japanese Lotus 3-4 inches in height. Leaves 18 ins across. Scented dark-rose coloured flowers.

DEEP MARGINAL PLANTS
Amongst plants with this habit are a couple

of gems which deserve a place in any tropical water garden.

Water Poppy *(Limnocharis humboldtii)*. This plant has smooth deep-green, glossy oval leaves which are borne on long ascending runners. Three-petalled golden flowers resemble the California poppy.

Water Snowflake *(Limnanthemum indicum)*. Closely resembling water lilies in general form, the white lacy flowers are born in profusion during the warmer months.

MARGINAL PLANTS

Taro or Elephants-Ear Plants. *(Colocasia esculenta)* is a giant herb with huge showy arrow-headed leaves. This, and other related species, needs to be planted in large pools. They grow best in wet soil in the margins.

Umbrella Palm *(Cyperus alternifolius)*. Large grassy marginals some six feet or so in height. There are also dwarf varieties. The name comes from the umbrella like inflorescence borne on the end of the long, slender stems.

Egyptian Paper Plant *(Cyperus papyrus)* Similar in growth habit to the above, but with huge mop-like heads. This plant can reach ten feet or more in height but there is a dwarf variety available.

Water Canna *(Canna species)*. Several species similar to the well-known Indian Shot plants of gardens but capable of growing in water. Showy flowers and imposing foliage.

FLOATING PLANTS

Floating Fern *(Ceropteris thalicroides)*. Only suitable for the warmest areas this bright green plant forms floating islands of finely divided foliage of typical fern configuration.

Water Lettuce *(Pistia stratiotes)*. Again only suitable for the warmest areas, this pale bluish-green plant is in the form of a rosette and grows up to 18 inches in diameter with long trailing white roots. Often used as a spawning medium.

Note: To this list of non-hardy aquatics may be added many of the plants listed under the hardy selection.

12 *SEASONAL CARE*

Depending on where you live, you may will need to make seasonal adjustments when caring for your Koi. The following advice applies to temperate regions.

SPRING (March-April-May)
Koi are at their most vulnerable in early spring. Day- and night-time temperatures fluctuate considerably, so keep the pond cover on at night to reduce wind-chill. Do not switch on venturis or waterfalls yet, but, if pump turnover has been reduced, restore it to full flow rate through sub-surface returns only. On milder days, sections of pond-cover may be removed to allow the sunlight to warm the water. When the temperature reaches around 10 degrees C (50 degrees F) pathogens begin to multiply and parasites are more active, but Koi immune systems will still be dormant. Fish in unheated ponds must not be fed until ambient temperature stabilises around 12-14 degrees C (53-57 F).

They can then be given sinking wheatgerm pellets – feed once, early in the day, to give them time to digest the meal before nightfall. Gradually wean them on to wheatgerm floaters and then on to a staple pellet. Watch for any abnormal feeding or swimming behaviour and bowl suspect fish for inspection, but remember that many pond remedies are ineffective at low temperatures –

Rock and water garden in the spring.
Photo: Dave Bevan.

any sick fish will have to be treated individually in an indoor hospital facility. Dosing the whole pond will only retard the recovery of the filter, so hang fire on this until late spring.

Feeding in itself puts a loading on biological filters, which may take time to kick in – help them along with either a liquid or bran-based bacterial preparation. Now is also the time to ensure your filters and pipework are sludge-free and that all your equipment is in good order. Check the lamps in UV units, valves for smooth operation and cartridges on tapwater purifiers. Are your test kits past their sell-by date, and do you have emergency pump spares? Has frost loosened any rocks or edging slabs, and do your filter covers need a fresh coat of wood preservative?

Test the pond water for ammonia and nitrite, and, if necessary, conduct large partial water changes to restore acceptable parameters. Zeolite in the filter is a good temporary ammonia-remover, but cannot be used in conjunction with salt. Winter water changes tend (wrongly) to be infrequent, and rainfall may have topped up the pond. Rainwater does not have the buffering capacity of the mains supply, so regular pH testing is especially important at this time.

The Koi pond in the summer.
Photo: Dave Bevan.

SUMMER (June-July-August)
Owners of heated ponds should not switch off the boiler, but adjust the thermostat to maintain a constant 70 degrees F. The rest of us can step up the feeding regime and begin to offer higher-protein growth foods. Perhaps purchase of an automatic feeder would be wise for those working away from home, so that Koi can dine little and often without subjecting the pond to ammonia surges.

As water warms, dissolved oxygen content falls but the fishes' oxygen demand rises. Activate surface skimmers and aeration devices in pond and filter, and keep any waterfalls or cascades running, especially at night. Dissolved oxygen measuring equipment is a sensible investment.

Ensure shading is in place over any pergolas, and consider how blanketweed should be tackled. It is best to attack the problem before it takes hold, as otherwise time that could be spent enjoying your Koi will be taken up removing the clogging algae – sometimes on a daily basis. Interpet Pond Balance, a liquid treatment, is effective. Good reports also come from users of pads made from barley straw or lavender stalks, while a well-planted vegetable filter will take up nitrates. The jury is out on electronic blanketweed controllers, which work well for some, but not all, Koi keepers.

Koi will flock-spawn in summer, generating a lot of organic material visible as a bubbly surface scum; large water changes are then called for, and fish must be checked for damage caused during the chase.

Any suspected health problem must be investigated swiftly, for pathogens are multiplying fast. Invest in a microscope and learn how to take and interpret mucus scrapes – sometimes protozoan parasites are very selective about their hosts, so that one or two Koi will become heavily infested while others remain clear.

If you take a summer break, the Koi will happily survive on natural food items, but it is best to have a knowledgeable person visit regularly to check that pumps and filter are working as they should. Leave the telephone number of your vet or fish health specialist, and a note authorising any treatment that may be necessary while you are away.

AUTUMN/FALL (September-October-November)
Climatic changes mean that early autumn can see the highest air temperatures of the year. Continue feeding a high-protein diet until the first cool spell, then reverse the spring feeding regime so that, by the time the food is tailed off, the Koi are on sinking wheatgerm. Fish in heated ponds are fed as normal.

A skimmer, if fitted, will deal with falling leaves, but netting off the larger debris reduces the workload on skimmer baskets. Pay particular attention to vacuuming and/or purging of bottom drains and filter settlement chambers so that the pond is largely free of organic matter. Trim the dying leaves and stems of any marginal plants. A pre-winter cleaning of the biomedia (rinsing in pond water only) may be called for, but

Continue to feed a high-protein diet until the first cold spell. Photo: Dave Bevan.

this should be done in stages so that the biomass is not affected.

Although the best-quality Koi are exported in late autumn, do not contemplate buying any unless you have a heated pond to receive them.

Before the temperature falls to 12 degrees C (54 degrees F) is a good time to medicate the pond against parasites if appropriate, and check that no fish has unhealed wounds, as tissue regeneration will soon cease. Sick Koi will go into winter in a weakened state and, if they do not succumb then, they will be especially vulnerable the following Spring. If you have any young Koi resulting from a summer spawning, these must be brought inside for their first winter, as should any fish under 6 ins bought earlier in the year.

An autumn bonus is that your Koi will be showing their best colours in the cooling water.

WINTER (December-January-February)
In ponds without supplementary heat, turn off or divert all aeration devices and make ready the pond cover. Giving Koi a short 'natural' winter is advocated by some, so the cover need not be installed until January. Resist the urge to feed the fish on warm days.

To save on fuel bills, heated ponds should by now have their covers in place – leave a small area open to the air so that gaseous exchange can take place. To what degree you heat determines how the Koi are managed. It is very dangerous to maintain an ambient water temperature around 50 degrees F, as the fish will be vulnerable to disease and use up energy reserves in active swimming. So either heat to 64 degrees F and feed them as for the rest of the year, or use the combination of cover and a low temperature setting to keep the water at 45 degrees F minimum for as long as the Koi are getting no food. After a month or so, the temperature can be slowly raised and feeding resumed.

The winter months.   *Photo: Dave Bevan.*

Long nights encourage lax maintenance, but unheated ponds should be checked daily and part water changes continued at the rate of 10 per cent weekly or fortnightly. Lag pipework from the water purifier to prevent it icing up. Approach the pond cautiously so as not to disturb the Koi. Be on guard against predation by herons, especially if natural waters locally have frozen over. This should never happen to a modern Koi pond fitted with an insulating cover.

SEASONAL CARE OF SUB-TROPICAL PLANTS

The climate in the region in which the garden is situated, is a summary of all the weather likely to be experienced in that particular place over a number of years. The pattern of activity and growth pertaining to a climatic zone will change almost imperceptibly as one zone merges with another.

The local topographic features and geology must also be taken into account. These often minor differences, even over a comparatively short distance, can result in micro-climates which greatly influence the types of plants which can be grown.

As with climatic zones, the seasons also graduate into one another and seasonal care varies greatly according to the calendar. As one approaches the equator, however, these seasonal differences become less. The fluctuations in temperature are marginal and the only real differences lie in the rainfall pattern.

Rainfall, or lack of it, is an important factor, inducing greatly differing growth patterns in the natural environment. Aquatic plants in artificial pools that are constantly topped up from the mains, or those that are spring-fed, often behave in a totally different manner to their wild counterparts.

Vegetative growth continues at a steady pace throughout the year, although the flowering cycle may be extended or remain the same as in other areas. However, this continuous growth does mean that pool husbandry is extended throughout the year with an almost continuous need for leaf-pruning and filter maintenance. When the water temperature is constantly at the optimum for the fish's metabolism, feeding patterns need to be more consistent, with no need to alter the ingredients or the frequency to suit colder winter conditions.

Aquatic plants from sub-tropical regions display seasonal resting periods as a response to drought conditions. Many perennials develop storage organs such as bulbs or tubers to tide them over these periods. Some are annuals and produce prolific seed to ensure the survival of the species. At these times, old and decaying foliage should be cut back and the debris thrown on the compost heap. At the same time, excess tubers should be severed from the rootstock and either used as propagation material or simply discarded.

Lotus are sensitive to frost and will die if the crowns of the tuber are frozen. The minimum winter temperature is 35 to 40 degrees if the plants must be moved indoors and kept cool. They must also be protected against rodents who are very partial to the tubers. Old biscuit tins are ideal for this purpose, but holes should be made in the sides and top to allow for ventilation. Damp sand or peat are suitable storage media. The same principles apply to tropical water lilies regarding winter treatment.

If plants are grown in containers, fertilizer tablets should be applied in the spring. Plants in very large enclosures, or which have the run of the pool, will flourish without feeding.

13 *SMALL KOI PONDS*

It is a sad but indisputable fact that most Koi sold around the world will be ending up (sometimes literally) in ponds totally unsuited to their needs. Through ignorance, or as a result of following incorrect advice casually dispensed at general aquatic outlets, purchasers are led to believe that Koi are merely larger versions of hardy goldfish or orfe, and require basically the same kind of care.

The proof that they need much more is evident every spring, when garden pond owners return to replace fish that have not survived even one year. Rather than laying the blame for the mortalities where it belongs – at their own door – it is less painful for them to believe that Koi are somehow 'difficult'.

Easy though it is to cite small ponds as killers of Koi, that is by no means the complete picture. True, the capacity of the typical ornamental pool can be measured in hundreds, rather than thousands, of gallons, and its depth is such that it freezes solid in winter and practically boils the fish in summer. There must therefore be a minimum Koi pond size. Anything much below 1,000 gallons and, no matter how well thought-out the system may be, the fish will still struggle. (There are countless examples of smaller Koi ponds which would seem to contradict this, but the line has to be drawn somewhere.)

Three constraints widen the gap between the ideal pond most Koi keepers would like and what they actually end up building: lack of space, lack of time and a limited budget. There is a very strong case, in certain circumstances, to opt for a smaller pond, properly constructed, rather than something huge and unmanageable – especially if its completion would hinge on cutting corners with materials and equipment. It is no use having 10,000 gallons of water if the funds for a decent filter system run out halfway through the project.

On the other hand, the smaller a body of water, the less stable it tends to be. Rapid fluctuations in temperature and water quality and a predisposition to blanketweed growth are potentially common drawbacks. So it is no use building a compact Koi pond as merely a scaled-down version of a larger one and still expecting it to work. It must be better in almost every respect!

REDUCING COSTS

This would seem to be at odds with the reduced cost factor, but genuine savings can still be made and funds diverted elsewhere. First, the pond can be tackled largely as a do-it-yourself project, cutting out labour costs. Hand-digging the holes for pond and filter saves hiring a mini-excavator and operator. Another major consideration is disposal of

Small Koi Ponds

spoil, which can be an expensive business. However, small amounts of topsoil can be redistributed over the garden and the subsoil used to construct a rockery/waterfall feature. Similarly with fibreglassing (one job best left to the professionals) – the unit cost per square metre does not vary much according to pond size but, fairly obviously, the smaller the area to be covered, the lower the bill.

AVAILABLE SPACE

What about would-be Koi keepers whose only restriction on pond size is the physical space available? Perhaps the only site is on a patio, which has to double for family barbecues. Length and width of a pond may be limited, but the third dimension – depth – can be capitalised upon in two directions, up and down. For example, a ground-level pond 8ft x 6ft x 3ft deep would hold approximately 900 imperial gallons. Dig down the extra foot, raise a wall and bring the water level another foot above the surrounding terrain and the capacity climbs to nearly 1,500 gallons.

The area taken up by a gravity filter on the same pond would be in the region of 8ft x 3ft minimum, but this is not necessarily wasted space – it can be a positive asset to the design of the garden. Covered by hinged decking, it will serve as a seating area or a display point for tub plants and Bonsai. The pergola built over it to counteract the effects of sunlight doubles as a support frame for climbing plants such as clematis, wisteria, miniature roses or honeysuckle.

Further integration of other, normally separate, water garden features into the scheme can be achieved; a conventional bog garden can be replaced by a vegetable filter, a great asset in the battle against blanketweed. This filter need not contain only watercress – Water Mint (*Mentha aquatica*), Japanese Iris (*Iris laevigata*), Umbrella Grass (*Cyperus alternifolius*), various rushes (*Butomus and Scirpus* spp.) will all assimilate nitrate, and annual sowings of Monkey Musk (*Mimulus luteus*) will provide a splash of colour.

EFFICIENT MAINTENANCE

In smaller Koi ponds, ease of maintenance is an absolute must – the moment any aspect of it becomes a chore, the temptation is there to skimp on essential jobs, and water quality and the fishes' health will quickly deteriorate. All filter chambers must be drainable to waste; all pumps must have isolating valves fitted either side so that they can be serviced or replaced without loss of water. The fewer pieces of ancillary equipment in the water,

Special consideration must be given to stocking a small Koi pond.

Photo: Barry James.

the better – submersible pumps, plus their hoses and cables, are a particular eyesore in small ponds. Larger filter systems can afford to be less than 100 per cent efficient and still function, but scaled-down versions must punch every ounce of their weight. The most important aspect is efficient settlement, which for today's small pond means a vortex.

These used to be exclusive to gravity-fed filters, as only a slow, steady inflow of solids-laden water is conducive to the particles spinning down to a collection and disposal point. Lately, though, pump-fed vortexes have appeared. These counteract excessive water velocity by stepping up pipe diameter from pump to entry point and employing a directional baffle within the chamber itself. While they are admittedly still not quite as efficient as the gravity versions, they will do the job.

Preceded by good settlement, almost any proprietary filter will perform the biological function in a small pond. It is hard not to make a case for the traditional bayed upflow design with transfer ports. GRP units are available with steeply-benched chamber bottoms, drain valves and pipework. These require only a level concrete base to stand on – patio slabs if above-ground in pumped mode, or a poured foundation for gravity-fed installation.

Such filters are normally sold as being suitable for ponds of a given capacity, but the makers' claims can be optimistic. Within the constraints of space, it is best to purchase the largest you can afford.

The other type of proprietary filter tends to sell itself on claims of maximum performance in the minimum amount of space, with more than one function carried out in each chamber. Typically, brushes will be deployed to trap particulate waste, and foam cartridges will intercept the finer particles while doubling as a biological medium. Some such designs are very efficient, incorporating spraybar or venturi aeration and valved discharge hoppers. Purpose-built vortex settlers enhance their performance. Other designs can look very imposing at first glance, but when you actually examine the space available for the media, and the limited dwell time they offer, they may not seem so attractive a proposition.

For Koi keepers on a strict budget, the much-maligned external box-type filter can be an option for the smaller pond – though only if preceded by one or more vortexes. In this format the filter is relieved of much of its burden of solids collection, and the foam sheets or cartridges will not need such regular cleaning in rotation, giving the biomass a chance to build up. Some upflow pump-fed models can be partially buried, and full gravity versions are also available, fed from a bottom drain or multi-level inlet.

If your small pond is gravity-fed it is likely to incorporate only one bottom drain, and thought should be given to the contours of the base to ensure that all the solids find their way into the filter. Rather than site the drain centrally, it is perhaps better to slope the base steeply (60 degrees) to one end of the pond and pick up water from there – the pond then acts as a giant 'hopper'.

TEMPERATURE

Given that small bodies of water warm up and cool down relatively fast, some means of artificially heating this type of pond should be considered. Electric heaters are initially inexpensive to buy, but their running costs can be prohibitive. Running a stainless steel heater-exchanger off the domestic gas central heating system is the preferred long-term option. Installation should be carried out only by an approved gas fitter. The quarterly bills will not go through the roof if the pond is also covered during the winter/early spring.

POND DESIGN

Pre-formed ponds are sometimes used to house Koi, but considering the price of these GRP units they are far from ideal. Their main drawback is lack of depth – rarely are they more than 30 ins deep, which is not acceptable to Koi. Nor are they necessarily a convenient option. Excavating the hole to accommodate them, then backfilling and levelling, can be more time-consuming than opting for a Butyl liner or blockwork construction in the first place. The fussier shapes should be rejected out of hand, as they are wasteful of potential water capacity and can, in the more extreme instances, obstruct flow around the pond and create dead spots. Only as header or subsidiary ponds do they have their place.

A clutter-free design is essential with all Koi ponds, but the smaller the body of water the more important this becomes. If a shed or outbuilding is reasonably close to the pond, a lot of the hardware can be housed inside, doing away with the need for visible dry pump chambers and compartments for UV units, junction boxes, mains purifiers, air blowers and so on. Security will be improved, the equipment will be protected from frost and, providing linking pipework and conduited electric cable is properly buried, safety will not be compromised.

APPEARANCE

Aesthetically, the appearance of a small Koi pond can be ruined by inappropriately tall adjacent planting or fussy ornamentation that draws the eye away from the water. That said, large surrounding rocks still have their place – smaller pieces do not look right, whatever the size of the pond.

INDOOR PONDS

Those of us with a conservatory may like to consider the benefits of an indoor display pond – here, small really can be beautiful. Providing the building's roof allows natural sunlight to penetrate, Koi kept indoors will blossom. The water temperature can be inexpensively kept high enough for the fish to feed year-round; there will be easy access to an electricity supply and mains drainage; poolside planting can include tropical or sub-tropical species and, above all, the Koi keeper can enjoy the fish all year round.

However, a full structural survey of the building must be obtained before work begins, otherwise you run the risk of subsidence or worse.

STOCKING A SMALL POND

Finally, the success or failure of any small Koi pond depends on the owner's restraint in stocking it. A safe rule of thumb for a filtered pond is 100 ins of fish per 1,000 gallons (some people work on surface area rather than volume but, providing the pond is 4 ft deep or over, the former calculation is more reliable). Filter manufacturers claim more Koi than that can be accommodated if a larger system is installed (i.e. a 4,000-gallon package on a 2,000 gallon pond), but in small bodies of water that can be a dangerous assumption to make.

Initial stocking should always be to a maximum of half the final recommendation, to allow for growth. Bear in mind also that three six-inch Koi will excrete less ammonia than one 18-inch specimen, due to the greater body bulk of the larger fish.

14 *POND SECURITY*

Koi are valuable creatures, sometimes in monetary and always in emotional terms. In a pond environment they are safe from attack by other, predatory, fish, but, unfortunately, still at risk from unwelcome air and land-borne enemies, both animal and human.

AIR-PREDATORS

In Britain, the main threat to Koi comes from cats and herons, although a surprising number of smaller birds will take young fish if given the opportunity. Crows, magpies and even blackbirds have been recorded doing just this, and it appears to be learned behaviour.

In other parts of the world, the list of predators can include snakes, egrets, raccoons, mink, martens, cranes and terrapins (known in the USA as 'turtles').

If you are in any doubt as to what is visiting your pond (most attacks take place at night or very early in the morning), the surviving Koi can give visual clues. Fish mauled by cats and other furred predators show four parallel clawmarks. Those that are victims of heron attack are more likely to have single stab wounds, inflicted by the beak, on their backs and flanks.

COUNTERMEASURES

Koi keepers, as animal lovers, will not countenance harming wildlife, but sometimes active or passive deterrent measures have to be considered when a pond is targeted. Dummy herons are not the answer – far from keeping other birds away, they can actually attract them, and there have been instances of the real heron trying to mate with its plastic counterpart!

The simplest tricks are still the most effective. Building a raised pond with an overhang defeats fish-eating grass snakes and nuisance amphibians. (Male frogs in the breeding season will sometimes clasp the head of a Koi, damaging the eyes. If the creature covers the fish's gills, it can suffocate it.)

Sheer-sided ponds make it difficult for birds that wade into the water to fish; they can still perch on the edge, but will have only one chance at a meal before the other Koi retreat to the bottom.

Heavy-gauge nylon fishing line strung at less than 6-foot intervals across a pond is another good defence against herons, whose wingspan is wider. A better tactic still, if the garden layout permits, is to stretch the nylon well above human head height so that it covers the pond and surrounding area.

If these measures fail, there are a number of commercial devices available to scare away predators. The simplest is a double tripwire strung on posts around the pond. When the

Pond Security

Netting can be used to protect Koi from the threat of herons and other predators.

Photo: Dave Bevan.

intruder (usually a heron) walks into this, it triggers a mechanical 'big eye' frightener which flaps open, and a percussion cap explodes at the same time.

More sophisticated are ultra-sonic transmitters activated by a passive infra-red detector. These emit sounds inaudible to the human ear, but unpleasant to cats and fish-eating birds. Similar detectors can trigger strobe lights, loud music, even spray jets of water. The drawbacks are that some of these can be intrusive to neighbours, especially if activated at night, and they cannot discriminate between your own domestic pets and other animals. Like car alarms, if they are set too sensitively they will constantly be going off, whereas on a more sleep-promoting setting they may let a marauder through.

DOGS

Having a dog on the property is one of the best predator defences, but the dog himself can damage a pond if he decides to go for a swim. And not all gardens are fenced well enough to prevent dogs from straying.

There is one device on the market in Britain and the USA which could provide the answer; a low-voltage cable is buried around the property perimeter and looped around any features (such as a pond) where the dog is not permitted to be. The animal is fitted with a special collar which emits an audible warning when he approaches the hidden cable. If he crosses it, a mild and harmless correction (similar to the static electric shock we might experience from elevator buttons or car doors) is administered. A short training period teaches the dog where he can and cannot go, after which he can roam the property apparently unrestricted.

SCARING DEVICES

Purely visual scaring devices tend to lose their effectiveness fast unless they 'do' something. The Japanese breeders use balloon-like inflatables in primary colours, with a huge eye decal, strung over their ponds to blow around in the wind.

Dummy cats or birds of prey may have a limited effect, too, but the best scarecrow I have yet seen consists of a day-glo orange inflatable man who periodically rises from a prone to a kneeling position, and bows to the accompaniment of a loud electronic wailing – not a solution for the smaller garden!

THEFT

Koi theft, like most crimes, is rarely planned. Opportunist thieves may simply be attracted to pondfish bigger than they have ever seen before, and steal Koi because of their size, not their quality. It is still comparatively rare

to lose fish in this way, and there are several things the Koi keeper can do to minimise the worry without spending a lot of money on security devices.

The most obvious strategy is to site the pond close to the house, in full view of a picture or conservatory window but out of sight of casual passers-by. Front-garden ponds are clearly most at risk from theft, vandalism and poisoning. If this is the only possible location, then some form of lockable grid may need to cover the surface, not only to protect the fish but to save lawsuits arising from children wandering on to the property and falling into the water.

FENCING

Without turning the pond into Fort Knox, it pays to invest in secure fencing or hedging. Solid garden walls are not recommended; far from acting as windbreaks they can encourage turbulent air currents and accentuate wind-chill over the pond. Good, intruder-proof hedging material includes

A lockable picket fence keeps small children away from the pond when adults are not around to supervise.

Photo: Nick Fletcher.

hawthorn, blackthorn, holly, laid hazel, beech, hornbeam, box, privet and pyracantha. Young *Leylandii* conifers are flexible enough to be pushed aside, but the trunks of more mature trees will form a post-like barrier if planted close enough together.

Where properties adjoin public areas, it is probably best not to site a Koi pond immediately adjacent to the boundary hedge or fence. It is not unknown for vandals to throw over toxic substances like bleach or detergent – clearly, the farther away from the wall the pond is, the less the risk of these finding their target.

It is illegal in Britain to place anything on top of a wall or fence that might injure an intruder, but, while that rules out broken glass and barbed wire, there is a harmless product now available consisting of strips of blunt, hard rubber spikes that will make attempts at climbing uncomfortable, whether the intruder is a domestic cat or a cat burglar.

ELECTRONIC DEVICES
Most electronic security devices for general home use will be of some benefit to Koi keepers, too. Movement and body heat-activated halogen lights are a favourite, though again 'light pollution' can alienate neighbours if the detector is on a sensitive setting. Recent developments include video cameras that link up to equipment inside the house and will either automatically switch to the video viewing channel if the owners are inside watching TV, or else record proceedings – even when the television set is switched off.

OTHER PRECAUTIONS
Inadvertently advertising the fact that you keep Koi is asking for trouble. Display personalised Koi numberplates (or car stickers proclaiming to the world that you love these fish), and thieves may well follow your vehicle and pinpoint where you live for

a future visit. Similarly, do not be too willing to tell strangers or casual acquaintances about your hobby. If a house caller should remark on your pond (usually along the lines that the fish must be very expensive – most non-Koi people automatically assume that they all are), play down the value of yours and try to convince him or her that they would not be worth the effort of stealing.

SHOW SAFETY
A danger time for planned theft of high-grade Koi is during a show; however careful organisers are not to link fish with their owners' names, word soon gets around as to who regularly attends the show circuit. As fixtures are advertised months in advance in the aquatic press, thieves will know when key Koi keepers are most likely to be away from home. Vigilant, trusted neighbours are a real asset under these circumstances (do not forget to give them your mobile phone number before you leave).

PHOTOGRAPHIC RECORDS
It is sensible to take photographs of all your Koi of any value, for two reasons. If any of your fish are stolen, you can take the pictures along to dealers in your area in case the thief tries to sell them on. And, if your fish are recovered, good recent photographs will confirm your original ownership, which otherwise might be legally difficult to prove.

INSURANCE
Insurance against loss of Koi, from whatever cause, is a tricky area; the few policies available carry high premiums and detailed exclusion clauses, so it is probably better to take your own preventative measures against the thief in the night.

CARE WITH CHILDREN
Finally, as mentioned earlier, pond security is a two-way concept – the pond needs

protection, but, equally, children need protecting from the inherent dangers of a pond.

Drowning tragedies are thankfully rare, but it is highly irresponsible to allow any small child unsupervised access to water. A toddler can be kept away from the Koi pond with a close paling fence with a lockable gate. This barrier need not interfere at all with the appearance of the garden, especially if the pond is designed along Japanese lines. The wood can be stained traditional red and black and actually add to the Oriental ambience.

Never rely on a flimsy wire-mesh cover to keep children safe from water. A foot can easily go through and the wire-mesh can actually make getting out of the pond more difficult. To be effective, a safety cover must be rigid (made of wrought iron or steel), built into the pond structure, hinged and lockable. But, if it is necessary to take such a drastic step, it may be better to postpone building the pond until the family has grown.

Ponds can be made child-proof using metal mesh, though this mesh would be a little coarse to offer full protection.   *Photo: Dave Bevan.*

15 *MATURING THE POND AND FILTER*

Efficient biological filtration enables Koi to live indefinitely in an enclosed environment. Without it, the pond would quickly become uninhabitable, due to a build-up of toxic ammonia.

THE NITROGEN CYCLE

In the nitrogen cycle (of which a working biofilter is a living example), waste matter is mineralised into ammonia (NH_3) and ammonium (NH_4^+). This is then oxidised by *Nitrosomonas* bacteria into nitrite (NO_2). In turn, the nitrite is broken down by *Nitrobacter* into the relatively harmless nitrate (NO_3), which is removed during regular partial water changes or taken up by plants in a vegetable filter. This is a simplification – the nitrogen cycle is only one of several taking place simultaneously in any pond (there is, for example, a phosphorus cycle), but it is the one that most concerns us here.

The beneficial filter bacteria (known collectively in a pond as the biomass) occur naturally in air and water, but, to colonise the filter and multiply to viable levels, they require nourishment, a constant supply of dissolved oxygen, and *time*.

The food supply for bacteria derives from organic matter; this is comprised of a mix of debris blown into the pond, uneaten pellets, decaying plants, small dead aquatic animals, and fish droppings. These eventually enter solution and are broken down by heterotrophic bacteria into ammonia. Additionally, ammonia is discharged directly into the water through the gills of our Koi and excreted as urine.

Neither biomass nor fish can survive in isolation; without the Koi, the autotrophic filter bacteria would not gain sufficient nourishment and would soon die back, and, without the bacteria, the Koi would be poisoned in a solution of their own waste. In order for this 'chicken and egg' situation to be resolved, a new pond and filter must go through a maturation process until fish and biomass are in a stable balance of mutual dependence.

When a pond is first filled there will be minimal or zero ammonia or nitrite in the water, and any nitrate present will have originated from the mains supply. The old-fashioned advice to switch on the filter, leave everything for several weeks and then introduce all the fish at once is fundamentally flawed, although some novice Koi keepers still think that if near-zero test readings are obtained after that time it is okay to proceed. What then occurs is commonly called 'New Pond Syndrome', which is a sanitised term for avoidable fish deaths.

In a typical scenario, all the fish go into the pond together and ammonia levels immediately begin to rise (detectable on a test kit a day or two later). At this early point there will be no nitrite present, because the Nitrosomonas bacteria will not have multiplied in sufficient numbers to oxidise the ammonia to the next stage in the cycle. Ammonia levels will continue to climb steeply while the bacteria establish themselves. After a few more days, however, as the Nitrobacter kick in, nitrite will register on test and levels will climb in parallel with the upward ammonia curve. Ammonia concentrations eventually peak and begin to fall while nitrite is still climbing. The second (nitrite) peak is reached days or even weeks after ammonia concentrations have fallen to safe levels, and only when near-zero readings are obtained for both can the pond be said to be mature.

Meanwhile, without intervention, the Koi will have died or been severely weakened from ammonia and/or nitrite poisoning. How can these casualties be avoided?

ESTABLISHING WATER QUALITY
There are two schools of thought. The first advocates a very gradual build-up of fish stocks, combined with daily testing and frequent water changes to dilute toxins. But there are several inherent weaknesses in this approach. It is time-consuming, because on each occasion that more fish are added, the stock/biomass balance is lost and there will be secondary rises in ammonia and nitrite while the bacterial populations catch up with the additional loading. This can occur even in established ponds, incidentally, if feeding rate is suddenly stepped up or a higher protein food is adopted.

Furthermore, it is unfair for fish to be present when toxins are above danger level; under this regime they inevitably will be, if only for the short intervals between partial water changes. Recognising this, it was once suggested that the first Koi into a pond should be inexpensive (in other words

THE NITROGEN CYCLE

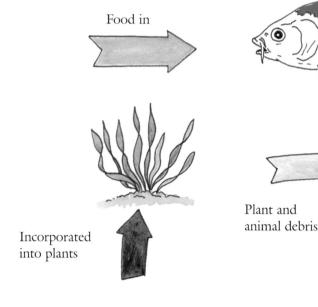

Food in

Plant and animal debris

Incorporated into plants

Oxidation by NITROBACTER bacteria

Nitrates NO^3

expendable) specimens.

The second method of maturation requires much more care and attention to detail, but it is neither open-ended nor seriously stressful to the fish; at the end of the process (a month or two) you will have a meaningful Koi population living in balance with the biomass. However, for it to work you must

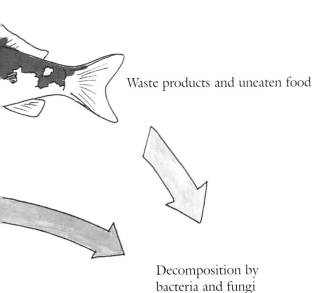

Waste products and uneaten food

Decomposition by bacteria and fungi

Under aerobic conditions

Ammonia
NH^3/NH^4

Oxidation by
NITROSOMONAS
bacteria

Nitrate test kit.

Photo: Nick Fletcher.

Sintered glass rings are an excellent filter medium, said to help in nitrate removal.

Photo: Nick Fletcher.

first invest, at the very least, in a tapwater dechlorinator, and preferably a purifier that will also remove metals and other common contaminants. Chlorine and chloramine are lethal to filter bacteria. You must also obtain reliable test kits within their sell-by date for pH, ammonia and nitrite, and preferably also for dissolved oxygen. The filter and aeration should be up and running, but not the UV.

Having ensured that the pH of the pond is between 7.2 and 7.8, and that there are no residual contaminants from the building process (e.g. lime from untreated mortar), introduce the fish in the usual way – floated in bags until temperature equalises inside and out. You then add a liquid suspension of live

ABOVE: Ballcock top-ups are preferable to the use of a hosepipe after part-water changes. Photo: Nick Fletcher.

LEFT: Dechlorinators in three sizes, with pre-filters. The units are filled with granular activated carbon.

filter bacteria into the biological chambers to begin the maturation process. While this is a great help, it is no substitute for time and care – it should be seen as seeding the biomass, rather than establishing it in one fell swoop. Another (riskier) way to do this is to add some mature media, i.e. a filter cartridge, from an already established system. This, however, lays your fish open to cross-infection. In the old days, people would even place a dead fish into the filter, or add a cup of urine, to supply the initial ammonia; enough said!

Instead of regular partial water changes, the pond is now fed a continuous supply of mains water through the dechlorinator/purifier, which should allow a minimum of 10 per cent of total volume to be exchanged every 24 hours. Now is the time to appreciate the built-in overflow, which should be piped to waste well away from the pond.

BEGINNING TO FEED

Once the Koi have settled in, you can begin to feed them. Daily tests should be made, and, once detectable ammonia and/or nitrite readings appear, a greater percentage of the water will need to be exchanged for fresh to keep them below danger level. The waste water is discharged from the settlement stages of the filter whenever necessary and the pond is topped up, after which the rate of constant feed through the purifier is increased. Additional seedings with the bacterial suspension are made according to the directions.

Taking pH readings throughout maturation is important, because the toxicity of pollutants varies according to the acidity or alkalinity of the water. Above neutral (pH 7.0), ammonia (NH_3) is more toxic, but nitrite (NO_2) less so. Below neutral, ammonium (NH_4^+) is less toxic but nitrite (NO_2) more so. To complicate the issue

Maturing the Pond And Filter

further, water temperature has a bearing on ammonia toxicity – the higher the temperature, the higher the percentage of NH_3 in a given total ammonia sample. This effect is more pronounced the more alkaline the water.

Your dissolved-oxygen test kit should be used daily during maturation to ensure that levels never fall below 5mg/litre, otherwise the fish will suffer. The capacity for water to take up oxygen falls as temperature rises. Bear in mind that filter bacteria are aerobic, so that heavy aeration in the biological chambers of the filter is just as important as in the pond itself. Vigorous aeration also helps to offset ammonia toxicity, though it is no substitute for water changes.

As filter maturation progresses, daily testing will reveal the need for fewer part water changes, and once readings stabilise out (near-zero ammonia and nitrite) the constant supply of new water can cease. From then on, the normal maintenance regime of periodically flushing the mechanical stages of filtration to waste and topping up through the purifier will suffice, and the UV unit can be switched on.

WATER TESTING
Regular water testing should still be carried out on a weekly basis; electronic meters are very quick and convenient, and this encourages their use. For the 10 per cent of so of male Koi keepers who are colour-blind, they are essential; people with poor colour vision cannot always interpret the comparison charts supplied with liquid or dry tablet test kits.

Even established filters will suffer occasional knock-backs from the use of medications, or when new fish are introduced. A danger time in unheated ponds is spring, when feeding resumes after a winter break. The filter bacteria population will have reduced, as virtually the only source of ammonia will have been that excreted from the fishes' gills – then, suddenly, an additional organic loading comes along. This is the time for a booster dose of liquid bacteria and larger water changes.

Another way of offsetting ammonia surges is to place a net bag of zeolite rock into the filter. This natural material absorbs the pollutant, and can be re-charged by soaking it in a strong salt solution overnight. Such chemical filtration should not be seen as anything other than a temporary measure, however, and zeolite must never be used in a pond treated with salt, or it will 'dump' its ammonia load back into the water.

This gravity-fed filter is housed under cover in an area equalling that of the pond itself.

Photo: Nick Fletcher.

The pH of a new pond can be expected to rise during maturation but should stay within the suggested parameters, otherwise Koi will be affected as the regulatory mechanism affecting the pH of their own blood is put under strain. A falling pH can signify a filter not working properly, or insufficient water changes; a buffer such as cockle or oyster shell can be introduced into the filter, but not before the underlying cause has been investigated.

There is probably no such thing as a 100-per-cent-efficient filter, as there will always be a residual ammonia level in pond water awaiting transfer to the biological chambers. Dwell time (the time it takes for water to pass right through the filter system) and turnover rate (the number of times the total pond volume passes through the filter in a given period) may be insufficient and lead to a rise in residual ammonia, in which case the pump and/or filter may need upgrading; meanwhile, feeding should be reduced.

QUARANTINE PONDS

Quarantine and hospital ponds need to be matured in just the same way as the main facility, as there is little point in moving a sick fish into a smaller body of water if all the parameters are less than ideal. Remembering that fish and filter bacteria are interdependent; it is best (once the vat is matured) to keep Koi in permanent residence, though they need not be the same fish all year round. If this is not practical, well-quarantined goldfish will supply the ammonia needed to maintain the nitrogen cycle.

As vats tend to be subjected to regular medication, it is especially important to monitor water quality; some chemicals, e.g. potassium permanganate, de-oxygenate the water, so heavy aeration in the vat and its filter will need to be maintained.

OZONISERS

All the above precautions apply to Koi ponds and vats filtered the traditional, biological way – but now there is an alternative set-up which permits heavy stocking and feeding from day one, with none of the worries of ammonia and nitrite build-up. The system will never be in universal use, for it is not cheap. However, given Koi keepers' love of technology, this is the direction the hobby could well take as we enter the next century.

The system centres around ozone (O_3), a gas that could be described as oxygen with an extra molecule. In this state it is very unstable, and seeks to revert back to O_2 by oxidising everything in its path. As we know, oxidation is the process used by nitrifying bacteria to break down ammonia and nitrite. In the presence of ozone, ammonia is oxidised into nitrate, oxygen, water and hydrogen; ammonium becomes nitrate and water, while nitrite is converted to nitrate and oxygen.

Ozonisers have long been used in marine aquaria and in fish-farming to kill pathogens, but in a Koi-keeping context they can do much more. Introducing the gas directly into the pond would be disastrous, of course, so the technology involves generating a measured amount of ozone (controlled by a redox potential sensor) into a heavily oxygenated reactor chamber incorporating a protein skimmer. Here the ammonia and nitrite are chemically changed and removed, along with the DOC (dissolved organic carbon) that we commonly call protein.

Ozone gas also kills all bacteria in contact with it, so it reduces populations of motile pathogens. Filter bacteria, being sessile, are not affected – as in a UV chamber, only the organisms passing through the unit are destroyed.

An ozoniser can be used in two ways – either as an addition to an existing filter system or, with modifications, as a direct

Combined ozoniser device and foam fractionator.

Photo: Nick Fletcher.

replacement. In the first scenario it is particularly useful in the summer months, ironing out pollution peaks caused by the combination of heavy, high-protein feeding and raised water temperatures. It will also kill the single-celled algae that cause green water, so no additional UV will be needed.

As a complete system, the ozoniser is teamed with a simplified gravity-fed mechanical filter (one or more vortex chambers fed from the bottom drain/s) to remove solids. There is no need for

subsequent biological chambers, as the ozoniser and protein skimmer combined will remove all ammonia compounds and return only oxygen-rich water to the pond. In this semi-sterile environment, Koi will grow rapidly and be less susceptible to protozoan parasite attack, while any minor wounds or split fins will heal rapidly. Water quality and clarity in systems like these is said to be impeccable, and the new generation of purpose-built ozonisers are attracting a lot of interest in the UK and Europe.

MAINTAINING THE POND AND FILTER

A properly-specified Koi pond is designed to be self-cleaning. Surface and sub-surface returns from the filter generate a circulatory current which brings solid debris within the catchment area of one or more bottom drains. If the pond walls and floor are smooth and free of blanketweed there are no obstructions to the process – the solids pass directly to settlement.

VACUUM SYSTEMS
However, many perfectly satisfactory Koi ponds function well without these refinements – they just need more input from their owners. An example would be a gravity-fed system which picks up water from an elbowed wide-bore pipe fed through the pond wall into the settlement stage. The business end is either meshed off or, more commonly, set within half an inch of the pond floor so as to draw off solids from the immediate vicinity. The action of fish putting solid waste into suspension means that sooner or later most of it will be pulled out, but to maintain pristine conditions some form of vacuuming system is appropriate.

For part-raised ponds a simple syphon can be set up – a length of 1.5-inch diameter rigid plastic pipe attached to flexible hose long enough to take the waste water to the nearest inspection chamber or soakaway. On to the rigid pipe can be fixed an extension handle, for greater reach and control. The whole assembly is submerged in the pond so that no air is trapped in the pipe, and the free end of the flexible hose is then covered with the palm of the free hand and brought smartly out and over the wall. Water should flow freely. Syphons are also useful in old-style above-ground settlement chambers with no independent drainage.

Small ponds can benefit from manual vacuums. The type favoured by the Japanese is especially good for removing fish droppings; when the handle is gently pumped, solids are strained into a collection bag and the water returns to the pond.

For smaller, shallow ponds, this manual pump-action cleaner is hard to beat.

Photo: Nick Fletcher.

Another type, for use in ponds up to a metre deep, is a variation on the valved stirrup pump. Here a flexible hose leads out of the pond, taking with it water and dirt.

The best pond vacuums, though, are the powered systems based around a surface swimming-pool-type pump. Complete kits comprise an extendable pole with vac brush head (for concrete or liner ponds), reinforced suction hose, the pump itself – sometimes trolley-mounted – and more hose to carry away waste water. Solids are intercepted by a removable strainer basket within the pump before they can reach and possibly damage the impeller.

If the filtration system is run off an external pump, then an arrangement of valves will allow the pondkeeper to hitch up a vacuum extension to it, an obvious money-saver. A useful adjunct to all vacuums is a long-handled soft brush to sweep debris towards a dirt collection point.

SURFACE DEBRIS

The pond surface can accumulate debris too, in the form of atmospheric dust and windblown leaves and twigs. The larger particles can be drawn off with a hand net, but for ongoing surface clarity most Koi keepers will opt for a constantly-operating skimmer. In its simplest form this can be a U-shaped pipe leading into settlement, both ends open, the one drawing from just below the pond surface being fitted with a sliding extension. This enables it to be raised at feeding time, preventing the ingress of pellets. Basic gravity skimmers work because, when the pump is running, the water level in the pond is always fractionally higher than in the filter but is trying to equalise with it.

Alternatively, independent floating skimmers powered by a submersible pump can be used in ponds where it is not practical to run another pipe through the wall of the filter chamber. One or more floating 'pots' with neutral buoyancy will self-adjust to pull water over their rim whatever the pond level may be, so (for example) they will compensate for fluctuations in levels from evaporation loss in hot weather.

Power skimmers are the most efficient option of all, but they must be incorporated at planning stage, as the weir and collection pot are built into the pond wall. These skimmers are identical to those found in swimming pools and are run from an external pump. Here again, a multi-port valve on the main system pump can determine when the skimmer operates. The mechanically cleaned water can be pumped directly back into the pond, but a better option is to feed it to a waterfall with header pool, which will encourage the finer solids to settle out.

DEALING WITH FOAM

There is another type of waste attracted to the water surface during the mineralisation of fine organic particles into ammonia. This is known as DOC (dissolved organic carbon). It cannot be taken out by mechanical means, and, at high concentrations, it 'flattens' the water surface, giving the pond a yellowed, slightly oily, millpool appearance, and encourages foam formation under waterfall returns. The problem is most evident in summer, particularly when Koi are on a high-protein diet and being fed several times a day. Although DOC can inhibit the efficiency of filter bacteria, its removal is desirable mainly for cosmetic reasons, and a foam fractionator may be the answer.

While tropical marine fishkeepers have long been using a scaled-down version of a foam fractionator known as a 'protein skimmer', hobbyists have until very recently had to get by with some form of home-made device. The simplest version, known as a co-current skimmer, consists of a vertical tube, part submerged in the pond or passive settlement chamber, with a source of air (a diffuser or airstone) at its base which drives an air/water mix up the tube. DOC is adsorbed on to the bubbles so produced, and foam or froth collects in a removable cup for regular disposal. A more efficient version – the counter-current skimmer – has pondwater pumped downwards into the vertical tube and aerated by a small venturi device. This gives longer air/water contact time. Even so, getting a foam fractionator/protein skimmer to constantly produce the reassuring froth is not always easy; even when it is fine-tuned there will be times when the device is generating no foam at all. This is nothing to worry about, and is merely a sign that the fractionator is doing its job.

There is now available in the UK a German-made commercial foam fractionator with an extensive air/water interface and long contact time, early test results on which are promising.

GREEN WATER AND BLANKETWEED

So-called 'green water algae' and blanketweed are primitive plants with the potential to be present in nearly all natural rivers, ponds and lakes. They contain chlorophyll, and, like most other plants, they photosynthesise, giving off oxygen during the day and carbon dioxide at night.

To thrive they need three things – warmth, light and nutrients – and during the spring and summer these conditions are met in Koi ponds to a far greater degree than in ponds which are heavily planted, and whose surfaces are shaded from the sun by the leaves of waterlilies.

Koi ponds tend, with a few exceptions, to be rather bare environments; in order for fish to be properly appreciated, water clarity is a prerequisite. Unfortunately, shade-free ponds receiving direct sunlight can warm up and turn the colour of pea soup virtually overnight. The third element required by the single-celled algae – nutrition – is provided in the form of nitrates (the end-product of biological filtration, often augmented by a high level in top-up tapwater) and phosphates.

Koi do not mind healthy green water – they will have spent at least one summer back in Japan in shallow mud ponds, benefiting from the host of tasty aquatic organisms arising from the algal base of the food chain. In conjunction with the trace elements found in the clay that lines these ponds, the murky conditions encourage good colour and skin quality, so the October netting is always a time of excitement as the breeders see for the first time in months how their Koi are progressing.

Until a few years ago, green water was seen as a sporadic nuisance to be endured, but something that would disappear as the pond achieved a 'natural balance'. This may have been what happened in unfiltered, planted ponds, but Koi systems are very unnatural in terms of the large volumes of fish supported in relatively small bodies of water.

Green water is sometimes confused with water containing high levels of particulate waste. The movement of the fish keeps this debris in constant suspension, reducing visibility down into the pond. The remedy is to step up flow rate, improve the mechanical filtration or increase the frequency of pond vacuuming.

There are two real dangers associated with true green water. At night, when carbon dioxide is emitted, the pond becomes more acidic (a very weak solution of carbonic acid). Quite dramatic pH fluctuations can occur in a 24-hour period; if these are suspected, the water should be pH tested first thing in the morning and just before dusk. A green pond can become oxygen-depleted, and in low-pressure conditions on a warm night fish can be killed.

Another disadvantage is that Koi cannot be seen clearly in green water, and signs of disease can be overlooked until it is too late to treat them successfully. So, one way or another, the green has to go.

ULTRA-VIOLET UNITS

Chemical remedies (mild herbicides) were and still are a recognised remedy, but they can be expensive to administer repeatedly. They can also retard the growth of higher plants. Dyes have been tried, too – they reduce light penetration into the water, but a bluish tinge gives an unnatural (and somewhat flattering) cast to the colours of Koi.

Luckily there is one complete answer to green water, and that is UV clarification. Ultra-violet light was first used in indoor aquaria to kill pathogens or at least reduce their numbers. It is still used in fast-turnover Koi quarantine systems for that purpose. Water is pumped past a UV light source encased in a quartz sleeve, when the kill rate will depend on several factors – the wattage of the lamp, the proximity to it of the bacteria or protozoa, the contact time (related to chamber size and flow rate), and the frequency of recirculation.

When the first UVs for Koi ponds appeared, it was felt in some quarters that they would kill not only free-swimming bacteria but those in the filter too, or else bring about a semi-sterile pond environment that would dull the fishes' immune systems. These fears proved groundless; the only organisms affected by UV are those in contact with the light source, and even if filter bacteria strayed from their source of food (they are in fact sessile), only a minute percentage of the total population would be destroyed.

What pond UVs do most usefully is disrupt the cell structure of the single-celled algae which bring about green water.

Individual cells are so small that even the finest filter medium will not trap them – they merely circulate round the pond and its filter system. After contact with UV light, however, the damaged cells flocculate, or clump together. These larger bodies can now be intercepted by open-cell foam or granular filter media, and, providing a UV of adequate wattage is run continuously, green water will no longer be a problem.

The great variance in wattages between units claiming to treat similar gallonages can be confusing. A rough rule of thumb of 10 watts per 1000 gallons is a starting point, but many less powerful units seem to perform equally well in a clarifying role, providing the tubes are renewed at six-monthly intervals. UVs are either mounted on top of external pump-fed filters or on the return side of the pump in gravity-fed systems. In both instances they must be pump-fed.

There are no dangers associated with properly-installed UVs, except that a working lamp must never be viewed with the naked eye – it can damage eyesight. If the pond is being medicated, the UV should be turned off for the duration of the treatment, otherwise it will degrade the chemicals before they have a chance to work. And should the pondkeeper disconnect the UV over winter (when green water is not a problem), exposed units should not be left in situ. Ice can form in the chamber and crack the quartz sleeve, which is an expensive item to replace.

DEALING WITH BLANKETWEED
With the pond rid of green water, another nuisance algae soon makes an appearance – blanketweed. The two rarely appear together, but once a pond ceases to be opaque, the filamentous algae take over where the single-celled types have left off.

It is often said (usually by Koi keepers who have got it) that good blanketweed growth is the sign of a healthy pond. Certainly a short

coating, like green baize on the pond sides, is attractive – the fish seem to like it too, either grazing it or feeding on the tiny organisms it harbours. Much less welcome is the long, stringy alga (*Spirogyra, Cladophora* and related species) that can grow literally before your eyes. It is unsightly; it harbours dirt particles that would otherwise find their way into the filter; it breaks off and clogs submersible pumps and bottom drains; and it is particularly rampant in areas of strong oxygenation and water movement, such as venturi returns, around airstones and at the base of waterfalls.

The vigour of blanketweed varies according to where you live – it is most prevalent in hard-water areas, as it uses calcium salts in its cellular structure. Pond construction method also determines how much of a nuisance it will be – blanketweed finds it more difficult to gain a foothold on smooth surfaces (such as fibreglass gel coat) than on liners or inexpertly rendered concrete.

Unless kept in check, it will interfere with water circulation, break away and clog bottom drains and filter intake pipework, and entrap uneaten pellets and fish droppings in its strands. When it decays in late autumn, it will increase the organic loading on the filters.

If chemical or electronic control measures are not used, or fail to work, it is all down to physically pulling out the stuff on a daily basis. Plain or electrically-powered 'twirlers' are only one stage removed from the old tactic of using a roughened stick, though they make shorter work of the job. In the longer term, it is probably best to invest in a product which creates conditions unfavourable for algal growth but is harmless to fish, higher plants and filter bacteria.

MANUAL REMOVAL
The first and most obvious control method is manual removal. Traditional roughened sticks

have been superseded by 'twirling' devices, some battery-operated, but the principle is always the same. Large balls of compacted algae can soon be accumulated, but the operator is bound to miss some.

CHEMICAL TREATMENT

Chemical treatments are legion: Clarosan, used for keeping swimming pools crystal clear, is a favourite. For best results, a sachet of the granules is suspended in a current, and replenished as required.

Blanketweed cures, of all things Koi-related, seem to attract the fringe element. There is little doubt that all work some of the time, for some people; but a 100 per cent safe and proven remedy still seems a long way off. Koi keepers most successful at keeping blanketweed at bay tend to use several control methods simultaneously.

MAGNETS

Powerful south pole-opposing magnets are sold as an adjunct to UV units and certainly seem to inhibit the build-up of limescale on their quartz sleeves. In some instances, they also reduce blanketweed growth, but success can be short-lived. It is almost as though the algae adapt to the changed conditions and comes back stronger than ever. Reversing the polarity of the magnets around feed pipework may give another temporary respite, but the process is time-consuming.

SHORT-WAVE RADIO

In recognition of this, domestic scale-inhibiting devices working on short-wave radio frequencies have appeared on the pond market. These, like magnets, allegedly interrupt the assimiliation of calcium carbonate by blanketweed, and, as soon as partial immunity is attained, the frequency is reversed at the flick of a switch. Later (and pricier) models incorporate computer-controlled random frequency switching.

It is almost impossible to assess the effectiveness of these devices, as many other factors may come into play in determining the rampancy of blanketweed growth. Users report everything from total and permanent elimination, through partial and temporary respite, to complete failure.

FILTRATION

Vegetable filtration can be an ally. The principles are described in more detail in another chapter, but to be effective such filters, planted with greedy nitrate-absorbing plants such as mimulus or watercress, need to be large in relation to the pond.

Some filter media, especialy sintered glass and ceramic by-products, are claimed to have nitrate-removing properties, taking the process of nitrification one step further by reducing the nitrate under anaerobic conditions to nitrogen gas. Again, the jury is out: unless they are placed in a bypass filter with low levels of dissolved oxygen it seems hard to understand how they can work, as good aeration is an essential part of biological filtration.

Tapwater purifiers can, however, help control blanketweed by removing nitrates in the mains supply before they reach the pond. It is noticeable that Koi ponds in which partial water changes are made straight from the tap seem to suffer most from filamentous algae – not to mention other ills! There are some purifiers which the makers claim are guaranteed to get rid of blanketweed, though it is significant that the cartridges responsible can actually release dissolved metals into the water. A sure sign of metals contamination is an algae-free pond, but this is a very high price to pay for being able to see the fish.

Finally, there are barley straw and lavender stalks – semi-natural blanketweed remedies that have been under test for several years and would seem to have considerable potential. The straw or lavender (free of pesticide contamination) is sold sewn into loose-weave cotton pouches or strips and placed in an area of the pond where there is flowing water, either a filter chamber or beside a venturi return. After a few weeks the organic material begins to decay, releasing enzymes which inhibit the growth of the algae. Of the two, lavender has been shown to be the more effective, but it can reduce dissolved oxygen levels and so should be used only in well-aerated ponds.

SHADE
Shaded Koi ponds tend not to suffer blanketweed problems as much as those exposed to direct light for much of the day. For ponds in open situations, a pergola is the answer. These structures not only add Oriental ambiance, but can be roofed over with greenhouse shading mesh. Depending

on grade, this can reduce light penetration by between 35 and 85 per cent. As light is needed for successful algal growth, the results are obvious. The mesh has a secondary cooling effect, too, and some designs of pergola can actually be walled in during the winter to form an accessible cover.

Owners of new ponds are often lulled into a false sense of security because blanketweed does not appear for the first year or two. Ponds where it never does appear tend to have large, efficiently designed filters, overhead shading, relatively low stock levels and sensible feeding regimes. It is better to control the algae as soon as the first signs of them appear; otherwise loose and decaying blanketweed will place a high organic loading on the pond and can lead to water-quality problems.

16 *BUYING KOI*

Koi keeping is not and never will be a cheap hobby – as those who participate know only too well. To the layman, though, the initial cost of building a proper pond and the regular bills for food, medication and, of course, electricity are all overlooked as attention focuses on the price of the fish themselves: "They cost a fortune, don't they?"

This idea is fostered by the huge sums of money exchanging hands in Japan, and, to a lesser extent, in the UK and elsewhere, for very special Koi indeed. These are fish purchased with the express purpose of being shown at top level, and winning. But they are in no way representative of the millions shipped around the world annually. The truth is, with Koi as with so many other things in life, you get what you pay for. In any event, the fish, glamorous as they may be, are rarely the main expenditure – at least in the long term.

Luckily there are Koi available to suit everyone's pocket. What generally happens is that newcomers are undiscerning, as long as the fish seem attractive and healthy. Metallic fish appeal more than the subtler varieties, which is why every pond seems to have at least one Ogon. As people grow with the hobby and visit more dealers and hobbyist ponds, they learn what distinguishes run-of-the-mill Koi from those of higher grade, and

may as a result end up unhappy with what they have bought to date. Developing an eye for good fish takes time and experience, but to fully realise the dream means digging down fairly deep into the pocket.

A lot of perfectly competent hobbyists are happy to remain with quite ordinary Koi, of course, and, if funds are limited, a sensible soul will realise that any spare cash should go towards improving the fishes' environment by upgrading the pond, rather than be spent on more fish purchases. Indifferent Koi kept under ideal conditions are far preferable to top grade fish in cramped and poorly filtered accommodation.

CHOOSING A SUPPLIER

Japan is the home of Koi, but many other countries with favourable climates are now producing fish for export: China, South Africa, Thailand, Cyprus, Singapore, the USA and, of course, Israel. Although parent stocks may be Japanese, the Koi (with exceptions, mainly in the case of Israeli fish) are volume-bred, so little if any culling takes place. Such Koi still find a mass market through garden centres, pet stores and non-specialist aquatic outlets, and size for size are no more expensive than goldfish – at least, they should not be. Even less exclusive than these general-grade fish are Ghost Koi, crosses between common carp and the metallic Ogon. Doitsu

Buying Koi

There are Koi available to suit everyone's pocket.

Photo: Dave Bevan.

Buying Koi at shows is a great temptation, but you can only do it if you have good quarantine facilities at home.   Photo: Nick Fletcher.

or fully-scaled, they are extremely hardy, sometimes quite colourful, and exhibit hybrid vigour which encourages rapid growth and good resistance to disease.

The number of specialist Koi outlets in the UK has risen to meet demand over the last decade, from a handful to literally dozens; the same is true of European countries (notably Belgium and Germany) and the USA. So finding a supplier is no problem. But with so many grades of Koi to choose from, from so many countries of origin, where do you make a start?

The first thing is to cultivate a relationship with a specialist dealer you can trust. Only those who major on Koi should be considered – if you want goldfish, go to a garden centre, but if you want Koi, go to a Koi dealer. The well-known people advertise regularly in the aquatic press, but a better pointer is personal recommendation – put a few questions to someone who has patronised a particular dealer over a period of time.

What is the service like – before and after purchases have been made? Is a full range of dry goods and Koi hardware carried? Are there regular imports of quality fish, in all popular sizes and price brackets? Have there ever been health problems with Koi soon after purchase and, if so, what has the dealer's response been?

The next step is to make a short list of Koi dealers and visit their premises, preferably midweek when they will not be so crowded. Use your eyes and nose. What is the state of the water and fish in the sales vats or ponds? Is every Koi in a saleable condition? Are nets/handling socks disinfected? Are purchased fish properly packed for their journey home? Are the staff helpful, without being pushy? And what is the standard of their advice? You may have to take along a more experienced Koi-keeping friend to help assess all these things.

WHAT TO BUY?
Whatever fish you choose, it is on the assumption that your pond and filter are matured (see previous chapter) and that, ideally, you have a good quarantine facility for new purchases. In other words, you are now building up your Koi stocks to the recommended level, allowing for further growth, and intend to keep these fish for the foreseeable future.

My personal opinion is that Japanese (or perhaps hand-picked Israeli) Koi are the only sensible choice, but overriding that sentiment is something even more basic; if you like it, and you can afford it, buy it. I prefer Japanese Koi simply because, long-term, they represent the best value for money.

To explain the price structure fully would take a book in itself, but Koi from Japan are available in degrees of excellence from 'general' through to 'show' and 'special' grades. Following each spawning the breeders make several preliminary culls, discarding the rejected fry and juvenile fish as being absolutely worthless; general grade Koi are the first to have any commercial value at all. The breeders do not retain them because they would merely take up space in their growing-on ponds that would be better occupied by Koi of higher quality, so they are sold on very cheaply in Japan, or purchased

A mixed bag indeed... Beginners should avoid buying Koi this small but should opt for 8–10 ins specimens as the minimum size.
Photo: Nick Fletcher.

by brokers and shipped all over the world.

These fish are often quite pretty, and of recognised varieties, though not of interest to serious Koi keepers. But they are arguably still superior to what is produced elsewhere in the Far East.

Moving on a year, the breeders continue to segregate fish worth keeping back from those they feel have reached their optimum commercial potential. These ex-Tategoi (now known as 'Tateshita') are all available for bulk purchase, but can be graded, either before leaving Japan or on arrival in the UK (the dealer will sort through and price up every consignment, which is bound to contain a best and a worst fish, and all gradations between).

Some of these Koi go on to win prizes at minor shows, and to the unpractised eye they can look almost as impressive as the top-flight fish. But the Koi that win National Championships are almost always individually priced and selected on visits to Japan, either by dealers or customers accompanying them.

Beginners to Koi keeping are strongly advised to choose middle- to high-grade Japanese Koi 10-12 ins long. These are hardier than the appealing babies and much more likely to survive their first winter, since no Koi bred in Japan will have experienced water temperatures lower than 55 degrees F before export.

The urge can be very strong to have most of your favourite Koi varieties represented in the first year of pondkeeping. But this is futile if, in order to achieve this goal, you are restricted by your budget to buying small fish which soon perish. A friend of mine, who had just purchased 20 small Koi each costing £18, said enviously of another Koi keeper: "I wish I could afford quality fish like yours." That person had just bought one 18-inch Showa for around £300! The moral is to build up your collection slowly with fish you really want and will like in years to come. As your tastes become ever more refined, you will probably, if you wish, be able to sell your original purchases back to your regular dealer – something you could not do with general grade Koi, however well they might have grown in the meantime.

It may seem heartless to sell on fish and replace them with better ones, in fact many Koi keepers cannot bring themselves to do it. But this is the only sensible way to steadily improve the quality of your collection.

Otherwise the pond soon becomes overcrowded. At best, this can mean that fish do not achieve their full growth potential, and, at worst, it can lead to deteriorating water quality and all the associated problems, such as outbreaks of bacterial disease. Do not be misled by the stocking density of dealers' vats – the fish are fed sparingly and their filtration systems are (or should be) oversized to cope with fluctuating Koi populations.

VIEWING THE FISH
When you go to buy Koi, give yourself plenty of time; it should be an enjoyable experience, not a rushed exercise. Start by browsing around the vats and ponds to gain an overview of what is available. First impressions are important, and you will soon have a mental list of possibilities. Now look more closely at those that have caught your eye – as far as you can tell, are they in a healthy condition? They should obviously be free of any marks or badly-split fins, but are they swimming evenly, with all fins spread? Is the respiration rate steady, or do they appear to be 'blowing'? If one gill cover is moving more than the other, reject the fish, as gill infection or damage is probably the greatest killer of newly-imported Koi.

Sometimes recent arrivals will skulk on the bottom of the vats, and one or two individuals will perhaps separate themselves from the rest. This is usually due to nothing more sinister than transit stress, but there is no point in subjecting such fish to further traumas with yet another journey and yet another change in water chemistry. If you like a new import (and it is not one of countless general-grade babies swimming together, virtually indistinguishable from one another), you may be able to leave a deposit with the dealer and pick it up in a month or two, when it has settled down. It is always better to miss out on a Koi than take it home when it is not fully fit.

ABOVE: This collection of top-quality Koi was built up gradually over a period of years.
Photo: Nick Fletcher.

TOP RIGHT: The Koi is steered towards a floating bowl or basket.   Photo: Keith Allison.

RIGHT: Closer inspection can take place once the fish has been bowled.   Photo: Nick Fletcher.

Once you are satisfied with your short-listed Koi you should ask the dealer to bowl them for you – this involves guiding them into a floating blue viewing bowl or basket where you can examine them at close quarters. Etiquette says you should not request this unless you are half-serious about a purchase. Ideally the viewing should be in strong natural daylight – if the Koi dealer's premises are indoors, he will happily move a bowl of fish outside for you.

You can now get closer to the Koi and look at the subtler points such as skin quality, kiwa (definition of scale edging where one colour meets another), and desirable/undesirable traits of particular varieties (such as a clear lustrous head in an Ogon – a plus point – or whether any red pigment has moved into the fins or tail of Kohaku – a demerit).

It is not fair, at least in the early stages of your relationship with a Koi dealer, to ask him/her what he/she thinks of your choice of fish. The dealer is hardly going to dissuade you from buying it, and will more likely reply

(with some justification) "If you like it, that's what matters."

What you can legitimately do is to ask details of the breeder if known, not so you can boast of having a 'designer Koi' but because bloodlines develop in different ways. Sometimes a Koi will be effectively 'finished' at 10 ins, while other apparently unprepossessing fish will change so as to be almost unrecognisable. This is especially true of Sanke where, in the case of one famous breeder's fish, almost all of the initially faint sumi disappears, only to come back later, strong and well-defined.

As a general rule, try and envisage what your Koi will look like when they are bigger. Red patterns (hi) often fade but seldom spread, whereas sumi (black) will grow, especially on Showa. So, if you buy a Kohaku that looks like a miniature version of a Grand Champion, remember that, as it fills out and the skin stretches, the hi will occupy less of the body area. It is better to buy 'hi-heavy' Kohaku and hope that the pattern divides pleasingly in later years. On the other hand, if you buy a young Showa with a good balance of hi, sumi and white skin it is likely that the sumi will continue to spread, perhaps to the detriment of its eventual appearance. Remember – hi goes, sumi grows!

The mix of Koi varieties you choose is up to you, but most hobbyists like representatives of the Go-Sanke (Kohaku, Sanke and Showa) swimming with Koi of contrasting colours. A pond full of Ogons alone would look very dull, but a bright metallic yellow or orange Koi perfectly complements the tricoloured fish. Similarly, few people would want exclusively Gin-Rin Koi, but one or two will set off their companions without this scale refinement. Some of the plainer Kawarimono (Chagoi or the black Karasugoi) only serve to emphasise the beauty of true patterned Koi.

To assist your choice, view a few ponds whose fish please you, and note down what varieties they contain, and in what proportion.

When you are close to making your choice, ask the dealer to run his hands over the fish and lift the operculum gently to examine the gills, which should be bright red, with no erosion or mucous covering. If all is well, the dealer will now double-bag your fish. You should lift the bag and examine the Koi from all angles against the light, paying particular attention to the belly, the fin roots and the mouth. Even at this stage, if you detect something amiss (such as an infected scale, an unhealed wound or a deformity) you are well within your rights to reject the Koi – a good dealer will understand. Only when the transit water has had a soothing disinfectant (Elbagin) added, oxygen has been blown into the space above the water and the bag has been sealed with elastic bands will the Koi be deemed yours.

KOI IN TRANSIT

All Koi in transit should be kept in the dark, so slide a black bin liner over the bags before placing them in insulating polystyrene fish-boxes. You can often obtain these from your dealer, but it is always as well to bring your own, just in case.

A few dealers will offer a short-term guarantee with their Koi, but they are the exceptions – after all, if a fish dies soon after purchase, who is to know the cause? Often it is poor water quality in the owner's pond. This is another reason for cultivating one Koi outlet, for once you are accepted as a conscientious hobbyist, you are more likely to obtain redress if something does go wrong. Your case will be strengthened if you bring back the dead fish with two sizeable samples of your pond water for analysis.

So far I have not mentioned quarantine, because it is a contentious subject. Some highly respected outlets sell their fish the day after they arrive, others isolate them for two or three weeks. The truth is, many diseases take far longer than that to manifest themselves and the responsibility of quarantining should always lie with the purchaser, not the dealer. That applies whichever quarantine method the dealer may adopt – prophylactic, where medication is added to the quarantine vat as a precautionary measure against protozoan parasites or potential bacterial problems, or passive, where the fish are merely kept under observation and medicated only if apparent need arises.

Once you get your Koi home, their transit bags should be floated, unopened, for about 30 minutes to equalise water temperatures. This applies whether they are being introduced to a quarantine facility or straight into the main pond. Some hobbyists like to dip new arrivals, in which case the fish and the water from the bag should be transferred to a container with an airstone and the required medication, already dissolved in a little pondwater, introduced. Common salt at up to 3oz per gallon for up to five minutes, while the fish are watched for any signs of distress, is often used, or enough potassium permanganate crystals to stain the water dark red – one gram per two litres for three minutes.

It is often said that pond or vat water should be mixed gradually into that already in the bag, to minimise any shock from differences in pH. In fact it takes many days for a fish to adjust to a pH shift, and so this mixing process is quite unnecessary.

Buying Koi

New fish should not be disturbed, nor should you attempt to feed them straightaway. They do have a tendency to jump, especially where the water is agitated, so net or cover over waterfalls and venturis for a day or two.

It is worth testing even well-established quarantine vats for ammonia, especially if more than one new Koi has arrived, since fish that have been a while in transit can 'dump' ammonia when transferred to cleaner water, and in a relatively small container this can burn fins and gills unless a large water change is performed.

WHEN TO BUY?
When is the best time of year to buy Koi? The very high grade Japanese fish come into the country after the breeders' mud ponds have been harvested in October, or early in spring when stocks retained under cover are on the point of going outside again. But introducing such fish into your own pond when temperatures are still fluctuating (spring) or starting to fall (late autumn) can be dangerous unless you have heating.

Koi to satisfy most hobbyists' needs are available right through the spring/summer 'season', and dealers increasingly make trips to Japan to select them. If the timing is wrong for you, they will often take a deposit and keep your fish for a period (charging a 'boarding fee' to cover feeding and the pond space they take up). This is a good way to buy what you want without compromising the fishes' health in any way.

17 DIET AND FEEDING

Wild carp, the ancestors of Koi, are predominantly bottom-feeders and their physiology reflects this – two pairs of sensitive barbules around a protrusible mouth are the typical trademarks of fishes that root around in the substrate of rivers and lakes. This is not to say that they will not take surface food; when there is a prolific hatch of aquatic insects, carp will be up there with the trout, sucking in the pupae and emerging adults.

Anglers know that carp can be caught on floating baits, but that these are not successful all the time. On warm summer days, carp close to the surface are frequently not interested in food and appear to be dozing. Only in the ornamental pond will they regularly take their meals off the top.

THE NATURAL DIET

The species *Cyprinus carpio* is omnivorous. In natural ponds, the carp diet includes filamentous algae, soft-leaved water plants, aquatic insects and their larvae and pupae, crustaceans of all sizes from *Daphnia* to freshwater crayfish, snails and their eggs and, at certain times of the year, the fry of their own and other fishes. In a typical head-down feeding position, when the carp are stirring up clouds of silt, feeding tends to be indiscriminate. Mouthfuls of mud with attendant flora and fauna are drawn in,

filtered through the gill rakers, unpalatable matter is blown out again and the rest, providing it is small enough to be crushed by the powerful throat (pharyngeal) teeth, passes into the long gut for digestion.

The more nutrients the water of the carps' wild habitat contains, the more edible matter will be available to be cropped by fishes close to the top of the aquatic food chain, at the peak of which are predatory species – pike, perch, zander and catfish.

CAPTIVE CARP

The growing-on mud ponds of Japanese Koi breeders replicate natural bodies of water quite closely, except that the aquatic predators are not present. Each year, before these ponds are refilled, they are limed to destroy parasites and then the substrate is raked and fertilised with phosphate-rich material such as chicken manure to encourage a bloom of unicellular algae. These organisms in turn support *Daphnia* and other small organisms which the growing Koi can feed upon. But the young fishes in these lightly-stocked ponds still need supplementary feeding twice daily – the natural food resource is not sufficient on its own.

It follows that in ornamental Koi ponds there is no reason to suppose that fish will live and thrive on their wits alone (and whatever crawls, flies or blows into the

Diet And Feeding

A Koi coming to the surface to feed.

Photo: Dave Bevan.

water). Our ponds are increasingly kept unnaturally devoid of plants, while stocking density is extremely high in comparison to Japanese summer quarters. The little natural food available is quickly eaten, which is why you rarely see insect life in a Koi pond. The filter chambers, on the other hand, are soon colonised by snails, fly larvae, freshwater shrimps and hoglice.

FLOATING AND SINKING PELLETS
The floating pellet or food stick is now on the menu for Nishikigoi the world over. It says much for their adaptability that coloured carp can quickly adapt to surface-feeding, although we must remember that they learn this competitive behaviour from fryhood. For all that, in any pond there will always be individuals that are reluctant to rise to pellets.

These fishes hang down in the water and presumably intercept surplus food expelled by their pondmates.

It is both pleasant and practical to feed floating food. Not only can we interact with our Koi as they greedily suck pellets from the fingers, but we can use the opportunity to spot anything amiss with them. This is the only time (unless the fishes are bowled) that we are able to view their flanks and bellies at close quarters and check for wounds or ulcers. And if normally extrovert Koi hang back from the feeding rush, it is a good indication that they are not well.

Early and late in the year, when the pond is cool, sinking pellets are substituted for floaters and the Koi quickly revert to their natural mode of feeding. Specialised Koi food manufacturers naturally want us to extend the use of their products – easily digestible wheatgerm sinkers are not just a sales gimmick but a means of nourishing the fish at times when a high-protein diet would cause more problems than it solved. But Koi food is nonetheless big business. It is not enough that our fishes remain in good health – their colours must be optimised and rapid growth promoted. As a result, basic diets are available alongside special colour-enhanced and high-protein foods to suit all grades of Koi, from ordinary family pets to potential show winners. It was not always so.

A MODERN KOI DIET

Older pondkeepers will surely recall the cardboard tubs of goldfish food that seemed to consist largely of bakery sweepings. For a treat, fish could be given dried 'ants' eggs', which were not eggs at all but pupae. Until

the late 1970s, pondfish were expected to subsist on this fare, supplemented by anything else we had the means or time to supply. While some elements were of real value, others were harmful, the classic 'wrong food' being white bread, high in carbohydrate. This does little for fishes except to make them fat.

When Koi began to gain in popularity their owners realised that traditional goldfish foods were not going to be enough to sustain them. Commercial pet nutritionists had not yet realised what a huge market lay untapped, so the fishes had to get by on a supposedly balanced diet of sweetcorn, brown bread, domestic table scraps and even trout pellets. Sweetcorn has plenty of bulk but little food value; like all 'wet' foods with a high moisture content it can rapidly pollute the water. However, Koi do not instinctively

One of the great pleasures of Koi-keeping is hand-feeding the fish.

Photo: Dave Bevan.

Some Koi become very tame.

Photo: Keith Allison.

know what is good for them, and find the taste of corn appealing. If it is given today it should be of a brand without added sugar. Wholemeal bread is still universally fed for roughage, but it can lead to eye protrusion in some Koi. Trout pellets are actively harmful, having a high-protein formula for rapid growth with no regard to good skin and body shape. The colour-enhancers in these pellets are of no benefit to ornamental fish, as they are there to tint trout flesh pink. All they do for Koi is impart that shade to areas of white skin.

Recipes for home-made composite Koi food to be oven-baked, cut into blocks and frozen can include fresh ingredients such as honey, shellfish, the white meat of chicken, flaked white fish and cereal binders. But the once-popular shredded beef-heart or indeed any red meat should be avoided, as the fats these contain will solidify at low temperature.

Prawns and shrimps, either shelled or in their natural state, will send Koi wild. They are the nearest thing they will get to river crayfish, and are seen as a nutritious treat. Dried or freeze-dried krill, sold to feed carnivorous tropical fish, can also be offered.

The best natural Koi food, their equivalent of a juicy steak, is earthworms – which can boast three times the protein content of red meat. As breeders of any ornamental fish

know, worms are excellent for conditioning the parent stock prior to spawning, and a great way of boosting the strength of languid fishes after a long winter in an unheated pond. Shredded worms are body-building nourishment for growing fry. Moreover, earthworms are absolutely safe, providing they are dug from soil that has not been treated with pesticides. The pathogens in soil and in fresh water are quite different, and cross-infection is impossible. The same benefit accrues from Koi foods of marine origin.

Worms can be cultured under a hessian sack, kept damp and seeded with old tea bags, potato peelings and vegetable scraps, or raised in 'wormery bins' sold for the purpose. There are many different species in the average garden, but those you dig from the ground are more palatable than the rather bitter 'tiger tails', redworms and brandlings found in compost heaps. Other garden insect denizens can be fed to Koi, even snails and slugs, but snail shells should first be cracked so that the fishes can extract the meat.

The vegetarian tendencies of Koi can be satisfied, in warm weather, with a meal of lettuce. The leaves have little food value but provide roughage. Fish take a while to recognise lettuce as food, but once they have they will soon rip a whole one to pieces.

SELECTION OF KOI FOOD

Large pellets (fed to large-size Koi) when the temperature is over 50 degrees F..

The smaller size pellet is used for small fish.

Colour enhancer (large pellets).

Koi sticks (colour enhancer).

Economy Koi pellets.

Economy Koi sticks.

SELECTION OF KOI FOOD

*Wheatgerm large pellets
(winter and summer food).*

Wheatgerm medium pellets.

*Spirulina small pellets
(food for red and black colouring).*

Fish flakes.

Fish flake and stick food.

Lettuce.

*Koi treats: Sweetcorn, orange
segments and earthworms.*

Photo: Nick Fletcher.

Orange segments, too, are a wonderful food
for Koi. The peel should be left on, and the
fish will noisily suck out the pulp, rich in
Vitamin C.

COMMERCIAL KOI FOOD

Today's range of prepared 'off the shelf' Koi
foods is wide and potentially confusing.
Besides flake, there are pellets, floating and
sinking, in grades to suit everything from fry
to adult Koi, and occasional 'treat' foods like
silkworm pupae or rapid-growth recipes
containing dried insects. These are typically
fed to condition up fish in the weeks before a
show.

Paying a premium price for Koi food may
improve colour and growth rate, and there
are even Vitamin C-enriched pellets which
claim to stimulate the immune system.
Almost all Koi food now available will suffice
as a perfectly acceptable maintenance diet,
however. What you pay above that basic
requirement will (or should be) reflected in
the sophistication of the recipe, its protein
content, the type and amount of colour-
enhancers, the refinement of the ingredients
and, in some cases, import costs. The snob
value attendant on some brands can push up
their retail price, too. As the saying goes,
'Caveat emptor' (let the buyer beware!).

A typical pellet recipe might comprise
wheat, wheatgerm and bran, maize gluten,
fishmeal, soya and animal protein, fish oil,
vitamins, antioxidants and colour-enhancers.
The four main constituents are protein, oil,
ash and fibre – their relative percentages can
tell us so much and no more, as (for
example) a high protein content is not in
itself a guarantee of quality. More important
is to know the ingredients from which it is
derived.

Protein content of Koi food can be
anything from 25 per cent to 50 per cent by
weight. Fishes need it for growth and tissue
repair, so fry foods and summer recipes
(when metabolism is fast) should contain the
most. Low-protein recipes are more easily
digestible but have less energy value.
Wheatgerm pellets (with vegetable-derived
protein) are a good compromise and so are
fed at the beginning and end of the
pondkeeping season. With its high roughage
content, the food stays in the gut for only a
short while; morning feeds are preferred,
giving the fish time to digest them before the
temperature drops with nightfall. It is
doubtful if feeding at low temperature can
harm Koi directly as, quite simply, they will
not eat unless they feel the need. The real
danger comes from uneaten food breaking

Diet And Feeding

down and overloading a filter whose bacteria are only ticking over.

Carbohydrates and fibre are additional energy sources to protein. Koi can suffer constipation, and fibre gives the necessary roughage to prevent it. Ash is perceived as a cheap bulking ingredient but it does more, in that it supplies the fishes with minerals and trace elements.

Oils and fats, a valuable energy source in Koi food, are known as lipids. Unlike saturated cooking fats which solidify when cold, they remain liquid at all times.

Added vitamins are a contentious issue. It is hard to make a case against including them in the diet, for it is known that deficiencies can bring about lowered resistance to disease and actually precipitate illness. On the other hand, it is difficult to attribute a sick Koi's condition to vitamin deficiency alone, as so many other factors can come into play. It is accepted that Vitamin A is essential for healthy eyes, while the B complex strengthens the nervous system and helps with growth. Vitamin C builds strong bones and builds resistance to infection, and Vitamin D is also cited as essential to good, even, growth rates. Some vitamins can be lost or their efficacy reduced in the mere processing of Koi food by the manufacturers, and this decline continues the moment the seal is broken on the container. To minimise the effect, food should be stored in cool, dry conditions in sealed opaque containers. It should never be fed once the sell-by date is past, or there is the added danger of oxidation.

QUANTITIES

Few Koi keepers are remotely aware how much their fishes eat on a daily basis, nor is it essential for them to know. They merely follow the instructions given on the packaging which, typically, will advise feeding, two or three times daily, as much as the fishes will consume in five minutes. This is obviously a variable feast. In summer it is quite possible for Koi to consume and digest six meals a day. This 'little and often' approach is better than feeding the same amount over one or two sessions, not least because it puts less strain on the filter. Using a feeding ring makes it easy to net off uneaten pellets in the unlikely event that the Koi begin to lose interest in their meal.

The same instructions will caution against feeding once the water temperature falls below 50 degrees F. This cut-off point is deliberately set on the high side, so that Koi keepers will not be tempted to offer the occasional token handful of pellets on mild winter days.

It is almost impossible to overfeed pondfish. If they eat too much they will merely pass more partially digested food from their bodies. This, though, puts more pressure on the filter.

Koi can survive on the daily pelleted food equivalent of less than 2 per cent of their body weight, but this intake will only be a 'maintenance' diet. The fishes will make little if any growth. Step up the feeding and the Koi will not only grow, but begin to lay down fat reserves to see them through their winter fast. Well-nourished females will be developing eggs for next season's spawning, and food-derived energy surplus to mere survival is equally essential in the weeks leading up to the act, as the eggs will then have a high yolk content to sustain fry in their first few days of life before the free-swimming stage.

Top Koi keepers want to promote the fastest possible growth, but not at the expense of body shape. It is not unusual for them to work out their fishes' food requirements to the nearest gram, taking into account the water temperature (which affects the speed of metabolism). Even then there is no guarantee that one or two greedy individuals will not overeat at the expense of the rest, although hand-feeding can help spread the rations. So, too, can the mixing of various pellet sizes. All too often the smaller fishes miss out because the pellets are simply too large to fit into their mouths. There is a case for feeding pond flake or fine granular food to young Koi for this reason alone, but it is an expensive option for adult fishes, which can go through a tub in no time.

COST
Floating food sticks seem universally attractive to Koi, and appear good value for money until you realise that much of what you are buying is air. The fishes have to take in high volumes to satisfy their appetite, and this accounts for their frenzied surface feeding. Grades vary from 'economy' (high in carbohydrate and ash, low in protein, and without colour-enhancers) to 'Koi' and 'growth'. The darker-coloured, denser sticks are equivalent to the better-quality pellets.

It is obviously cheaper to bulk-buy Koi food, but you should avoid having any left over at the end of one season and using it the next – it will have lost most of its vitamin content and may have oxidised, especially if not properly stored. Fish club members can buy a large bag and divide up its contents so that nothing is used after its sell-by date.

SEASONAL FEEDING
Sinking pellets tend to be fed when water temperature is low. The reasoning is that the fishes, down on the bottom of the pond, will need little effort to reach them. In extreme cases, it is thought that a Koi can use up more energy swimming up to the surface for a pellet than that pellet gives back. Sinkers are usually, though not always, of an easily-digestible wheatgerm formula which passes quickly through the gut. The disadvantage is that it is harder to see when you have overfed sinkers, and netting out the surplus can be a chore.

Sinkers have a place in summer feeding, too; mixing a few in with floating pellets benefits bottom-dwelling tench (in a mixed-population pond), or those Koi with a built-in reluctance to come to the surface.

HOLIDAY ARRANGEMENTS
It is often asked whether Koi will come to any harm if they are not fed for days, or even a week or two, while their owners are on holiday. The answer is almost certainly 'no'. People who show their Koi routinely starve them for up to a week before the event, so that there is less waste excreted into their transit bags and the show vats – but greenish droppings indicate that the fishes have been

If you are going away, it is a good idea to have someone responsible to come and check on your fish.

Photo: Nick Fletcher.

Diet And Feeding

cropping blanketweed as a substitute for their pellets.

On the other hand, it is always advisable to have a friend or neighbour check on the pond in the owner's absence, if only to make sure that the pumps are still working and that the bottom drain has not clogged. It will do no harm to make up 'ration packages' of pellets to be fed during these visits.

AUTOMATIC FEEDERS

In families where both partners work, particularly during the summer, an investment in an automatic feeder will ensure that the Koi are fed little and often. There are a few models purpose-made for ornamental fish, but most on the market are adapted from commercial applications in fish-farming. They all consist of a lidded hopper filled with pellets and some means of dispensing them at regular pre-set intervals. This mechanism can be clockwork, mains-powered via a computer, or even work from solar panels, which need only daylight (not direct sunlight) to function.

The alternative is a 'demand feeder', activated by the Koi themselves. When they nudge a pendulum on the hopper base, reaching to just below the pond surface, a predetermined quantity of food falls into the water.

For Koi fry, regular meals are essential. Because their food is so fine as to resemble dust it can be loaded into a clockwork aquarium feeder suspended over the rearing vats. Such a feeder will have holes in the base of the hopper, and a slowly-roating disc flush up against it. When holes in the two marry up, the food is released. Alternatively the food drum itself revolves; for both types of clockwork feeder it is vital the food is kept bone-dry or it will not run freely.

18 DISEASE AND PARASITES IN KOI

By Paula Reynolds

BACTERIAL DISEASE
AEROMONAS

When several Koi in a pond develop red marks or ulceration, bacterial disease is likely to be the cause. Ammonia and nitrite in the pond water, a lack of pond hygiene (particularly in the filtration system), or the introduction of an infected fish without prior quarantine are all possible reasons for an outbreak of disease. Quarantining does not guarantee a healthy fish – disease can still become a reality, regardless of how long you isolate a new Koi. The practice merely minimises the risk of spreading parasites and disease. The stress associated with transportation is a major factor in the development of health problems, and allowing time for acclimatisation can considerably reduce this.

Coping successfully with bacterial disease in the short term can involve a lot of medical attention for the infected Koi. In the long term, re-infection is common, and preventing a new outbreak is not always straightforward. A minor bacterial problem can develop following a period of poor water quality, but the Koi may respond to a series of small, frequent water changes. The immune response in the fish themselves can heal the problem without a great deal of intervention by the Koi keeper.

In more serious cases where water quality is not the cause, a pond bactericide can be tried, but only if the filter can tolerate this without loss of biology. However, when disease is affecting the fish internally, treating the pond will not cure the problem though it may help to limit its spread. The topical treatment of ulcers can help prevent secondary infection in the body, and can improve minor infections – however, when disease is internal, nothing that you put into the water or on to the body will work.

The bacterium *Aeromonas salmonicida* is mainly responsible for initiating ulcerative disease in Koi. However, in the Koi pond, it is the secondary *Aeromonas hydrophila* complex that is isolated in bacterial cultures. *Aeromonas* species can be very harmful to Koi, causing high rates of mortality. Taking a swab from a lesion then sending it to a laboratory for culture and antibiotic sensitivity testing is normal practice, although the information is far more reliable when obtained from the kidney of a recently deceased fish that has had a full post-mortem examination.

A report on this investigation can then be taken to a veterinary surgeon. Most vets will not undertake aspects of fish health care outside their personal field of expertise. While not wishing to advise Koi keepers about other types of disease or pond management problems, some vets are prepared to oversee the administration of antibiotics to bacterially infected fish. The vet's knowledge of the safe use of antibiotics can be vital to the success of the treatment. If bacterial disease recurs there may be an environmental cause, and you may need to seek advice from an aquatic consultant.

BACTERIAL GILL DISEASE

Mixed species of bacteria are frequently isolated from the gills of fish suffering from bacterial gill disease. A culture is required to identify the pathogens involved if antibiotics are to be tried. Some antibiotics become toxic to fish when used in solution as a bath, so it is advisable to take professional advice. While, in the early stages, it may be possible to arrest the development of bacterial gill disease, once the gill tissue becomes swollen or hyperplastic, survival is unlikely. Overcrowded ponds, which are unhygienic and low in oxygen, are a common cause of bacterial gill disease. High levels of ammonia during transportation, or poor water quality in a new pond, are other possible factors.

Once the gill lamellae are damaged, bacteria and fungus become secondary invaders. Placing infected fish in a well-oxygenated salt solution of half an ounce per gallon, together with Acriflavine, can help. Benzalkonium chloride is also effective against some types of gill disease.

TUBERCULOSIS

'Mycobacteriosis' is the correct term for tuberculosis in fish, and many species of fish living in variable climates around the world are susceptible. The disease is progressive and infected fish lose weight and become lethargic, possibly developing skin abnormalities. This disease can only be diagnosed and treated professionally, and, while treatment can be successful, the recovery rate is low. However, the actual incidence of mycobacteriosis in Koi is rare, and the signs of the disease described can equally apply to many other health problems. Koi keepers frequently blame tuberculosis if Koi fail to thrive when, in fact, genetics and intensive farming methods are to blame.

FUNGAL DISEASE
SAPROLEGNIA

Most water-borne organisms are harmless to Koi, living alongside them in perfect harmony. Even those organisms that are a potential threat require appropriate conditions before mounting an attack. The

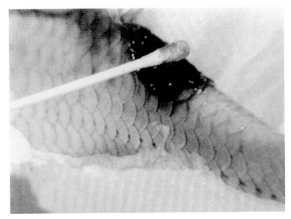

A swab being taken for culture.
Photo: Paula Reynolds.

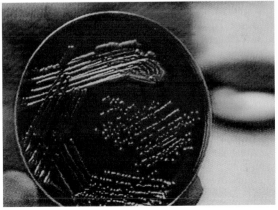

A petri dish containing agar showing a bacterial colony.
Photo: Paula Reynolds.

numbers of parasites present, the general wellbeing of the fish themselves, the water quality, and its temperature, will all influence the situation. We term this kind of organism an 'opportunistic parasite'. It waits in the guise of a friend and, the minute the opportunity exists for it to become parasitic, it takes up residence, on the body or internally, and starts to live off the fish. This usually occurs when the parasites recognise some weakness or deficiency in the host fish. Fungi are just such organisms.

The study of fungi and allied organisms is termed 'mycology'. It is an extensive science, as fungal disease can affect all living things. Fungi are multicellular organisms and many species are found in all types of aquatic environment, including, of course, the Koi pond. When fungal patches are observed on Koi, you are dealing with an opportunistic organism causing a secondary health problem. An entry portal will have already been created on the skin of a susceptible host fish – by injury, parasitic damage, or even an ulcer. The fungus invades the wound, using it as a source of nourishment and therefore reproduction. Saprolegniasis is the most common fungal disease of the skin and gills of Koi or goldfish. However, if the disease is investigated, other species of fungi are often implicated in infections.

Saprolegnia can appear rather like tufts of grey- or even yellow-tinged cotton wool. The colour changes are caused by matter in the water that becomes trapped in the mycelium, which is the collective term for the fungal hyphae which form the thick filamentous growth. A patch of fungus normally grows radially, and the area enlarges as the fungus reproduces by spore formation. Once the fungus has penetrated the outer skin or epithelium, and is attacking deeper into the dermis, it can interrupt the control of body fluids. This obviously threatens the circulatory system of the fish, so it is potentially a serious disease if left untreated.

Skin damage also creates an entry point for bacteria and viruses into the body, as these too live in water. The inflammatory response begins whenever body damage occurs, and all sorts of substances travel to the injury site and focus their activities on protecting the fish against any foreign matter or disease-causing organisms gaining entry to the body. The ability of the fish's immune system to deal with a major invasion of pathogenic organisms depends on the conditions in which the fish lives, and particularly the water temperature. However, *saprolegnia* is active at far lower temperatures than many other harmful organisms.

The most important consideration whenever fungus is observed is to find out why there was an entry portal in the skin that allowed the fungus access to the body in the first place. Unfortunately, fungus is thought by many hobbyists to be an inevitable disease in fishkeeping, rather than secondary to an underlying cause. It is also important to bear in mind that a fungal growth can collapse in air when Koi are netted for a closer examination. It is the water that supports the fungus, creating its fluffy appearance. Out of

Fungus attacking a body lesion.
Photo: Paula Reynolds.

water, fungus is often mistaken for other skin conditions.

If you observe fungus on just one Koi, the most likely reason is that the fish has injured itself, and fungus has invaded the wound. However, if you see fungal patches on many Koi, then the probability is that there are parasites on the body damaging the skin and creating entry portals. So curing the fungus will not necessarily remedy the underlying problem, and you need to investigate more thoroughly. Poor water quality can impair the protective potential of the mucus layer, making the Koi more vulnerable to fungal disease. It is common to see fungal patches on injured Koi, those damaged by parasites or those suffering the lesions associated with certain diseases.

However, dramatic environmental changes can also result in fungal disease, the Koi developing what appears to be a thick covering of fur all over the body. Moving fish into a new pond with significantly different water chemistry, without any gradual acclimatisation, could result in this response. Initially, the mucus layer may have been seriously affected by the environmental change and its protective properties diminished. It is the stress reaction, and hormonal changes occurring in response to the new environment, that will influence whether or not the Koi will succumb to the fungus.

While minor infections do respond to treatment, Koi seriously infected by fungal disease seldom survive. Sometimes, what may appear to be a small patch of infection is so deep into the tissues that the fish will not recover. It is important to discover the underlying cause of the fungal infection before you use any medications, as they all have side-effects.

Chemicals should always be used with caution, particularly if poor water quality is the reason behind the vulnerability of the Koi

to the fungal infection in the first place. Malachite green has good fungicidal properties, but it is a toxin and should only ever be used in ponds where optimum conditions are prevalent. If the pond pH is low, or there is a high level of organic matter in the pond, malachite green is not a suitable treatment. Many pond treatments pose risks when water temperatures are high, and this applies to malachite green.

BRANCHIOMYCOSIS

Saprolegnia is also found in the gills of Koi as a secondary invader, following parasitic infestation or bacterial gill disease. Branchiomycosis is a fungal disease affecting the gills of carp and some other species. Unless it is professionally identified, any fungus observed attacking the gill filaments is far more likely to be *Saprolegnia*. However, *Saprolegnia* is likely to invade gills already compromised by branchiomycosis, in most outbreaks in which there is more than one species involved.

The disease is usually found in overcrowded aquatic environments where higher water temperatures, high levels of dissolved solids and low oxygen content are other predisposing factors. Most ponds provide healthier conditions than this, so it is not a disease common in Koi keeping.

It is usually younger Koi that figure highest in the mortalities during an outbreak of branchiomycosis, due to the overstocked nature of some fish farms where the disease is more prevalent. However, the disease is seen in newly-imported Koi when conditions are conducive to it, and all Koi, irrespective of maturity, can succumb. Older Koi will nevertheless have acquired more natural immunity to disease in general.

It is the blood vessels in the gill lamellae that are under attack in branchiomycosis. The fungus penetrates to a degree where tissue fusion results. Thrombosis develops in the blood vessels, and, ultimately, the secondary lamellae responsible for diffusion can no longer obtain enough oxygen from the water passing over them to sustain life. Vascular necrosis is the result, and mortalities are usually very high unless early treatment is implemented.

When buying newly-imported Koi you may inadvertently select a fish with a background history that makes it a candidate for the development of fungal gill disease. Insufficient preparation for transportation can result in over-exposure of the gill to ammonia and other influences during transit. This may not be apparent initially, requiring the necessary trigger factors. Quarantining all new Koi prevents the spread of this type of disease.

Gill diseases in general do not respond well to any medication, irrespective of whether they are fungal in nature or due to some other cause. The damage has invariably already been done before the signs are observed, but isolation in high oxygen can help, and salt at half an ounce per gallon can be beneficial. If fungus is observed attacking the gill filaments, a fungicide such as malachite green can be tried in conjunction with salt at half an ounce per gallon. When isolating Koi in a hospital tank, adequate oxygen is essential, especially for fish with gill problems. There are other products around specifically for gill treatment

that your dealer can advise on, although once the gill is seriously infected there is very little treatment that can be attempted with much hope of success.

The decision to isolate fish suffering from any type of fungal infection is not straightforward – we must regard all infected fish as a 'factory' producing fungal spores which are naturally infective. This is not a healthy situation for any Koi in the pond so far unaffected. They, too, risk infection if they are injured, and can even become compromised by the sheer scale of the problem if the outbreak of the disease is a major one and the conditions less than optimum.

If a fish is isolated too soon before an appropriate diagnosis of the underlying condition has been made, that fish may receive treatment for only the fungus, without regard to the underlying cause. This can jeopardise the health of all the Koi in the pond.

VIRAL DISEASE

Viral disease infects all living things, including fish. Unlike bacteria that attack a specific part of the body, viruses attack individual cells. The signs of disease that develop vary according to the particular virus, and specialised histopathology is required for an accurate diagnosis. However,

Saprolegnia sp, Branchiomyces sp. and necrotic tissue.   *Photo: Paula Reynolds.*

These gill filaments are too pale.
     Photo: Paula Reynolds.

the research that is needed to give us a better understanding of viral disease in ornamental fish is currently regarded as uneconomic, and it will be many years before we will be able to cure such diseases.

Acknowledging that there are serious and uncontrollable viral diseases known to be affecting Koi leaves us with prevention as the only safeguard. Our aim is to prevent a Koi most likely to be carrying a virus from being introduced into the pond. Newly-imported Koi and fish from open waterways or coarse fisheries pose the highest risk of carrying not just viruses, but disease generally. Quarantine cannot ever be regarded as foolproof when it comes to limiting the spread of disease, but it can minimise risks of a total wipe-out.

CARP POX

The correct term for the disease known as carp pox is 'cyprinid herpesvirus'. As the name suggests, it is not a disease confined to Koi, but can affect all members of the carp family. The virus is of the same type that causes the cold sore that has plagued the human population for years. While we can alleviate cold sores by topical applications, there is no effective treatment for carp pox in fish.

The disease first presents itself as a white, glossy tumour on the skin or fins. It is frequently described as resembling a drip of candle wax adhering to the body. Being able to multiply fastest at low temperatures, carp pox is more prevalent during winter. Infected Koi are usually young – with maturity they develop antibodies that later protect them from the virus. Mature Koi that are observed with the familiar white growths have possibly not been subjected to the disease earlier in life, and will ultimately be able to ward off infection.

Isolation is recommended for most unwell fish, principally to limit the spread of disease. In the case of carp pox this is not practical.

The sheer numbers of fish infected by the virus can be difficult to house out of the main pond, and, as most Koi will be carrying the disease anyway, it achieves little in the way of prevention.

It is more appropriate to leave all the Koi in the pond, making use of the isolation tank for any fish that becomes very run down by the disease. This is unusual, as most Koi cope well with carp pox infections. However, should a Koi develop growths all over the body and become lethargic, there is a case for placing it in the hospital tank in half an ounce of salt per gallon, and slowly raising the water temperature until the fish appears more comfortable. This will probably be at a water temperature around 55-60 degrees F. By then the white tumours may have diminished, although this virus has adapted to survive at higher temperatures.

Sometimes, carp pox presents as a layer or plaque on the body, rather than as a tumour. The colour of the growth can also vary, and is frequently seen to turn pink or red. This is not a cause for concern and simply implies that the root of the growth has invaded a nearby blood vessel and some bleeding has taken place into the tumour. Fish with a carp pox infection do not always thrive, and the growth rate can be slower. However, as the disease affects mainly young Koi, and then only in winter, it is not regarded as a major health problem. It is seldom ever serious enough in any fish to require isolation, and mortalities from it are extremely rare.

SPRING VIRAEMIA OF CARP (SVC)

This disease is better known to Koi keepers as SVC. Mainly a European problem, there do not appear to have been any cases of this disease in the US, although confirmed cases have been reported in Australia

In the UK, it is not a disease found in the Koi pond, thanks to the strict control on fish importation. While this legislation has

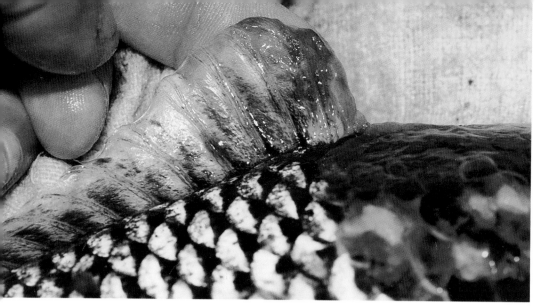

Carp Pox on the dorsal fin and body of an otherwise healthy fish.

*Photo:
Nick Fletcher.*

protected Koi in the UK for many years, we cannot become complacent about this serious disease – illegal imports from uncertified sources are a growing risk factor. SVC is often mentioned in the media, which fuels speculation and causes concern to the Koi keeper. As it is a notifiable disease, the Ministry of Agriculture, Fisheries and Food (MAFF) has to be informed of any outbreak. In its early stages, SVC can resemble other health problems. The chance of it ever occurring in a Koi pond is so rare that hobbyists need to ask themselves a few questions before jumping to wrong conclusions and wasting the valuable Ministry resources:

1) Have I recently purchased any Koi? If the answer is 'not for over a year', then forget SVC. If the answer is 'yes', remember that Japan, Israel and many other countries have to provide proof that their fish are free of SVC – so check the origin of the Koi.
2) What time of year is it? If it is a hot summer day, then forget SVC – this is predominantly a disease found in cooler water temperatures.
3) Has my pond been contaminated by the introduction of wild carp, or by fishing nets or other equipment used in open waters or coarse fisheries? If the answer is 'no', then SVC is not threatening your Koi, but they may have a problem that requires professional advice.

Bear in mind that there is more chance of a breeding a Grand Champion Koi in your pond than of getting SVC!

COMMON KOI PARASITES
There are several parasites affecting Koi that are observable with the naked eye.

LERNAEA (ANCHOR WORM)
Signs: Parasite protrudes from body; resembles a thin white fish bone; the wound created can appear inflamed; severe infestations can cause secondary problems.

Lernaea burrow under scales anywhere on a fish, leaving only the rear end of their bodies exposed. The shape from which their common name is derived is thus not immediately obvious, as most of the parasite is embedded in flesh. If an anchor worm is removed with tweezers, a close look will reveal the anchor end. If it is missing, half the parasite will still be in the flesh of the Koi and a second attempt at removal will be required. These are delicate parasites and can easily break while being extracted with tweezers.

After intact removal, dab the wound with a bactericide suitable for topical application – some bactericides are for pond treatment only. Checking the whole body of any Koi on which an anchor worm has been found is advisable, as they are masters of disguise. Frequently, they are spotted close to fins and can easily be mistaken for a fin ray that has lost its fine membrane.

As it matures, the anchor worm continually changes its form in order to perform new functions – we term this process 'metamorphosis'. All embedded anchor worms are female. The male fertilises the female and then dies, its role in life over. The fertilised female burrows into the flesh of the host fish in order to lay her eggs safely. She continues to metamorphose, and develops the anchor apparatus after she is embedded in the fish. The ovaries then move position down her body. Just before the parasite is about to produce her eggs, the yellow egg sacs can be clearly seen on the reproducing female. It is inside these paired sacs that the eggs themselves mature. The sacs are shed and the new generation of anchor worms breaks free from them.

At this early stage, the young anchor worms (known as nauplii) are oval. Water temperature has a great deal of influence on their development, but, about 50 hours after birth, they moult to become metanauplii. Then begins a series of stages in which the organism is termed a copepodid, and each developmental stage has a number. The worms reach sexual maturity at the sixth copepodid stage, and that is when the fertilisation of the female takes place and she seeks the host fish. It is only the female parasitising a Koi that you will be able to observe – other stages of this complex life cycle are invisible to the naked eye.

Larger Koi are less affected by the anchor worm until the numbers parasitising the fish are high. It is also possible that disease can

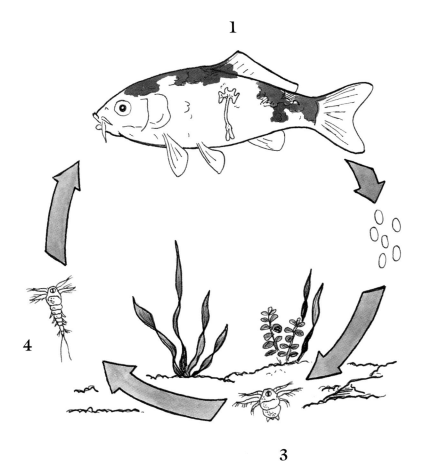

1

2

4

3

Anchor worm life cycle.

KEY
1. Adult female anchor worm in skin (not to scale).
2. Eggs released into the water from egg sacs.
3. Free-living juvenile stage.
4. Later juvenile stages are parasitic. The adults mate and the female develops a wormlike shape.

find access via the wound created. Fry and smaller Koi are far more vulnerable to anchor worm, but, in the garden pond, the Koi keeper is likely to identify the parasite before it becomes serious.

While quarantining all new Koi helps to prevent parasites being introduced into the pond, this particular one can defeat the process. One or two anchor worms do not constitute a problem, nor does it mean that the parasite is breeding in your pond. The parasite may simply need removing and the area topically treating. There is no need to use chemicals in the pond on finding the odd anchor worm. In Japan, *Lernaea* are not regarded as a serious pest unless the infection is severe.

Lernaea infestation has been known to cause a marked behavioural change in some fish species, but not in Koi. Neither does it affect the appetite of infested Koi in the way other parasites can. In cases of heavy infestation, or when secondary disease occurs, there will be greater reaction. There may be some localised irritation, but that is usually the full extent of the problem.

ARGULUS (FISH LOUSE)
Signs: Easy to observe, mistaken for black spots; lethargy; food refusal.

The fish louse does create disinterest in food, even when relatively few 'lice' are present. If the infestation is heavy, the Koi may be irritated, scratching on objects or on

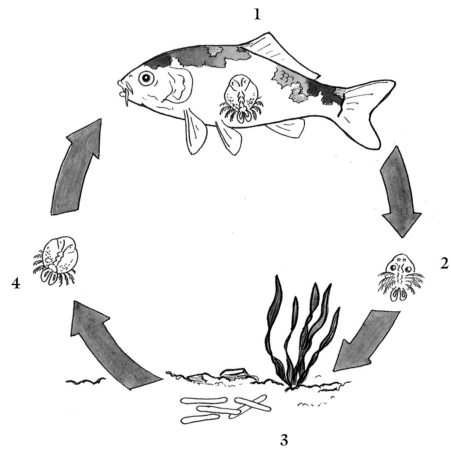

Fish louse life cycle.

KEY
1. Adult lice clinging to skin using suckers (not to scale).
2. Mature female leaves fish to lay eggs.
3. Eggs are laid in long capsules.
4. Juveniles pass through several stages before becoming adult.

the bottom of the pond. Red marks caused by the action of the parasites can become visible on the body. Sometimes behavioural change is observed before the parasite is actually seen.

Fish lice are the commonest of the larger visible parasites found on Koi. They are usually spread by purchasing already infected fish or aquatic plants. Adults are easy to spot on the body of Koi when they move, although their dark grey coloration can be a good camouflage on any multi-coloured fish. Within the Koi varieties, there are many good hiding places for lice – try looking for *Argulus* on a Shiro Utsuri!

The juveniles are very hard to see with the naked eye, but in an examination bowl you can easily see them swimming in the water around the fish – returning at intervals for a snack and then detaching themselves once more. The fish louse looks rather aggressive, and possesses some good attacking as well as defensive mechanisms. The body is flat and oval, but broader across the middle; males and females appear very similar. The eyes are located on either side of the head. *Argulus* has four pairs of legs, which are for swimming only. The parasite clings to the body of the host fish with numerous barbs, hooks, spines and suckers. These various appendages and the cup-like suckers can cause some damage to the body of the Koi, but *Argulus's* best weapon lies in the mouth.

This mouth is a complex apparatus that enables the organism to feed as it glides over the body of the host fish. The mouth cavity contains the mandibles, which equate to our jaws and are situated on the ventral surface. The stylet is located between the mandibles, its purpose being to stab and then inject the host with an anticoagulant. This substance ensures that the blood flow is continuous for the parasite, as blood is the main nutrition of *Argulus*. The flesh-piercing stylet creates not just the possibility of anaemia, but also the

risk of secondary infection by bacteria, virus, or fungus. *Argulus* spreads disease from fish to fish as it moves on to new hosts.

Fish lice lay eggs on objects in the pond; these are sticky and will adhere to the bottom of the pond or other surfaces. Their life cycle, in comparison with other crustacean parasites such as the anchor worm, is simple, as many of the metamorphic stages take place inside the egg itself. The complete life cycle can take up to 100 days, but this will be influenced by the water temperature and other environmental factors. It is not likely that the numbers of fish lice will diminish in the pond environment without resort to chemicals to eradicate them, although, when temperatures decrease, so does the rate of reproduction.

PISCICOLA GEOMETRA (FISH LEECH)
Signs: Brown worms clinging to the body of a fish.

Observing a leech making a meal of the blood supply of a favourite Koi is the ultimate nightmare. Worse is the knowledge that more leeches lie in wait to attack if you intervene to remove one individual. Leeches are harboured by objects in the pond, especially plants and their containers. In fact, plants are often the source of the initial introduction of these pests.

Many organisms resemble the fish leech, and some may indeed be members of the same family. They may be found on plants or in the filtration system, sometimes in very high numbers. The size and colour of these worm-like creatures will vary with the species, but they are commonly grey, brown or even red. However, unless the organism is actually attached to the body of the Koi, it will not be a fish leech.

Piscicola geometra is the most common leech found in the garden pond, and therefore the main problem for the Koi keeper. It can be seen firmly attached to the fish, its body expanding and contracting. The colour of the body will vary, depending on how recently a meal of blood has been digested. Through a magnifying glass, or sometimes (with larger specimens) via the naked eye, *Piscicola geometra* can be seen to have a geometric, banded body pattern – hence the name.

The health risks that pertain to all parasites with the ability to damage the body or gills of fish apply to the leech – potential secondary infections and the actual transmission of disease. Just like the fish louse, the leech feeds on blood, which situation, depending on the severity of the infestation, carries the added risk of anaemia. Certain parasites carry and transmit specific conditions, and the fish leech is known to carry organisms that in turn parasitise the blood and major organs of fish.

The problem in eradicating leeches from the Koi pond is the cocoons. These are what we would term eggs in other species, and they harbour the next generation of leeches – they are long and thin and a rather dirty grey colour. The cocoon cannot be permeated by certain chemicals, which is why control of this parasite is so difficult. The cocoon can take three months or longer to hatch out, depending on temperature (which is a major influence). At the onset of the leech infestation, you will have no idea how many cocoon generations there are or the variable times at which they will all hatch, and this makes control still more difficult.

Once the parasite is in residence in the Koi pond it has to be eradicated as soon as possible, otherwise it will breed out of control in the unnaturally favourable environment of the pond. The only alternative to chemical control is a total pond

Fish leech life cycle.

KEY
1. Adult leeches feed on fish blood for 2-3 days at a time (not to scale).
2. Leeches leave the fish to digest or to lay eggs.
3. Leech eggs laid in cocoons attached to rocks and plants.
4. Newly hatched leeches need fish to feed on.

clean-out, ensuring that all objects, from submersible pumps to statuary, are removed and sterilised. Discarding plants in ponds infested with leeches is essential – lilies are beautiful, but they are a common carrier of leeches. Many Koi keepers are not enthusiastic about pond plants, as the Koi do tend to spoil them. However, water quality can be improved when plants are part of the environment.

When the pond cleaning is completed, the keeper will have learned the hard way how to identify the cocoon. It is not likely that a Koi would be returned to the clean pond with a leech still attached, but do remember that the gills and mouth need checking. Any Koi that have been damaged by leeches may need topical treatment with a bactericide.

ERGASILUS (GILL MAGGOT)

The incidence of *Ergasilus* in the gills of imported Koi has been greatly reduced by better parasitic control measures on the part of those farming the fish around the world, although it is still an active parasite in other species. Closely related to the anchor worm, this parasite was once a big killer of Koi. Unlike *Lernaea*, it is found in both the gill cavity and in the mouth of infected fish. Its common name arises from the white egg-sacs laid by the female which, outliving the male, parasitises the fish. *Ergasilus* is a bloodsucker, and anaemia can result from an infestation. But it is the damage done to the gill filaments which brings about the highest incidence of mortalities.

The following parasites which affect Koi require a microscope for observation.

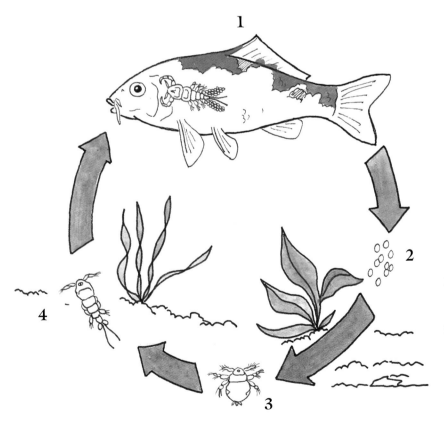

Gill maggot life cycle.

KEY
1. Parasitic females attached to the gills (not to scale).
2. Eggs are released into the water from the prominent white egg sacs.
3. Eggs hatch into free-living juveniles.
4. Later juveniles must find a host fish to survive.

GYRODACTYLUS (BODY FLUKE)

Signs: Depending on severity of infestation, fish may flash and flick, but will not refuse food unless secondary problems occur.

If parasites are causing a problem, the fish will scratch continuously at any time of day. The occasional twitch is not necessarily a sign that flukes are the problem. The body fluke does not kill fish directly, and is not regarded as a serious parasite. It is secondary problems that can become life-threatening, should the number of flukes increase and damage the skin. The body fluke attaches itself to the skin of the Koi and holds on with an attachment organ known as the 'haptor'. Situated at the caudal or rear end of the parasite, the haptor consists of two large hooks with smaller hooklets surrounding them.

There is a sucker at the anterior end of the body but, unlike other flukes, *Gyrodactylus* has no eye spots. It feeds on cellular debris, blood when it can be obtained, and other tasty morsels found in the mucus layer or in the epithelium. The hooks can be damaging to the Koi, particularly when there are large numbers of *Gyrodactylus* on the body. The resulting skin abrasions can all too easily become invaded by bacteria, fungus or viruses. These disease-causing organisms live in pond water, awaiting the opportunity to invade a host fish. In biological terms, the site at which disease enters the body of the fish is known as the 'entry portal', and many pathogens rely on other organisms to create this entry point for them.

The body fluke gives live birth directly on to the body of the fish, rather than laying eggs. Being an egg can be a risky business when you live in water. Nature got around this problem well by ensuring that the young fluke is born with its 'clinging on' apparatus ready for action, and the genital system ready for reproduction. It is fascinating to observe *Gyrodactylus* down the microscope, as one to three future generations can actually be seen

in development inside the uterus. Flukes do not always remain on the original host fish, and are transported to a new host through body contact. There are more then 100 species of body fluke found in the various aquatic environments, but the one most commonly found infesting the Koi pond is *Gyrodactylus elegans*.

DACTYLOGYRUS (GILL FLUKE)

Signs: Prevalent at water temperatures around 65-70 degrees F; operculum may protrude; refusal to feed and lethargy in the latter stages

Dactylogyrus, the gill fluke, is related to *Gyrodactylus*, the body fluke. The two are similar in many respects, particularly body shape, but some physical variations make for easy differentiation. Under the microscope, the gill fluke can clearly be seen to have eye spots at the front end of the body. *Dactylogyrus* is oviparous, or egg-laying, and therefore the uterus is not observed internally. The eggs are sticky so that they can adhere to the gill filaments, and they hatch at a water temperature of 68 degrees F. Many eggs do not survive and are washed out of the safety of the host gill. Obviously, the gills of fish nearby become a new host, and thus the infestation is passed on. One or two gill flukes pose no real threat, particularly at low temperatures. However, *Dactylogyrus* is a more serious parasite than *Gyrodactylus*, and, if many breeding adults have been observed microscopically, chemical treatment may be the only option.

The gill function is vital to the survival of the Koi, and gill flukes can be very destructive to the gill filaments. Both bacteria and fungus commonly invade tissue damaged by flukes, and when large areas of the filaments are affected they become fused together. Then cellular death of the gill tissue occurs, preventing diffusion, and the fish dies. Fish with an advanced gill fluke problem may exhibit gill covers that protrude as the filaments swell. They may also spend time in the outflow of a venturi or at the base of a waterfall, although this behaviour can indicate many other possible conditions.

ICHTHYOPTHIRIUS MULTIFILIIS (WHITESPOT OR ICH)

Signs: White spots resembling a sprinkling of salt; lethargy; refusal to feed; Koi hanging under waterfall or pond surface; high mortalities.

Koi are very hardy fish and can survive an outbreak of whitespot as long as remedial action is taken before secondary disease strikes and gill damage becomes too great. The parasite is commonly introduced by unquarantined Koi, and all new fish pose the same risk, as whitespot can be carried sub-clinically. The parasite is commonly triggered by transportation and handling, or when fish are placed in a water temperature lower than they have been used to, even if acclimatisation has been carried out. The life cycle is complex and, depending on the number of organisms, three consecutive treatments may be required to interrupt it.

Water temperature can have a major influence on the efficacy of the chemical in use. A lot of microscopy would be required to be accurate about the interval required between each chemical treatment – at 55 degrees F possibly four days apart would be successful. While there are other methods of controlling whitespot which are claimed to be successful – such as raising the temperature – this is not at all practical in the Koi pond, and could have all manner of side effects. Chemical control using a product specifically aimed at whitespot is the best approach.

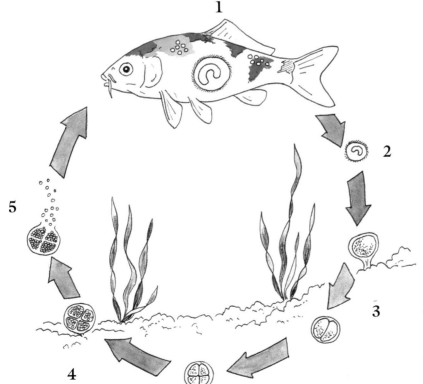

KEY
1. Individual cells beneath the skin (not to scale).
2. Mature parasites.
3. Parasites enclosed in a gelatinous capsule.
4. Each cell divides to form 1000 or more infective stages.
5. 'Swarmers' must find a host in 24 hours.

White spot disease cycle.

CHILODONELLA

Signs: Clamped fins; respiratory distress; excess mucus; lethargy; high mortalities.

This protozoan parasite is found on many species of freshwater fish. Mortalities may be high before the parasite is diagnosed, so there is very little time for diagnosis and treatment. Clamped fins, lethargy and respiratory distress are the only signs. Viewed microscopically, the parasite is oval, vaguely heart-shaped. It moves with a slow, gliding action in a circular motion. The organism dies soon after leaving the host, and, after death, appears rounder in shape.

TRICHODINA

Signs: In severe cases, lethargy; excessive mucus; respiratory distress.
In minor cases, slight build-up of mucus.

Trichodina are ciliates identified microscopically. Sometimes called the 'Mexican Hat', they also resemble a catherine wheel. When highly motile they resemble a flying saucer, being round in shape – the denticular ring can clearly be seen. There are three genera and many species, all with variations of form.

Under good pond husbandry this parasite rarely gets out of control, and a low level is common on Koi. The use of chemicals should be avoided unless the problem is severe, as it can make the situation worse. It is far more important with this parasite to consider how it was triggered out of control. There is usually an environmental reason to be found.

ICHTHYOBODA (COSTIA)

Signs: Lethargy; refusing food; excess mucus; high mortalities; commonly found on stressed fish.

Microscopically, the parasite resembles a comma doing somersaults, but it dies off under the heat of the microscope light. When one fish is stressed for any reason, that fish is sometimes the only one found with *Costia*, and isolating it and medicating accordingly is all that needs to be done. However, in other situations the whole pond becomes infested, though this is uncommon unless you are dealing with greatly stressed or newly-imported Koi. Koi dealers will see more *Costia* than the Koi keeper. *Costia* does seem to be able to recognise the weakness in the host fish very quickly, and survivors of a *Costia* attack are rare unless it is caught immediately in its early stages. It affects both body and gills, and all parasites attacking the gill are serious. This parasite is active all year round, but more common and more likely to become a problem at higher temperatures.

19 DISEASE RECOGNITION AND TREATMENT

By Paula Reynolds

When Koi are feeling unwell their behaviour will change. As we have seen in the previous chapter, they may single themselves out from the other fish, hover under the waterfall or pond surface, refuse food or become lethargic. The Koi keeper may observe erratic swimming or a failure to maintain buoyancy.

These signs merely indicate there is a health problem – they are not an aid to an actual diagnosis. Knowing what is wrong, and whether the problem can be cured, depends on further observation for more specific indicators such as flicking, scratching, skin reddening, swelling, raised scales, ulceration, protruding eyes, excessive mucus or other skin abnormalities.

INTERPRETING SYMPTOMS

Flicking and flashing can indicate a water-quality problem; nitrite, particularly, is a major irritant of Koi. In all too many cases the hobbyist fails to appreciate that nitrite is the cause, and an inappropriate chemical is introduced to the pond which only adds to the problems for the Koi.

Skin irritation also induces flicking and can be due to a high number of parasites on the body. This behaviour does not tell the Koi keeper which parasite is involved, but, when combined with lethargy and loss of appetite, it is an indicator that parasites are responsible. Fish lice, anchor worms and leeches can seen with the naked eye, while other parasites require the use of a microscope, an essential tool to the Koi keeper.

Ponds can easily become contaminated, which opens up many possible causes of irritation and changed behaviour, heavy metals being among the commonest pollutants .

Red marks on the body of a Koi can result from a bruise or be a response to an environmental change. They cannot be ignored, as they could be the first sign of bacterial disease.

A wound on one Koi may be an injury, but, when several fish all have the same type of lesion or ulcer, this usually indicates bacterial disease. If a larger area of the body or the vent is red, this too suggests a bacterial infection.

Raised scales are commonly caused by bacteria attacking the scale pockets, but this can be a localised problem which responds to topical treatment.

Although fungi live in all ponds they can only cause secondary disease; the skin of a healthy fish cannot become infected. Therefore, when fungal growths are observed, there is an underlying cause that has to be investigated. Fungus growing from a wound on one Koi implies that a fish has

RECOGNISING PROBLEMS
Photos: Paula Reynolds.

A Koi killed by nitrite poisoning and its secondary effects.

This Koi has an ulcer on the pectoral muscles.

A wound on the mouth – prompt treatment is essential.

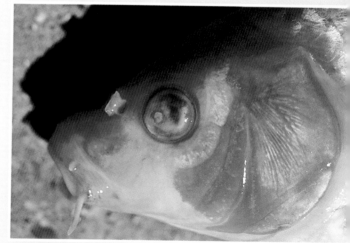

A cloudy eye can indicate bacterial disease.

Bacterial erosion to the surrounding skin, now affecting the eye.

injured itself, possibly on a sharp object in the pond, and fungus has gained entry to the body via the wound. When several Koi are all infected with fungus, then there may be an underlying parasitic cause, or a health problem occasioning damage to the body and allowing the fungus an entry point.

COURSES OF ACTION

Lumps, bumps, growths, tumours and other abnormalities have so many possible causes that professional diagnosis is needed to determine if the disease is infectious to other Koi, and if the condition is treatable. Of course, Koi can develop many unsightly skin lesions that are not necessarily life-threatening.

In the case of an internal tumour, it is advisable to let the fish live out its days as long as it is feeding and behaving normally. Surgery requires specialist skills, and very few tumours can be surgically treated in Koi.

Infectious disease can prove hard to control. For example, there are strains of bacteria causing ulcerative diseases which spread quickly when the temperature is conducive. A hospital tank can be valuable, and, if a fish is moved from the pond in time, cross-infection can be prevented. The success rate in treating serious bacterial disease may depend on getting good advice from the outset.

Parasites and poor water quality are both common causes of gill problems, but the condition will generally affect many, if not all, the Koi in the pond. A gill condition observed in only one Koi is more likely to have other causes. Gill tissue can heal, and Koi do recover from minor gill problems such as minimal exposure to ammonia. The edge of the gill filament can become ragged in mature Koi, and missing gill tissue does not always imply fish will not survive. However, every gill filament should be deep red, with no discoloration. Serious gill

disease is usually incurable, and attempts at extending the life of an affected Koi may add to its suffering.

Euthanasing any Koi in obvious distress (one that is unlikely to survive in the long term), is the only humane option. However, a Koi that is active and feeding – despite any obvious health problem that cannot be remedied – is still enjoying life, and should be allowed to do so. Quality of life for any animal is far more important than duration.

DEALING WITH COMMON KOI HEALTH PROBLEMS

Sometimes an ailment affects only one Koi, and will not be passed on to the other fish. But identifying this fact poses problems for the Koi keeper. In general, parasite problems should be treated in the pond. Bacterially and fungally infected fish need isolation to prevent the spread of disease to healthy Koi unless the whole pond is already infected. Koi with minor wounds can be left in the pond if responding. It is the unusual that causes concern and gives rise to the need to isolate.

Your hospital tank should be filtered, and an airline is essential. The water should be tested regularly, as the filter may not be fully biological. Provision to change water frequently may need to be made, either via a purifier or with conditioned water. So place the tank near a tap if possible. Heating a hospital tank should be done gradually, with the starting temperature being the same as that of the current pond. While heating improves the immune response and aids wound healing, take care not to allow a bacterial or parasitic problem to worsen by providing too high a temperature. At around 60 degrees F, Koi have a greater ability to fight disease. The following list can help in emergencies when there is no time for a proper diagnosis.

1) Many Koi are listless and exuding a high level

of mucus. There is a slight reddening of the body. Nitrite is the most common cause, although other pollutants are equally possible, as are parasites. While reddening suggests infection, bacterial disease seldom attacks all the fish at once, and, in this case the symptom is more likely to be due to irritation. Check all water parameters, particularly nitrite. Take mucus smears to eliminate parasites. If neither is the cause, isolate one or two Koi in a tank not filled from the pond to prove whether the pond water is contaminated.

2) There are white lumps on several Koi.
If the growths appear glossy and wax-like, then the condition is most likely the viral disease, carp pox. This disease causes a white tumour or layer to form on the body or fins. There is no treatment necessary, as it is a disease of cold water which diminishes as temperatures rise. Mature Koi resist the disease, which is not regarded as serious.

3) Koi are lying on the bottom of the pond, sometimes inclining to one side.
Possibly due to chilling of the swimbladder – affected Koi can be placed in shallow, salted water that is slowly heated. An improvement may be observed after three or four days, but, as secondary problems can affect the swimbladder, you should seek professional advice.

4) Several Koi have patches where the scales are raised.
Possibly a minor bacterial infection of the scale pockets. Either isolate the affected fish and treat it topically, or treat the pond if several Koi are all showing the same signs. If there is no improvement within a few days, seek professional advice.

5) All the Koi are mouthing at the pond surface, or are under the waterfall.
Possibly the level of dissolved oxygen in the pond water has dropped – this can happen in very hot weather – or the fish may have a parasitic infestation that is affecting the gills. The possibility of something toxic in the water cannot be ruled out. Increase the aeration of the pond – if you cannot do this, play the hose on the pond surface. Chlorine will be the least of the problems in such an emergency. Changing water may improve the problem if the pond has been contaminated. Examine a fish, looking in gills and over the body generally, and take a mucus smear if possible to rule out parasites. If the fish appears normal, place it in a hospital tank in high oxygen and observe it. If it improves, you know that the pond water and not disease is the problem.

6) The Koi are refusing food and are lethargic. Many of them are swimming near the surface of the pond – new fish have been introduced recently.
Whitespot is the most likely possibility. The spots are not always visible before the behaviour of the fish changes, but, equally, it could be another parasite, and a toxic substance could give the same indications. Net one or two Koi and examine them closely for spots. When whitespot is advanced, the Koi may appear to have been sprinkled with salt. Treat the pond for whitespot without delay, as this parasite kills.

7) The Koi are listless and are spending a lot of time on the bottom, although the weather is warm. Some of the fish are developing black spots.
The most likely cause is fish lice – catch a Koi and view the body close up. Fish lice are very easy to identify – seek a dealer's advice on treatment if it is indeed lice. If the black spots are more like black cysts when viewed close up, and are attached to the fish and not moving, seek professional advice.

8) *One Koi has an open wound on its side which is irregular in shape.*
Possibly an injury rather than disease. The wound should be topically treated and the pond scrutinised for sharp objects.

9) *Four Koi have ulcers which have been topically treated, but are not improving.*
The numbers involved suggest bacterial disease; isolate the affected fish and seek professional advice.

10) *Several Koi have patches of raised scales.*
Possibly a localised bacterial infection. If the condition is extreme in one or two Koi, isolate them in salt and bactericide, or treat the pond with bactericide if several Koi are all showing the same signs. The patches can be topically treated.

11) *The Koi flick and jump, especially night and morning.*
This behaviour is taking place at specific times, so it will be due to the water chemistry and temperature changes that take place in all ponds at night and in the morning. If the Koi had a parasite problem, they would be flicking and flashing continuously, not intermittently. No action needs to be taken as long as the jumping is restricted to these times of day. However, if the problem gets worse, seek professional advice.

12) *There appear to be a two or three small bones protruding from the body of a newly-purchased Koi.*
This is most likely anchor worm – remove manually from the body with tweezers and then dab the area with topical bactericide. The pond does not need treating unless the problem becomes serious.

13) *The body of a Koi is bloated, the scales are standing out and the eyes are protruding.*
Dropsy is the most likely condition – not a disease in itself but a sign of many possible health problems. One affected Koi can be placed in a solution of salt and bactericide. The salt is essential to attempt to reduce the fluid. If many Koi are suffering from the condition, seek professional help.

14) *A material resembling cotton wool (cotton) is growing in tufts from several Koi.*
Most likely a fungal infection which is secondary, attacking skin that has been damaged by parasites or injury. Take a microscope smear if possible, and treat the pond if a parasite problem is found to be underlying. Your dealer can advise on products, and you can also check the section below. If only one Koi is affected, it is far less likely that there is a pond problem. The fungus may have gained entry to an injury and the Koi may respond to being isolated in a product with bactericidal and fungicidal properties.

TREATING A WOUND, INJURY OR ULCER

Skin damage by parasites or sharp objects such as plant baskets, as well as the ulcers resulting from disease, can all require topical treatment. Koi keepers are sometimes reluctant to net fish in order to treat a wound, as it is a stressful procedure, so assess the lesion beforehand.

WHEN TO INTERVENE
• The wound has been caused by a heron, a cat, or a sharp object in pond.
• Several Koi have ulcers.
• An injury has not healed of its own accord, although the water is warm.
• Fungus is growing from a wound.
• A lesion appears minor but the fish is not behaving normally.
• A lesion is more inflamed, deeper or wider than it once was.

GUIDELINES FOR TREATMENT
Photos: Paula Reynolds.

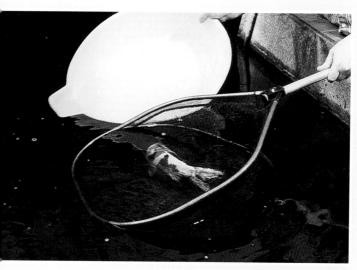

Use a net in the water to guide the Koi into a bowl.

This Koi has a lesion on the nose which requires treatment.

A Koi under sedation.

Only when a Koi loses equilibrium in anaesthetic should it be taken out for treatment.

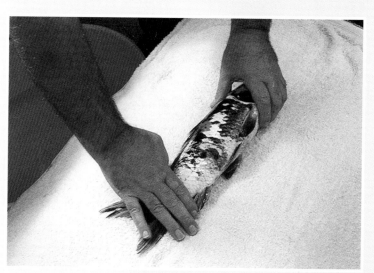

The fish is placed on a wet towel prior to treatment.

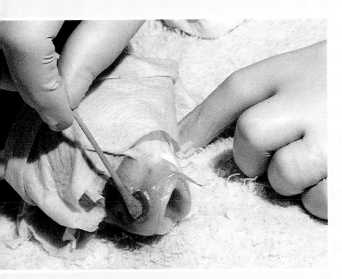

Treating the wound.

The Koi coming round after the anaesthetic.

- A lesion is not healing due to low temperatures (over-wintering in a hospital tank may be required).

Intervention by the Koi keeper is not always necessary – wounds and injuries can heal naturally, but this process can be delayed during seasons when water temperature is low. In summer, minor abrasions are far less likely to require treatment. Lesions that are part of a disease process are less likely to heal without medication, although this depends on the type of infection involved.

When only one or two Koi develop a wound, the possibility is that these are injuries. If, however, several Koi develop wounds at the same time, then they may be suffering from a bacterial infection. The wounds on such fish are more likely to be ulceration, and this is caused by disease.

While they may respond to topical treatment which will help to prevent secondary infection, most bacterial diseases are more successfully treated by using antibiotics with professional guidance. Any Koi with an open lesion should always be isolated in a hospital tank containing salt at half an ounce per gallon, and a bactericide. Whenever Koi are hospitalised, provide

plenty of oxygen and monitor the water quality regularly.

It is less stressful to sedate Koi before carrying out a full treatment. There are many substances that will do this, but, in the UK, the licensed fish anaesthetic is MS222. This can be obtained from a pharmacy that retails veterinary products, or direct from a veterinary surgeon. The pharmacist cannot provide advice on the use of the substance. The vet has a higher responsibility in law, and may ask to see a fish to satisfy himself there is a genuine need for the substance.

As well as the anaesthetic and the topical medication, tissues for drying and disposable gloves will be needed. A baby-changing mat makes a safe work-surface and this can be covered with a clean towel dampened in pond water to keep the Koi wet while out of water. If you prefer to carry out the treatment without sedation you will need another pair of hands to restrain the fish in a wet towel, exposing only the wound. Keep a towel for exclusive Koi use, and soak it in disinfectant before it is laundered.

NETTING
There are all sorts of nets on the market designed for specific sizes of Koi – injury can

result from their inappropriate use. Never chase a fish around the pond for hours with a net. You will only cause exhaustion and stress. If the shape or size of the pond creates a problem, a drag net is required. A bowl is also essential, and most Koi keepers favour a baby bath. Never lift the Koi clear of the water in the net, but minimise damage by using the net to guide the Koi into the bowl. Do not over-fill the bowl with water, but use just enough to cover the dorsal region of the fish. Cover the bowl before you remove it from the pond; the fish will be less stressed and less likely to jump out if the bowl is darkened.

SEDATION
Introduce the anaesthetic to the bowl and replace the cover if the Koi is still lively. The fish will gradually succumb to the anaesthetic and eventually turn on to its side. The time this takes can vary – in warmer water the process will naturally be quicker. When the Koi has been on its side for half a minute, you can place your hands under the fish and gently raise it clear of the water, keeping your hands over the bowl. If the Koi starts to flip its tail, then return it to the bowl and repeat this procedure until the fish becomes sedated enough for you to carry out the treatment.

The hobbyist does not require the fish to be fully anaesthetised in order to topically treat a wound. All that is needed is mild sedation, so do not expect the Koi to be motionless.

WOUND TREATMENT
When using topical sprays, protect healthy skin, eyes and gills with a damp towel or tissue. The wound should be cleaned initially with a mild wound-cleaner, and dabbed dry with tissue. Next, a bactericide is applied and allowed to remain in contact for a few seconds. The wound should then be well dried before a final layer of either a cream or a wound-sealer is applied, but do not use

both at once or they will not adhere. For subsequent treatments there should be no need to clean the wound again – the bactericide and sealer should be enough. During the final treatment, possibly only the antiseptic cream will be required, and there may be no need to sedate the Koi.

RECOVERY
After treatment, the Koi can be carefully carried back to the pond or hospital tank in either the damp towel or the treatment mat. Once it is back in the pond, do not handle the fish at all – allow the Koi to recover from the anaesthetic naturally by supporting it in a net held in fast-moving water. The rich supply of oxygen is all that is needed to revive the fish, but recovery time will vary with temperature and the general condition of the fish itself. Even if the Koi does not right itself immediately, there is no need to intervene. As long as the gill movements are getting stronger all the time, be patient.

It is rare for there to be any problem with the recovery of Koi following sedation. Only if the fish fails to show any gill movement at all should you introduce oxygen into the gills with a gentle back-and-forth rocking motion. This must be done very slowly or it will be counterproductive, and can even cause gill damage if carried out too fast. You cannot ram oxygen into the gills – it has to be taken up from the water, and that is a slow process.

Aim to carry out a topical treatment only once a week with a minor wound. More serious lesions may require attention at three-day intervals. Stress, and the side-effects of the anaesthetic, make greater frequency undesirable. Avoid re-opening a wound, or preventing the healing process by over-treatment. As they heal, most ulcers and injuries will turn white around the edge of the lesion. Later, as with a scab on human skin, the wound will take on a very glossy appearance.

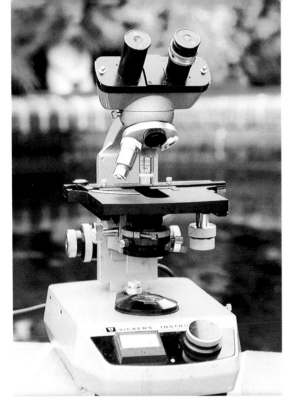

A good microscope is essential in disease and parasite identification. This is a reconditioned hospital model. Photo: Nick Fletcher.

ROLE OF THE MICROSCOPE IN KOI KEEPING

Many organisms, generally referred to as parasites, have the potential to cause health problems in fish. Those that live externally are termed ecto-parasites, those living inside the fish are known as endo-parasites. Koi living in the confines of a garden pond rarely suffer problems with internal parasites. The body and gill parasites that most commonly bring about health problems fall into two categories – those that can be seen with the naked eye, and those that require a microscope to aid identification.

For the Koi keeper, an expensive microscope is not a necessity – a magnification capability of x400 will be more than adequate. Children's microscopes are the least expensive, but the hardest to operate. A better-quality secondhand hospital microscope can be a good option. A model with a built-in light source is preferable to one requiring a torch.

Binocular models make for easier viewing than monocular types, and a mechanical substage allows more control of the glass slide during viewing, though it is not an essential feature. Without a mechanical control, the slide has to be moved by hand, which can be difficult for the inexperienced.

It is perfectly possible to care for your Koi without taking mucus smears which are then viewed microscopically. Without this aid, however, it is likely that the Koi keeper will have to resort to the use of chemicals more frequently than a hobbyist who owns a microscope. Such Koi keepers will also need to develop observational skills, and learn the subtle variations in behavioural pattern that occur with each parasite infesting the pond. The microscope is a great help in preventing the needless use of chemicals in the Koi pond, as it takes the guesswork out of pond treatment.

All fish will carry some parasites, and the life-cycle of these microscopic organisms will vary with the species – water temperature has a major influence on their reproduction level. *Trichodina*, for example, is commonly seen at low levels in mucus smears, but its presence does not imply there is a health risk; pond treatment is not required. However, when the fish are showing signs of behavioural change such as lethargy, while at the same time a higher level than normal of *Trichodina* is observed, the possibility is that the parasite has now changed its normal pattern of activity and is multiplying by fission. The reproduction rate of the organism in this instance will be far higher, and chemical intervention will be required before the parasite gets out of control.

To take a mucus smear, you need only restrain a fish carefully in a net – there is no need to sedate a fish for this procedure unless you want to examine the gills. Using a blunt-ended but flexible tool that is not going to cause injury (a lolly stick is an option), remove a very small amount of mucus from the body, possibly from more than one area. Place this on a glass slide and cover it with a cover slip – a little water may be required, depending on the thickness of the mucus. There is no need for staining – the basic smear will be adequate for the needs of the hobbyist.

The axilla is the shallow depression into which the pectoral muscle folds when the pectoral fins are held against the body, and is a common site for body parasites. The gill fluke often strays out of the gill opening on to the body. The body fluke can find its way into the gill cavity, although you will seldom see a high number of strays of either type, as they prefer their own territory. Determining how many parasites seen in a mucus smear actually constitute a health problem is not easy for the novice, but experience can be gained by taking smears from healthy Koi as well as from those with parasite problems. It is important to assess the level of parasites in the pond properly, and this can be achieved only by taking a mucus sample from several Koi. Samples will also be more representative if taken from different areas of the body. One Koi that is run down will naturally carry more parasites.

Understanding why parasites are triggered into changing their behaviour and reproductive methods can help the hobbyist to prevent them becoming a health risk. Fluctuations in any water chemistry parameter can be enough to initiate a parasitic infestation. A nitrite level that has gone undetected, or a dramatic rise in pH, could cause body flukes to multiply. A too sudden drop in temperature could trigger an outbreak of whitespot, an organism frequently introduced to ponds by failure to quarantine. All fish carry some parasites subclinically, and even the use of chemicals cannot eradicate organisms in that state – they are hidden, awaiting the appropriate moment to attack.

The pond should not only be free from fluctuations but should also be hygienic, and the fish fed a diet appropriate to the species, including some natural foods to ensure that the mucus layer will be in condition to protect the fish from attack. The stable pond is the optimum environment. Parasites are opportunists which recognise the weakness of a host fish, and utilise that vulnerability to their own advantage.

GETTING HELP WITH A HEALTH PROBLEM

Taking a cat or dog to the vet is nowadays as commonplace as a visit to the doctor. However, deciding where to go when your fish are not well is not so straightforward. The fact is that most Koi health problems are not directly linked to the fish themselves. The pond and the health of its inhabitants are uniquely linked in a way not seen in other branches of animal welfare. Many aspects of both the design and construction of the pond and filtration system can have the potential to create health problems. The novice fish keeper lacks knowledge and experience, and frequently fails to seek advice. The skills of a qualified aquatic consultant can prove valuable at the outset of the hobby, so that the proposed pond is built to provide an optimum environment from day one for the fish that will live in it.

For instance, turning a goldfish pond into a Koi pond is going to be successful only with knowledge of the pitfalls and the compensating factors that need consideration. Most newcomers to the hobby would not realise that Koi excrete far higher levels of waste than goldfish, and they therefore fail to appreciate the vital role of both mechanical and biological filtration in any pond that is going to house Koi. When problems are continual, it is likely that either the pond or its management is to blame, and good professional advice should be sought.

A specialist Koi centre should be able to offer good advice on basic health matters when water quality or even parasitic problems are suspected. When serious health problems are a factor, the dealer may refer a customer to a fish health consultant or a fish pathologist, depending on what appears to be wrong. In the case of bacterial disease, your local vet may be able to offer advice and prescribe antibiotics. While not specialising in fish, a veterinary surgeon does have a great deal of knowledge about infection generally, and this can be successfully applied to the treatment of bacterial disease in fish.

A water analysis could reveal that the pond water is unsuitable for the long-term wellbeing of the fish. Chlorine, heavy metals and other contaminants can be removed by water purification, and a water-purifier manufacturer will offer advice to prospective customers on which unit is right for their specific problems. Joining one of the many Koi-keeping clubs or societies offers the opportunity to turn the hobby into a social activity, and gain from the experience of others. There are so many sciences within Koi-keeping that are highly specialised, and it has to be appreciated that no one source can ever provide the diversity of information, and knowledge and advice required.

GUIDELINES FOR THE USE OF CHEMICALS

1) Chemicals should only be used in the Koi pond to cure a known health problem, never as a matter of routine. Medications can never replace good management, and there are no miracle cures.

2) Calculate your pond gallonage accurately in advance – overdosing can kill; underdosing fails to work.

3) Always follow the instructions on the container of any pond remedy. The dose level of a medication is based on its concentration, which does not appear on the bottle, and will vary with the brand. For example, malachite green and formalin are both available in

variable formulations, so using some brands at the generic dose in the list that follows would not be appropriate.

4) Test the water to ensure that all parameters are normal before introducing a medication. If ammonia or nitrite is already polluting the water, a chemical will make matters worse. A pond treatment used in a pond in which the pH has fluctuated could kill all the Koi. Re-test the water following treatment to ensure that the filter is still biologically effective.

5) Switch off the UV whenever chemicals are used, as it can weaken their effectiveness.

6) Ensure oxygen is adequate before using a pond medication. The dissolved oxygen level will become lower as the water temperature rises, and chemicals will lower this even more. It is advisable not to treat the pond on a hot day.

7) The argument for switching off the pond filtration system while using a medication is a negative one. The presumption is that it will prevent loss of filtration biology due to the action of the chemicals. However, consequences of a die-back in the filter due to

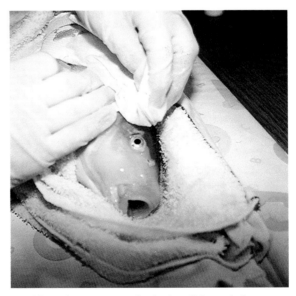

Rubber gloves protect both the fish and the keeper during all procedures involving contact between the two.   *Photo: Nick Fletcher.*

the reduction in oxygen supply could well equal any loss attributable to the chemical. Filter media will all vary in this respect, as some, more than others, will have the structure to best protect the organisms during the presence of a chemical. Bypassing the biological filter during a treatment is yet another possibility, but this too can only work in the short term. If sequential treatments are required, the filter will be bypassed for so long that some die-back will be inevitable. Some stages of the life-cycle of certain parasites may well be in the filtration system anyway, although this depends on the organism and the way the filter is designed.

8) Always measure a pond treatment into a watering can (kept exclusively for pond use) that has been pre-filled with pond water. Then distribute evenly all around the pond.

9) Many of the products used in fish health are toxic to humans. Disposable gloves and protective clothing are recommended; the eyes, too, are vulnerable. Those with asthma or who are concerned about respiratory problems should wear a mask, particularly when dealing with powder products, or when formalin is in use.

10) Store all the chemicals used in Koi-keeping with lids secured, away from children and pets, and in a location where it is cool, dry, and dark.

11) Many chemicals become either toxic or ineffective with age, so check the shelf-life with the manufacturer. Test kits, too, can give a false reading if out of date.

12) Allow time for chemicals to break down before repeating a treatment, or using an alternative product – with most chemicals this takes from three to seven days. Never mix products without checking safe combinations.

The products listed below are in common use for the treatment of Koi, although not all are licensed for that purpose. The branded products represent only some of those currently on sale. The generic products are available at some aquatic centres, or can be ordered from a chemist.

CHEMICALS USED IN THE TREATMENT OF KOI

MS222 fish anaesthetic (licensed Thomson & Joseph Ltd)
Dose: 1 gram in 10 litres of pond water, or as directed.

Full anaesthesia is not required by Koi keepers, but mild sedation can make topical treatment easier. Buffering the solution should not be required unless the carbonate hardness of the pond water is below 150mg $CaCo_3$ or 8.4 Gdh. Do not use with salt or other chemicals in the water. Obtainable from veterinary surgeons, veterinary pharmacies, and some chemists.

Sodium Chloride (common salt)
Dose: Long-term in hospital tank 1/2 oz per gallon (14 g per 4.55 litres) until improvement. Short-term bath 3 oz per gallon (84 g in 4.55 litres) for 5 minutes.

Use salt that is additive-free, cooking salt for example. The dip is not a substitute for the long-term bath. Stronger dips can be used for stubborn parasites, but Koi can become unconscious in strong salt dips, so seek advice. Salt can be used in conjunction with many other products such as bactericides, but does not safely mix with formalin or potassium, for example. All fish with any body damage benefit from living in salt.

Used to treat (short-term): Wounds or injuries; eye infections; body and gill parasites when the pond itself cannot be medicated for any reason; as a pick-me-up for lethargic Koi.

Used to treat (long-term): Dropsy; bacterial infections; any open body lesion.

Malachite Green and Formalin
Dose: Malachite green, 1 ml:17.6 gallons (81 litres); Formalin, 15 ml:220 gallons (1001 litres).

Malachite green is used with formalin to protect the fish because formalin alone removes the protective mucus layer that can harbour parasites. The malachite green is bactericidal and fungicidal and so reduces the risk of secondary infection. Salt should not be used with formalin. The above doses apply to the generic substances only.

Used to treat: Whitespot; *Chilodonella*; *Costia*; *Trichodina*; body and gill flukes.

Three treatments at seven-day intervals may be required for some parasitic infestations.

Acriflavine
Dose: 2 ppm for a generic powder, or as per instructions for a bottled formula.

Acriflavine for aquatic use must have a neutral pH. Long-term exposure can cause sterility, and is unsuited to fry; it can be used with salt.

Used to treat: General bacterial infections; wounds; ulcers.

Potassium permanganate
Standard dose: 1.5 grams per 220 gallons (1001 litres). Dissolve well before use.

This chemical, unlike many others, is still effective below a water temperature of 50 degrees F. Potassium permanganate can have adverse reactions, forming toxic manganese dioxide. It should not be used in ponds in which the pH is high or unstable, or in a pond which has a high level of organic matter. It does not safely combine with salt.

Used to treat: Bacterial problems; very stubborn cases of *Trichodina*, where it can prove more effective than other parasite remedies.

Chloramine T
Dose: 10 grams per 1000 gallons.

Used mainly as a bactericide, but some grades can be impure. Higher dose levels should be used with caution.

Used to treat: Patches of raised scales; gill disease; *Costia*; body and gill flukes.

Benzalkonium chloride
Dose: 1 ppm, repeat at two-day intervals.

Used to treat: Bacterial gill disease (and for general disinfection purposes).

Koi Anti-parasite FS (Interpet Ltd)
Used to treat: Parasites with free-swimming stage to their life-cycle. *Costia*; *Chilodonella*; Whitespot; body and gill flukes (not for use with all species).

Ark-Klens (Vetark)
Used to treat: Bacterial infection of the skin and gills (and for general disinfection).

Paradex (Lincolnshire Fish Health)
Dose: 100 ml per 1000 gallons.

Used to treat: Fish lice; leeches; body and gill flukes. Re-treat when juvenile stages of the life-cycle are observed. Suitable for Koi and goldfish only.

Medifin (Tetra)
Used to treat: General parasitic infestations and bacterial disease.

Pond Pride 3 Parasite Control (King British Aquatics Ltd)
Used to treat: Whitespot; *Costia*; *Trichodina*. This product was originally sold as WS3.

Myxazin P (Waterlife Research Industries Ltd)
Used to treat: Finrot; ulcers; general bacterial disease. Also effective against fungus and protozoa.

Bioxyl (Lincolnshire Fish Health)
Dose: 100ml per 1,000 gallons.

Used to treat: Bacterial infections and injuries; fin erosion caused by water-borne bacteria; some types of ulcerative disease can be prevented by sequential use; lowers the risk of secondary septicaemia.

Protoban (Vetark)
Dose: Formulated as a five-day treatment.

Used to treat: Whitespot; *Costia*; *Trichodina*; *Chilodonella*; some effect on flukes; lowers pathogenic bacteria levels.

Combat (Lincolnshire Fish Health)
Dose: 10 grams per 1000 gallons.

Used to treat: Myxobacterial infections; Columnaris; raised scales; wounds; ulcers; general gill conditions; Costia; Whitespot; body and gill flukes.

Pond Pride 8 – Open Wound Control (King British Aquatics Ltd)
Used to treat: Open wounds; injuries; ulcers; helps prevent septicaemia.

Tamodine (Vetark)
Used to treat: Topical treatment of ulcers and injuries.

Aquaswab (TAP Ltd)
Used to treat: Topical treatment of wounds and skin disorders.

Koi First Aid Kit (LFH)
Used to treat: Contains products for cleaning and treating all skin lesions.

ANTIBIOTICS
Legally, antibiotics can be obtained only on prescription and used under professional guidance. Antibiotics create side-effects and it is better to predetermine the appropriate drug for a specific disease by a sensitivity test rather than guesswork. The abuse of antibiotics by those producing Koi, as well as by hobbyists, has now limited their effectiveness and increased the need to obtain proper advice. Feeding antibiotics to Koi is less effective than a course of injections, which provides the correct therapeutic dose.

There is very little benefit from antibiotic baths and they are unsuited to treating serious systemic infection. Minor skin infections may respond, but some antibiotics become toxic to fish when used in solution. Do not adapt an antibiotic in a powder form for injection, or feed the injection formulation. There are many antibiotics not suited to Koi or no longer effective. Below is a list of some currently used in sensitivity testing. Temperature, among other factors, can influence the frequency of use, and can vary the treatment regime recommended.

ANTIBIOTICS FOR THE TREATMENT OF BACTERIAL DISEASE IN KOI
Oxytetracycline: Dose varies with brand – now less effective in Koi.
Gentamyacin: Injection; 4 mg/kg of Koi body weight every other day.
Chloramphenicol: Injection; 40 mg/kg as directed; less effective in Koi.
Potentiated sulphonimide: Injection; brands vary; 30 mg/kg every other day.
Enrofloxacine: Injection; 10 mg/kg every 2nd or 3rd day as advised.
Oxolinic acid: 10-12 mg/kg in food; now more successful in goldfish.

There is great concern about the environmental impact of using antibiotics to treat ornamental fish. Bacterial resistance is now a serious problem in human medicine as well as in aquatics. Refusal to supply antibiotics to Koi keepers may become a reality in future. The use of all chemicals should be seen as a pond management failure, and disease prevention, rather than cure, should become accepted practice – for the very good reason that it is far more successful.

20 *INDOOR QUARANTINE*

Building a Koi pond can be a stressful experience. Quite apart from the expense (invariably exceeding your wildest estimates), there is the strain on the back and on family relationships, as every moment of spare time is swallowed up by the project. The last thing you might feel like doing, as you finally run in the water and find to your relief that there are no leaks and that everything works as it should, is to turn around and start work on yet another pond project. Sorry – if you are at all serious about Koi keeping, a quarantine/hospital pond or vat is not an optional refinement, it is a must.

THE QUARANTINE DEBATE

Without being alarmist, there are more reasons today to be wary about the health of imported fish than at any time in the past. This is despite the fact that our understanding of Koi health care has improved dramatically; shipping procedures are better and speedier; and diagnostic techniques are becoming ever more sophisticated. It is almost as though the minute enemies of Koi have regrouped to tip the odds back in their favour.

Parallel cases involving human patients are always in the news – we hear of mysterious bacterial diseases that resist known antibiotics, or viruses for which there is no known cure. In the Koi world, stories abound of a few dealers and many more hobbyists suffering apparently inexplicable 'wipe-outs', whatever the country of origin of the Koi. The majority of such incidents could almost certainly be traced back to known causes stemming from human error or carelessness – such as metal contamination in mains water or stalling filters – if thorough investigation were to take place. The temptation is always there, when Koi die, to blame something outside our comprehension and control, rather than to admit that the fault lies with us.

However, as with all things unexplained, from UFOs to Bigfoot sightings, there are nuggets of truth to be sifted from the spoil heaps of falsehood. It really boils down to this – sooner or later, without the safety net of home quarantine, an apparently healthy Koi may arrive in your pond and trigger a problem of epidemic proportions which the rest of the fish may or may not survive.

This statement is at odds with the thinking of a minority who advocate all new fish going straight into the main pond. It is as if obtaining Koi from reliable breeders and/or reputable dealers is an insurance against the unthinkable happening. But a health problem is no respecter of persons or of fish pedigree. Arguably, Koi with an undistinguished bloodline are best able to cope with ailments because they are closer to their wild ancestors, and have not been bred for colour and pattern at the expense of hardiness.

The reasoning behind the 'no quarantine' approach is sound in only one respect – unless the quality of water in the facility is equal to or better than that in the main pond, and unless the fish can enjoy a stress-free existence in their temporary quarters, the whole point of quarantining is lost. A spell in a cramped vat may itself bring on stress-related ailments, and fish dying under these circumstances could well have been in perfect health when first introduced. The Koi keeper may tell himself that he has saved a problem from spreading to his other fish when, in reality, he has brought on that problem in the first place.

NEW FISH AND SICK FISH

It is difficult to provide a stress-free environment for large new Koi without building, effectively, a whole new pond of 3,000 gallons or more, and lack of space and funds inhibits this possibility for most of us. There are, however, a number of Koi keepers belonging to the 'no quarantine' school of thought who nevertheless maintain a hospital treatment vat, so it is not idleness that motivates them – merely the triumph of hope over a bitter experience they have yet to encounter.

The mere act of mixing Koi from different environments may trigger problems, even if all the fish appear healthy before coming together. In a long-standing community of fish, each individual's immune system has geared itself to resisting latent ailments carried by its fellow Koi; this enhanced immunity develops whether or not there has been an actual disease outbreak. Even one new fish may disrupt this balance; both parties are at risk, as the newcomer is also left wide open to ailments present at background level in its pondmates. It takes some time for this threat of potential cross-infection to diminish – the analogy might be that of Victorian missionaries or explorers who passed on 'mild' infectious diseases which proved fatal to tribes who had built no resistance to them.

In a perfect world, hobbyists would have two facilities to back up the main pond – one to quarantine new fish, the other for medication for sick Koi. In practice, one facility usually has to perform both functions, though ideally not simultaneously! If yours is not up to supporting big fish, then, quite simply, big fish should not be purchased unless your dealer is prepared to quarantine them for some months in a lot of water and treat them for any problems arising during that period.

It is worth detailing a few instances where, without back-up, Koi would be in trouble:

1) Small fish purchased early/late in the season, not destined for a heated pond.
2) Fish requiring long-term medication with a remedy that does not work at low temperature.
3) Any fish needing lengthy medication when the main pond has been treated with salt.
4) Home-bred Koi facing their first winter.
5) Any fish with fin/tissue damage that needs water constantly over 60 degrees F before regeneration can take place (again unless the main pond is heated).

SITING

Quarantine ponds are almost invariably sited indoors – sheds, outbuildings, even a spare room in the house. The spare room may sound an attractive proposition but condensation may occur. The warmer the ambient air temperature, the less supplementary heating will be needed, and so the building should be well insulated and draught-free. It should ideally receive some natural daylight through a window or skylight, but then the panes should be double-glazed to cut down heat loss. This can be done with bubble-wrap, polythene or polycarbonate sheeting, depending on budget.

Permanent mains electricity must be installed, complying with all the safety regulations, and it helps if a drain is nearby – if not, waste water can be routed out of the shed by an arrangement of pipes – more of which later.

The great majority of quarantine/hospital ponds are above-ground. One advantage of this is that gravity settlement can be installed and the pump can be sited outside the pond. This is one less piece of equipment that the fish can rub against. If the pond is raised off the floor on blocks it can incorporate a bottom drain, with any taps and valves easily accessible. Otherwise, the option is a midwater inlet – but the pipe feeding the pump must be protected with a foam block to prevent small fish swimming into it. Central heating pumps are useful on quarantine vats, but only if the body is of phosphor bronze, otherwise any salt will rapidly corrode it.

Both gravity set-ups will involve cutting through the liner, however, and, even with proper tank connectors bedded in mastic, this can bring about weak spots. It is relatively easy to keep a small body of water clear of solids by regular vacuuming, especially since blanketweed will not be a problem indoors. Pump-fed filtration is therefore the usual choice.

The disadvantage of ponds not in-ground is that they lose heat fast unless proper steps are taken to insulate the walls and cover the surface when access is not required. This does not apply if the building is space-heated, but few of us can afford that luxury in a garden shed.

CONSTRUCTION

As with outdoor ponds, several methods of construction present themselves. For permanent installations, a blockwork shell raised off a level concrete floor with a liner fitted inside is popular. Otherwise, large free-standing containers can be pressed into service, as long as you are certain they are made of non-toxic materials. Recovered containers may be cheap, but their use is inadvisable unless they have previously been used for water or foodstuffs storage. Vats made of glassfibre, ABS (Acrylonitrite-Butadiene-Styrene), PMP (Polymethylpentane), PP (Polypropylene) or HDPE (High-Density Polyethylene) are safe, but PVC can occasionally leach plasticisers into the water.

Circular vats have no corners in which sick fish can hide, and they promote good water circulation and minimal solids build-up. But they are wasteful of space. Square or rectangular tanks can butt right up to a wall, providing that clear access is left on at least two sides.

There are even commercially-built quarantine ponds available with partitioned integral filtration chambers. While these are neat in appearance, and require minimal installation, in-pond filtration is not ideal if the medium is gravel or Canterbury spar – this is difficult to clean. It is better to have external filters utilising media such as foam or matting, which are light and easily removeable.

SIZE AND MATERIALS

As to the size of your quarantine/growing on pond, the bigger the better. A rectangular vat 10ft x 6ft x 3ft deep, filled to within six inches of the brim, will hold 936 imperial gallons – there are many facilities smaller than this, but around 1,000 gallons is arguably the break point between a successful system and one which will bring about more problems than it solves. If the depth dimension can be increased, obviously less floor space will be needed. So a vat 6ft square, 4ft 6ins deep (again with a six-inch gap above the water) would hold nigh on 900 imperial gallons. Limitations could be placed on depth by the height of the building and that of the Koi keeper, and any hollow blockwork construction more than two courses high should always be reinforced with steel rods and progressively backfilled with lean concrete mix as the walls are raised up, otherwise it might not withstand the outward pressure of water.

Once the shell is built, it can be insulated with polystyrene sheeting – do not forget the floor. As an alternative, drill into the blocks, fit battens and fill between them with rolls of loft insulation before fixing sheets of plywood on to the wooden framework with countersunk brass screws.

The liner can now be laid in. Butyl or reinforced PVC off the roll can be used, but a box-welded liner is the best choice, as it will fit snugly into the shell without creases or pleats (potential dirt traps). Tuck the top edge of the liner over the insulation before capping off the pond perimeter. Wooden planks, painted with polyurethane varnish, give a neat finish.

The pond should be covered, to prevent fish jumping out and to conserve heat at night, and the best way to do this is to have a hinged frame of netting over battens on a rope and pulley. This can be secured out of the way when access is needed. By incorporating a rebate into the wooden pond edging, polycarbonate sheets (double-glazing offcuts) can also be slid over the pond when required. These have excellent insulating properties.

Two or three 300W aquarium heater/stats can be hung vertically in the water from a wooden crosspiece to maintain the required temperature, their cables secured by taking a half-turn around plastic-covered screw-in cup hooks.

One or more compact 'header tank' filters of the type used in small garden ponds can service the quarantine pond. Downflow versions are best, where the water passes through sheets of foam and then through plastic biomedia before returning to the pond by gravity. Obviously these filters will need to be mounted above water level, on blocks or a sturdy table or bench. An in-pond submersible pump circulates the water through them. This is one instance where a fountain pump is just

as suitable as a solids-handler; in either instance the intake will need to be protected by a foam cartridge to stop small fish being drawn in. The filters act purely biologically, all solids being vacuumed from the pond.

Jubilee clips securing the pump hose must be cushioned to prevent damage to Koi.

A compact UV steriliser in line between the pump and filter will help maintain the clarity so essential if fish are to be closely observed, but UV treatment must never continue if the vat is being medicated with anything other than salt. The ultra-violet light quickly degrades chemicals such as malachite and formalin or potassium permanganate before they have a chance to work properly.

SIPHONS AND DRAINS

For cleaning a quarantine vat, a manual siphon is quite adequate. It is easy to make your own – a length of 1.5-inch diameter rigid pipe is attached to a flexible hose long enough to be fed into the nearest drain, and to make it easier to manoeuvre the business end around the pond bottom, the pipe can be tied to a pole. If your drain is too far away, an alternative is to clip a length of four-inch drain piping to a wall of your shed and lead it outside to a sump (a diamond core drill will make the necessary hole through a brick or blockwork wall). The pipe should be gently sloped to take the flow, and at the point where the siphon hose enters a section is cut away. The 'blind' end is capped, and, when not in use, another cap should be pushed into the outlet point so that rodents cannot use the pipe as a run into the shed or garage.

The sump into which waste water is piped is simply a hole 4ft-6ft deep, in the bottom of which is a layer of hardcore topped off with coarse gravel. Ideally, the hole should be brick-lined, although plastic bins with the bottom cut off can be used instead to prevent the sides collapsing. The sump should be securely covered when not in use. The long-term viability of any sump is determined by the permeability of the underlying soil and the height of the water table. If a sump is not practicable, vat water can be siphoned into a large vessel containing a submersible pump with a float switch, which will transfer it to the nearest sewer inspection chamber.

It is absolutely essential to know the exact gallonage of your quarantine pond, which should be filled through a water meter and tapwater purifier. Take a length of broom handle and as the vat reaches (for example) the 250-gallon, 500-gallon and 750-gallon marks, wrap a piece of waterproof tape around it. Do the same when the vat is full. The broom handle, stood upright at a predetermined point on the pond floor, can now act as an accurate measuring stick, doing away with the need to use the water meter every time you refill or perform a part water-change. It will also assist if, for example, your vat is salted and you want to know how much to replenish to keep the salinity constant after changing some of the water – though a salinometer should be used as back-up.

FILTERS AND PUMPS

Supplementary ponds are no different to any others in that their filters have to go through the maturation process. Liquid or freeze-dried bacterial booster products are more economical to use in relatively small volumes of water, but the only way to maintain and nourish the filter bacteria populations once established is to keep some Koi always in residence, and feed them! If the vat does need to be drained down and refilled, filter maturation will have to be started from scratch.

Good aeration is essential in a quarantine facility. One of the larger aquarium pumps adapted and sold for pond use will be ideal. Airlines (and all pipework and electric cables) should be run tidily through clips along the wall at the far side of the vat – in a confined

space it is essential to be orderly or you risk tripping over equipment. Nets, for example, should be stored upright or, if too tall, in slings hung from the shed or garage roof, out of reach of rodents.

HYGIENE AND EQUIPMENT

The whole point of a quarantine facility is to keep the Koi within it entirely separate from those in your main pond, to prevent cross-infection. There should be no transfer of water between the two; nets and Koi socks should be thoroughly sterilised after use; and any fish with suspected parasitic infestation being moved indoors for long-term treatment should first be dipped.

The shed housing the quarantine facility is very often also the place where treatment of sick Koi takes place, as this will involve minimal moving around of fish. All medications and associated equipment such as baby changing mats to lay the fish on, swabs, test kits, gram balances and even your microscope, should be stored in damp-free cabinets under lock and key.

Similarly, because sick fish recover best with the least possible disturbance, the shed should be locked when not in use. This discourages casual visitors from wandering in to look at them, or children coming in and dabbling their hands in the vat water. It is a safety precaution that will protect fish and small humans alike.

Under some circumstances it is permissible to mix growing-on Koi with those undergoing treatment, but you must be selective. Koi with minor physical damage that is not infected will benefit from the warmer vat water and pose no threat to others, but never mix healthy fish with those suffering from ulcers, dropsy, wasting disease (Fish TB), fungus, fin-rot or bacterial gill disease. Common sense should tell you what is safe to put together but, if in any doubt, do not do it! It is better to lose one fish than several.

21 HANDLING KOI

Like all bony fishes, healthy Koi are covered in a layer of mucus which has mildly antiseptic properties and protects the skin to some degree from attack by parasites or pathogens. Any breach in this mucus, particularly if the skin is damaged at the same time, lays the fish open to bacterial or fungal infections.

THE MUCUS LAYER

Healthy mucus is thick and elastic, and flows freely over the skin. Some fish in poor health, or males as they approach spawning, have only a thin covering and the skin can feel dry and almost like sandpaper to the touch. Obviously, such Koi are especially prone to damage during handling.

Minor injuries, if sustained in good-quality water at a temperature at or over 60 degrees F, will usually heal themselves. Koi do bump themselves, or rub off mucus while 'flashing' against the pond bottom – behaviour which is often, but by no means always, associated with external parasites or high nitrite levels. Sometimes Koi do this after feeding, or at certain times of the day, and only if the flicking is continuous is there likely to be a problem.

The mucus layer can be breached by protozoan parasites, and even more easily by crustaceans such as fish lice (*Argulus*) and anchor worm (*Lernaea*), luckily not often encountered if proper quarantining is carried out. The site of the small penetrative wounds made by these pests can again become inflamed and infected. Even so, an unbroken mucus coat offers a degree of protection.

Koi keepers must therefore ensure that whenever the need arises to handle their fish, it is done in a way which causes them no stress or damage. Above all, the mucus layer must remain intact and no scales must be dislodged – this applies whether the Koi is a six-inch baby or a Jumbo. The golden rule is that the fish must not leave the water longer than is absolutely necessary, and that handling is done calmly yet confidently.

NETS

Koi must never be lifted bodily from the water in a net – nets are used purely to guide the fish into a suitable receptacle, usually a floating bowl or basket.

Net frames should be circular, and the soft knitted mesh should form a shallow pan shape so that Koi cannot dive deep into the material and snag hard fin rays. Similarly-shaped nets are sold to anglers for the purpose of landing fish, but the handles of these are usually of a flexible material such as glass or carbon fibre, designed to bend under the weight of the catch. A Koi net handle, whether of metal or wood, should be rigid and in one piece.

There is a wide selection of nets available. Make sure the net you buy has a greater diameter than your biggest fish.

Photos: Keith Allison.

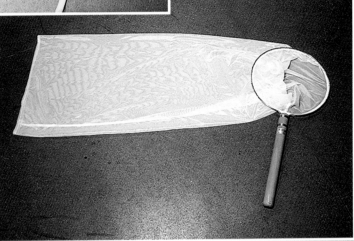

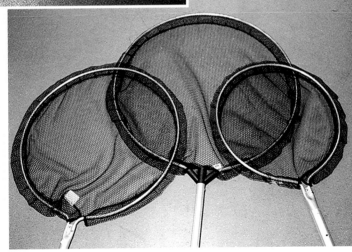

When deciding on the size of net to buy, aim for one with a diameter greater than the length of your biggest fish. The handle should similarly be as long as possible and preferably stretch the width and/or depth of the pond, though this is not always possible. Large ponds may need two people, each with a net, to effect a capture.

Some nets are easily detachable from their handles by means of a spring-loaded catch, but this sort of union is not as strong as a permanent fixture. It goes without saying that there must never be any projections from fastenings that could injure fish.

With their robust handles and fine mesh, Koi nets offer considerable resistance through the water, and so chasing fish is rarely successful. The technique is to lower the pan gently into the water and very slowly bring it up under the chosen Koi as it is facing you.

Once there, raise the net up and towards you, running the handle through your hands, keeping the fish's back under water but at the same time tilting up the rim adjacent to its head to discourage a sudden forward rush. As the Koi moves around in the net, you will have to constantly adjust this angle.

Generally, larger fish are much more sedate than little ones, and females better behaved than the more athletic males. But 'rogue' individuals that react violently to attempts to net them are present in most ponds. After a while you get to recognise these and can almost tell when they are about to jump clear of the net. Anticipation of these aerobatics does not always prevent them, however. After an unsuccessful netting attempt, wait a few minutes for the fish to calm itself before trying again.

Very large ponds defy conventional attempts to net Koi, and for these a variant of the drift-net once used to catch North Sea herring is brought into play. It consists of a fine-knitted mesh, slightly wider and deeper than the pond, with floats along the top edge and weights along the bottom. The sides of the net are fastened to sturdy poles. Starting at one end of the pond, two people draw the net gradually forward with the Koi swimming before it, until a small area at the other end is partitioned off. Koi can then be pan-netted and bowled in the usual way.

Nets are often used to move sick fish, and so should be disinfected after each application in a strong solution of potassium permanganate. Do not forget to wipe down the handles as well as immersing the mesh. If possible, invest in two nets – one exclusively for poorly Koi. Never, if you are also an angler, use your landing net on your Koi – this is a sure way to introduce pathogens to the pond, since all coarse and game fish carry disease-causing organisms, if only at background level.

After dipping your nets, the best way to store them is either propped mesh-end uppermost against a wall or, if the building is not tall enough for the handle, on a rack suspended from the ceiling – this can simply be a sling made from strong cord. Both strategies keep the net out of the way of any rodents present in outbuildings.

FLOATING BOWLS AND BASKETS

Koi bowls in which fish can be studied before purchase, or examined in the home pond, simply float on the water's surface. Before attempting to net a Koi, position the bowl within reach and tip it so that it part-fills with pond water. Transferring Koi into these receptacles is best done by two people, one inclining the net towards the bowl, the other tilting the bowl towards the net. Once the fish is safely in the bowl, the net should immediately be dropped down in the water and removed. In a confined space it also helps to have a third person making sure that the unwieldy net handle does not poke out windows or eyes!

Floating baskets, which are sold with detachable lids, have slatted bottoms allowing water through, so they are self-levelling. They are more convenient than a bowl, but not so good if the fish is being photographed. (Incidentally, for photography a rectangular bowl is much better than a circular one in which fish tend to swim in circles, hugging the perimeter).

A fairly recent development are circular meshed holding nets with a floating rim and a weighted base. These allow ingress of pond water and are useful for dealers segregating sold Koi awaiting collection, or when a customer is selecting 'definites' from 'possibles'. A cover net prevents fish jumping back to join their pondmates.

TRANSPORTING KOI

If a bowled Koi needs to be removed from the pond (for example, to travel to a show or

NETTING AND BOWLING
Photos: Keith Allison.

Stress must be kept to a minimum during handling procedures, so take your time when catching the Koi.

Guide the net towards the basket.

The Koi should be transferred to the basket without being lifted out of the water.

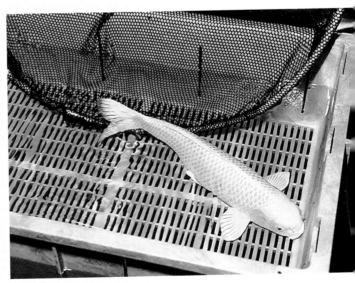

The Koi is safely in the basket.

to undergo topical medication), the tool to use is a 'sock'. This is best envisaged as a long cylindral mesh, open at one end and secured at the other around a circular rim attached to a short handle, shaped a bit like a table-tennis bat.

The rim of the sock is guided over the Koi's head while the other end is held tightly closed with the free hand. Once the whole fish is inside the sock, it is lifted clear of the water. Larger Koi can suffer internal damage under their own weight, so the hands at either end of the sock should pull against one another while the fish is inside, so that the mesh is kept nearly horizontal. In the case of very large Koi, a second person supporting the abdomen may be advisable.

The socked Koi is released through the open end, head-first – never let it go the other way, as this may dislodge scales.

At Japanese-style shows, another way of moving Koi short distances is in double polybags. Two members of the benching team carry these, the person at the free end of the bags twisting them closed with a turn around the hand so that even if he/she stumbles, the water and fish will not be spilled.

MANUAL HANDLING

Finally, there is manual handling – a sight common on videos of the All-Japan show and guaranteed to evoke gasps of disbelief, especially when the Koi is very large and valuable. The technique is practised at shows where a Koi has to be moved into an adjacent vat, but, although the knack is easily learned, bodily lifting of Koi is best left to the experts – usually dealers.

The first step is to mildly disorientate the fish by manually guiding it in a half-circle to the left, then to the right. The fish's head is turned towards the handler's body and, for a right-handed person, the left hand gently cups the fish around the anal fin and the

right hand does the same in the region of the pectoral fins – both thumbs point away from the handler. The idea is not to grip the Koi, but to cradle it in a balanced way so that, if it thrashes or flexes, the hands will go with the motion.

Any panic or nervousness on the part of the handler seems to be communicated to the fish, so the best handlers are always well-practised, confident, quick but laid back!

BAGGING KOI

The plastic bag did not come into common use until the late 1960s, when it opened up the Koi hobby worldwide. Fish could now be air-freighted in relatively small volumes of well-oxygenated water and survive flights of well over 24 hours with few losses.

When you buy Koi, your dealer will automatically double-bag the fish for you, but it is essential to know the technique if you are moving yours around to shows.

One bag is dipped into the pond, gathering enough water to comfortably cover the fish (usually a quarter to a third of the total bag volume). The first bag is then slipped into another of the same size, the weight of water ensuring a snug fit. The rims of the bags are rolled down two or three turns to form a floating 'collar' and the netted Koi is guided inside.

The bags are lifted clear and taken to a valved oxygen cylinder. Air is squeezed from the inner bag and the oxygen line inserted above the water – grip the rim of the bag around it to form a seal. Gas is now gently released to blow up the bag. Withdraw the line and twist the free end of the inner bag several times until the bag is taut. Double the twisted end over on itself and secure tightly with two strong elastic bands. Fasten the outer bag in the same way.

If the Koi is travelling any distance, a soothing agent called Elbagin can be added to the bag water, along with a little salt to

BAGGING KOI
Photos: Keith Allison.

A plastic bag is used to transport the Koi.

Patience is required to manoeuvre the fish into the bag.

The Koi is safely in the bag.

The Koi is inspected at close quarters, and from underneath.

Pure oxygen is pumped into the bag.

Careful handling techniques will ensure that valuable Koi reach their destination undamaged and without suffering stress.   Photo: Nick fletcher.

promote mucus flow and ease osmotic pressure.

SOPHISTICATED TRAVEL
The last word in Koi transport is used by Japanese dealers/breeders and some dedicated hobbyists with valuable fish. It consists of a free-standing soft plastic vat with a zip-over cover, usually carried in a lorry or on the back of a pick-up truck. Oxygen from a cylinder is conveyed through an airline to protected airstones in the transit water; there is nothing on which the Koi can injure themselves. They travel in the dark and arrive unstressed at their destination.

22 BREEDING KOI

By Tony Staden

One of the pleasures – and frustrations – of keeping Koi is that these fish are always full of surprises. Trying to breed them is no exception to this rule.

Goldfish and Shubunkins can be spawned within a few hours of a planned programme, but it is not so with Koi. Even after a lot of careful planning, male and female Koi will sometimes swim around the spawning tank enjoying their own company, and do nothing sexy until days later. Suddenly, when you least expect it, they will expend all their passion and, by the time you have found out, they will have dined at leisure on their own eggs. Or, without any preparation, and long before you have anticipated their being ready, they will flock spawn and confound your breeding programme. Some seasons they may just refuse to breed at all.

FLOCK SPAWNING
Most Koi keepers sooner or later experience flock spawning in the community pond, especially if there is a good growth of blanketweed and other plant material to stimulate the females to lay their eggs. Eggs can be collected from such unplanned events, and raising the offspring can provide lots of entertainment. They will be very varied, and a few may well be interesting, though not of the highest quality.

Flock spawning is also an excellent time to take stock of your fish and see which ones are actively involved in the chase, which females are laying eggs and which of the males are trying to fertilise them. I always find it useful to make records of individual Koi on these occasions, as there may be only a few good spawners in the community pond and this is the best time to identify them for future seasons. Usually a good spawner is consistent year on year. All the other hangers-on, chasing around, are merely waiting for the eggs to appear so they can have breakfast.

If you are content to spawn your Koi in your existing pond and you do not want to disturb the fish any more than you need, make sure you keep the pond reasonably free from blanketweed and any other spawning material until you are ready. If fish spawn on blanketweed it makes it very difficult to collect and move many of the eggs.

SPAWNING MATERIAL
When you judge the time to be appropriate, put in spawning material that can be easily handled and moved, once the eggs cover it. I use nests of brushes. These are made from 4cms/1^1/2 ins drain waste-pipe made into a square with sides of about 80 cms/32 ins (more or less, depending on the size of the fish and that of the container into which the eggs are going to be moved). Brushes are tied at intervals around this; their free ends

are tied together at the 40 cm/16 ins point, and a lead weight is added. This forms a very convenient nest – the waste-pipe floats while the weight holds the middle down.

A nest like this can be easily anchored in a pond (and Koi like attached spawning media, whatever it is). The fish swim up between the brushes and spawn in the cradle. The eggs often get lodged well inside the brushes, where other fish find it difficult to get at and eat them. The eggs stick to the brushes sufficiently to enable the whole assemblage to be carried and moved from tank to tank, as required.

Koi do not like to spawn on fresh brushes – they seem to prefer it if they have been in the pond for at least 24 hours. So, if you have ideas about removing nests as they fill with eggs and putting more in, stagger the sequence accordingly. These nests enable the Koi to swim into the brushes to mate, and a relatively good rate of fertilisation often ensues. If the fish have not used the nests within a week, remove them, wash them and return them to the pond.

SELECTIVE BREEDING

If you have much choice in selecting fish for breeding, take care and do not use misshapen, over-fat or poorly coloured Koi. Show winners are not the best, either. They may not be good spawners, nor producers of quality offspring; they may damage themselves and even die in the process. If possible, use fish that are not too large; 35-45 cm is a good size range.

Concentrate on choosing Koi that have a nice body shape and desirable colours. The males are usually more slender than the females (but not always) and have larger pectoral fins. In the breeding season they may develop tiny white spots on the gill plates and pectoral fins. These will cause them to feel rougher to the touch than the females. Some Koi are simple to sex, but I

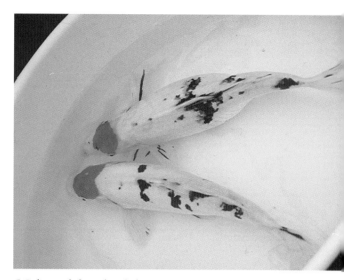

Male and female of the same variety. The female is plumper and has smaller pectoral fins.
Photo: Nick Fletcher.

have been fooled many times by the shape of a fish into thinking it was a female when in fact it was a male, and vice versa. This is where watching fish spawning and making notes comes into its own.

If you want to produce Kohaku or Sanke (or any other specific variety), it is useful to know the parentage of the fish used for breeding. Preferably, they should be proven breeders from a known strain, and there should be evidence of the quality of the offspring that the strain produces. Colour combinations are worth thinking about, but Koi genetics are complex, and an Orenji Ogon from one source may be quite different genetically from an apparently identical fish from another breeder.

Kohaku and Sanke may be bred together, when the resulting fry will show a very wide colour range. Kohaku on their own give yellows mixed with whites, reds, Bekkos and a relatively small percentage of – Kohaku! Adding Sanke to the mix results in anything from blacks and browns to white fish, plus some recognisable Kohaku and Sanke.

When choosing parents, good strong colours and acceptable body shape are

INHERITANCE OF SCALE PATTERNS IN KOI

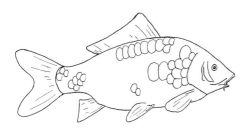

Mirror Koi: Breed true, but may arise from other crosses, e.g. lined x lined.

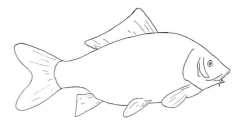

Leather Koi: When bred together give Leather and Mirror types.

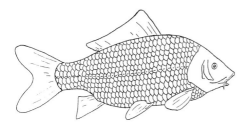

Scaled Koi: 'Pure' strains breed true. Strains from mixed parents give some Mirrors.

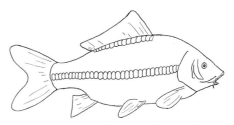

Line Koi: Never breed true. Always give some of all four types.

important, but pattern is not – it cannot be passed down from one generation to the next.

It is probably best not to mix parents if you seek a particular variety and you want to breed from your own offspring in the future. The exception would be with varieties like Ai-Goromo, which are a cross between Asagi and Kohaku. Japanese breeders have spent many generations trying to perfect particular Koi strains and, of course, the genetics of these can be wrecked by one outbreeding cross. Unless the parents have a comparable genetic make-up, mating Ogon with Ogon can be a disaster, as the offspring are often of very poor quality.

Shusui tend to give a fair number of other Shusui, but there will always be 25 per cent or more Asagi-like fish (with normal scales). The only thing you can be sure of with Koi breeding is that the offspring will throw up plenty of surprises.

SCALING PATTERNS

The inheritance of scaling patterns is well known, and, if the genetics of the parents are ascertained then the scaling of the offspring can be forecast with some certainty. There are four such scale patterns in Koi: an all-over covering of normally-sized scales; line scaling, where a double row of large scales runs down the back of the fish with sometimes a row along each flank; mirror-scaling, entailing a variable number of different sized scales, some of which can be very large and reflective (these are not prized by the Japanese Koi breeders and are usually culled out early); and leather scaling, where the fish may lack scales altogether.

The most prized varieties of Koi – normal-scaled fish and line-scaled fish like those in the drawings – can be bred with their own kind or with one another. Scaled fish from good stock usually breed true. Line-scaled Koi bred with one another never do, and will always throw up a mixture of all four scale patterns.

A pure-bred scaled fish crossed with a line-scaled Koi usually produces 50/50 scaled and line-scaled offspring, but, if the parents are breeders from a mixed and unknown source, a much more diverse mix of youngsters will result. Leather Koi are often very beautiful, but only a few appear as a result of selected crossings. Quality-bred scaled fish breed true, but not all scaled fish are genetically 'pure' – they may carry a recessive gene, and, if two such fish are mated, some mirrors may appear.

BREEDING TECHNIQUES

When the potential parents have been selected, the males and females can be separated, the males going into the spawning tank. The Koi must be fed well with the best-quality food to bring them into condition – chopped meaty foods like earthworms are excellent. How many eggs a female will carry is determined the previous summer and autumn, and good feeding from early April onwards will encourage them to grow in size but not in numbers. Large eggs in turn lead to strong fry with plenty of yolk on which they feed for the first few days after hatching.

Inducing Koi to spawn in our climate is something of an art. Of course, they can be injected with carp pituitary extract (unlike the goldfish group, they do not respond to gonadotrophins), or they can be stripped by gentle pressure, stroking along the abdomen towards the vent. But it is much kinder to the fish to allow them to decide when to spawn.

A water temperature of 18 degrees (64 F) and rising, coupled with a spell of high pressure and sunshine, often triggers the fish if water quality is good and there is plenty of spawning material to stimulate the abdomens of the females as they pass over it. When you are ready, put the spawning material into the tank containing the males, 24 hours before the females go in. The best time for them is the evening before an anticipated spawning. Two or three males to each female is the ratio for the best degree of fertilisation. If the fish are ripe and conditions suit them, they will usually spawn the following morning.

Tony Staden with a nest of brushes which he uses for breeding Koi.

Spawning is very vigorous, and tens of thousands of eggs are laid. These are very small at first, but rapidly swell to about 1mm in diameter. They are transparent, and a faint yellowish-green colour. Being adhesive, many will stick to the spawning medium. Spawning may continue for several hours; when the fish have finished they will probably start to eat the eggs. Certainly, any camp followers going round behind the spawning fish and looking interested will be eating any available eggs. Infertile eggs will turn white within a few hours, but do not be put off by the sight of so many in this condition – it is quite usual for only a small percentage to have been successfully fertilised, and these will stay clear and nearly invisible.

CARE OF THE EGGS

If the eggs are to be transferred to a hatching tank, the spawning material can be removed with them *in situ* and gently dipped into a dilute solution of malachite or methylene blue – at the same water temperature as the spawning water – to discourage parasites. If the parents are removed, leave the eggs where they are.

Providing you have plenty of very gentle aeration and water is circulating, do not worry about the infertile eggs. These soon become covered in a fungus called *Saprolegnia*, which looks like fine white whiskers. Fertile eggs will be hard to see while they remain transparent, but, after five or six days (depending on the temperature), the dark eyes of the embryos will show through the egg membrane. Hatching time is variable, and the whole brood will take two or three days to hatch after the eyes appear. The fry wriggle out of the membrane and rapidly attach themselves to any underwater object, including the sides of the tank, where they hang tail-down. Over the next day or two they absorb their yolk sacs and do not feed until they become free-swimming.

Eggs are prone to being eaten by many organisms found in Koi filters and pond water, including: *Asellus*, the water louse; freshwater shrimps; snails; and flatworms. So it is best to use carefully filtered, 'mature' water for spawnings and bringing on the eggs. Micro-organisms are essential for the raising of fry, in particular protozoa and rotifers, so do not adopt sterile tactics. On the other hand, do not take water straight from the Koi pond or filter, as this will always contain small invertebrate predators which will decimate the fry. Keep the water in a holding tank with gentle aeration for about two weeks at 20 degrees C (68 F) or more, and in this time most species detrimental to egg and fry survival will have died.

I find that the dead eggs provide lots of food for micro-organisms, and these in turn are eaten by the fry. But, should you fear that the water may become polluted by the total mass of dead eggs, and you wish to remove the fry to another tank, many can be siphoned off at this stage with the careful use of a large-bore pipe.

The dead eggs will rot nicely, and micro-organisms will feed on the *Saprolegnia* and the bacteria attacking the infertile eggs. Any other organic debris on the brushes/spawning media will experience a similar fate and provide good food for the fry. However, as soon as they are free-swimming, the fry must have additional food.

FRY FOOD

There are several proprietary fry foods on the market. Grinding down pellets in an electric food mixer is an alternative option, but be careful with coarse grades of pellet as they may not blend well. At this stage, fish feed by choosing particles of a suitable size. They do not consider taste or content.

Hard-boiled egg yolk is very useful, as the particles will fit easily into the mouths of fry and are of good food value. I go about preparing it in the following way: boil the egg for 10-12 minutes; remove the shell and the white; squash the yolk through the fingers into warm water, so that a yellow liquid is obtained; and put this into an ordinary hand-spray (1-litre size is ample). Spray a little of this mixture twice or three times daily over the fry tank. If they are feeding properly, the yolk will be easily visible in the semi-transparent stomachs of the little fish. Particles not eaten get trapped in the brushes and provide more food for the micro-organisms. Live food, such as newly-hatched brine shrimp, rotifers and the young of *Cyclops* and *Daphnia*, are excellent, but it can be difficult to guarantee these with any consistency.

Correct feeding is very important at this stage. Large hatches of fry soon die of starvation if there are not enough micro-organisms to go round, and no other food is given. A complete wipe-out can result within the first few days. To avoid pollution, provide gentle aeration and arrange for the water to flow through a filter bed.

A brood of young Koi, approximately four months old, at feeding time.

Photo: Tony Staden.

The fry grow rapidly and, soon, quality cat, dog and Koi pellets can go into the grinder to give them some variety. You will probably find that the young hang about the brushes, where decaying food particles are generating the vital micro-organisms.

After about four weeks, with regret, I remove the brushes, trying not to carry too many fry with them. At this stage, I do not mind if the water is not crystal clear, but, if there are any signs of pollution, it is time to move the fish to new quarters.

GROWTH AND CULLING

Growth of the fry is very uneven. They will range in size from very small to about 2.5 cms (1 in). The larger ones may become cannibals – you will see the tails of their smaller brethren sticking out of their mouths. Separate these cannibals – they grow very rapidly and can be fun to raise on their own. In any event, grade the fish by size from time to time, selecting those you want to keep.

Big heads, bent bodies, kinked tails and undesirable colours may be evident early on. The Japanese success in producing quality Koi lies in their rigorous culling and colour selection from an early stage. A very large number of fry are produced, but, within three weeks, all the offspring which show no evidence of their true variety are discarded. A second and third cull takes place as the fish grow, and only a very small percentage of the original spawning will be allowed to attain 10 cms (4 ins).

By September the largest fish from your home spawning may be up to 15cms long, but there will be many not half that size. At this time, the colour of the Koi is well established, though there may well be more changes to come as they grow larger. Quite often the best-coloured fish do not grow as rapidly as the rest, and may need to be nurtured separately. Fish under about 10 cms (4 ins) do not overwinter well outside, unless they are of the hardier varieties such as Shusui.

From the time of hatching, a small percentage of the fish die each day. Casualties tail off as they get larger until, by the time they are a few centimetres long, there are few further deaths. It is a common mistake to try to raise too many fish in a limited space. The result can be an almost total wipe-out from disease or starvation. So, given that a surprising amount of colour and scaling detail is evident after very few weeks, select only the fry that are most appealing and give them your full attention.

They may not be show-winners, but 'home- bred' Koi still engender a feeling of pride in their owners. Just occasionally, something quite unique emerges from the gene pool.

23 KOI APPRECIATION

apanese Koi breeders have a unique attitude towards their fish, born of a long association with them in their daily lives. Before Nishikigoi, carp were produced for food, and so, over many generations, Koi in one form or another have been bound up with the business of making a living, or even winter survival in the remoter areas of rural Japan. Incidentally, the word 'Koi' can legitimately be used across the board, even when describing uncoloured ancestral fish, since it is simply the Japanese for ... carp! Using the term 'Koi Carp' is akin to calling a German Shepherd a 'dog dog'.

STATUS OF THE CARP IN JAPAN

The qualities of carp, actual or imagined, have always elevated them above the status of mere cold-blooded creatures in Japanese culture; their strength and tenacity are reflected in paintings and on porcelain, with stylised examples shown battling up waterfalls to reach their spawning ponds. Carp are popular subjects for 'Netsuke', the small carved and often humorous wooden and ivory figurines originally made to act as toggles securing personal possessions around the sash of a pocketless kimono. Even today, parents of sons hang out Koi-no-bori (carp 'streamers' or static kites) to celebrate Boys Day, in the hope that their offspring will in some way inherit the desirable characteristics of carp.

The head has nonetheless always ruled the heart where Koi in Japan are concerned – particularly when the peasant rice farmers acknowledged the forces of hard economics and breeding ornamental fish became more lucrative than rearing carp for food. The Japanese 'love' of Koi has always been very different to the Caucasian sentimentality we display towards members of the animal kingdom. This explains why, in Japan, breeders will readily cull millions of deformed or substandard fry after each spawning. Even the top Tategoi, which represent the pinnacle of the Koi breeder's art, are retained only to the point where they will realise the greatest cash return. The best fish command professional respect, which is not to be confused with an emotional response.

'HANAKO'

That the Japanese are not uniformly so objective about Koi is illustrated by the attitude of a pioneer amateur Koi keeper, Dr Komei Koshihara, who owned a very special red carp 'Hanako' which had been cared for by several generations of his family. The Koi was allegedly 226 years old at its death in 1977 – almost certainly this was a gross, if well-intentioned, overestimation arrived at by drawing the wrong conclusions from scale readings, but there is no doubt that this was still a venerable fish.

The Ultimate Koi

Dr Koshihara would regularly visit the hand-tame Hanako in her remote pond when, if we are to believe his account, man and fish seemed equally delighted to see one another. "Although a fish, she seems to feel that she is dearly loved, and it appears that there is a communication of feeling between us. My greatest pleasure is to go to my native place two or three times a month and keep company with Hanako," the doctor wrote. He even penned haiku poems to the fish!

AN EXPANDING MARKET

When Japanese Koi keeping moved from being the preserve of the rich to the hobby of the ordinary citizen, appreciation of the volume-bred fish was at a rather low level – buyers had no real yardstick by which to measure good against bad and the breeders could sell all they produced, knowing that someone would find their Koi attractive. But, as tastes refined, which they did rather quickly, the market changed. The number of breeders fell, but the quality of the fish from the remainder improved, not only to satisfy Koi keepers in Japan, but also in response to

stiffer competition from abroad, notably Israel. Since then, Japanese Koi have remained several jumps ahead of the rest in the quality stakes.

Israeli Koi farming still concentrates largely on volume-bred fish, with some culling, though this is nowhere near as stringent as that practised by the Japanese. Higher-grade Israeli Koi are now being produced, too, to the extent that Israeli Ogons and Bekkos are almost impossible to tell apart from those bred in Japan. But the fact that ordinary-grade Israeli Koi still find a ready export market suggests that, worldwide, the level of appreciation is still quite low. This is borne out by estimates that, of the millions of Koi imported annually into the United Kingdom, only five to ten per cent are from Japan.

THE APPEAL OF KOI

What, then, is the universal appeal of Koi, and how do people come to spend thousands of pounds and dollars on a branch of fishkeeping not noted for being easy, or even in accord with the shrinking dimensions of the average garden?

Pond visits are a great social occasion for Koi keepers, and a forum for the exchange of ideas.

Photo: Nick Fletcher.

Koi Appreciation

The story usually starts with an ordinary goldfish pond, dug in an attempt to provide a better home for fish won at fairgrounds and crowded into small bowls. Gradually, stocks are built up in this shallow, poorly filtered but goldfish-friendly environment until the owner comes across his or her first low-grade Koi – usually at a garden centre. One or two are purchased with high expectations but they die within a few weeks, having first reduced the ordered collection of water plants to a shredded mess.

At this point the pondkeeper either gives up on Koi or returns to the garden centre, to be told that these fish require a pond at least two feet deep and of 500-gallon capacity – and the same type of filter as before, only bigger! This situation is extreme, as the standard of advice at non-specialist outlets is not as poor as it once was. But 'proper' Koi keeping is a minority interest which some retailing staff are still struggling to come to terms with.

Rare is the Koi keeper who builds an effective pond first time round. More typically he/she will bring out photograph albums charting the progress of successive excavations, each larger and costlier than its predecessor. However good the latest effort is, it never fully satisfies – partly to blame for this are ongoing innovations in Koi-related equipment, which can appear to render a pond out of date before it is half completed.

KOI CHARACTERISTICS

Good or bad as they may be in quality terms, all Koi share characteristics that endear them to their owners. Cyprinids are not the most intelligent of fish – this honour going to families like the cichlids, which pair up and exercise brood care in a number of interesting ways (including retaining their eggs, and subsequently the fry, in their mouths). Given the chance, Koi will eat their own eggs!

Fishy rocket scientists they are not, but Koi are bright enough to learn to recognise their owner and come to the pond's edge to take food from the hand. They are not true shoal fish, but they swim around in groups and appear to spend more time with some of their pondmates than others, almost as though friendships are being forged.

There appear to be introverts and extroverts in any pond – Koi keepers can always tell you which fish will be first up to the food, which ones spend the majority of their time near the surface and which tend to skulk around near the bottom, even when in bursting good health. For some unknown reason, Chagoi – the tea-coloured Koi which grow huge – have the friendliest disposition of all, and adding one to your collection can make the other fish much more outgoing. Mix orfe with Koi, on the other hand, and the sedate carp will take on their skittishness.

All fish are alleged to have a calming effect on their owners, something old-fashioned dentists were well aware of when they installed an aquarium in their waiting rooms. When gas was the only anaesthetic, the sight of a few guppies and angelfish would soothe the patient so that he did not need so much nitrous oxide to put him under – and so the tropical fish paid for their keep. Koi ponds in the grounds or indoor foyers of fast-paced corporate headquarters arguably fulfil the same function, offering employees a respite from the cut-throat world of big business.

Koi, especially large ones, have a serene way of swimming and a dignity of bearing which contributes to their mystique, but it is their huge array of colours in plain or metallic form, and in limitless combinations, that first attracts the beginner.

LEARNING THE BASICS

For new enthusiasts, the metallic fish exert most appeal – the classic variety of the Japanese, the red and white Kohaku, being passed over in favour of more 'obvious' Koi.

The frequently quoted Japanese saying 'Koi keeping starts with Kohaku and ends with Kohaku' may well be applicable in their country of origin, but certainly not elsewhere. Invariably, in Britain and the USA, Yamabuki (yellow) and Purachina (silver) Ogons, or the bi-coloured metallic Hariwake, are popular first choices. There is nothing wrong with such fish, of course, and they are relatively inexpensive to purchase, but a pond full of these varieties alone would soon cease to please the eye.

At this early stage, the hobby of Koi keeping now seems to divide between a majority who are happy simply with 'pet' fish and those who desire to improve the standard of their collection. For the latter, the learning curve is steep and involves acquiring a surprising number of Japanese words describing the basic Koi varieties and their many variants. There is nothing snobbish about this; it is just a form of verbal shorthand, very useful if you are trying to describe to a dealer the fish you want netted from a well-populated vat.

As an example, a beginner might say: "I'd like that sparkly-scaled red and white fish with two big patches of red on its back, another on its head and those cute red lips." A more seasoned Koi keeper would pinpoint the fish in question as a "Gin-Rin Sandan Maruten Kuchibeni Kohaku"!

'Gin-Rin' describes the scale type; 'Sandan' means a three-step red (hi) pattern; 'Maruten' indicates that one of these steps is in the form of a separate marking on the head; and 'Kuchibeni' is the Japanese word for 'lipstick', which describes perfectly the small amount of hi on the mouth.

ALL THINGS JAPANESE

Learning Japanese Koi terminology can be the first step to developing a deeper interest in all things Japanese; their culture, their religion and their gardening styles, all of which are bound together in traditions going back thousands of years. This is why Bonsai culture comes naturally to Koi keepers – not only do the little trees add ambience to a formal pond, but they typify the same long journey towards unattainable perfection upon which every aspiring owner of good fish will embark.

The Koi keeper's first trip to Japan, if it takes in the mountainous Niigata prefecture where the best fish are bred, will be a revelation. Going hand in hand with the beautiful, wild scenery will be a unique blend of the old and the new, even today far removed from the fast-paced lifestyle of the capital, Tokyo. For the rural Japanese, modern technology is a servant, not a master. Even the wealthiest breeders live modestly and have respect for their fellow men, which is why crime in the remoter parts of Japan is virtually unknown. Where else could ponds holding fish of inestimable value be left safely unattended?

CHANGING STANDARDS

A broad definition of Koi appreciation is keeping fish you personally like – never forget this, or you may be lured into buying expensive examples just because you have been told that they fulfil most of the criteria for excellence. Like language, the appreciation of Koi is a living thing and constantly changing. If anything, standards are becoming less rigid. As recently as 10 years ago, for example, Kohaku were supposed to conform to ideals of pattern etched in stone. Otherwise superb fish were written off for show purposes if, for instance, a head hi marking came down over one eye, or if hi went directly into the wrist of the tail without a break of white skin. There were even ideal percentages of red and white laid down, and Koi showing 'unbalanced' patterns were demerited, too. Before photography, there were Japanese 'pattern books' of painstakingly painted fish showing their evolution towards the required standards.

This has come round full circle, so that nowadays judges look for uniquely-patterned Koi. Standard step-marked Go-Sanke rarely take the top awards, but, if a fish has (for example) a head marking resembling a crown, a Bonsai tree or a character from Japanese calligraphy, it will attract the judges' attention. Of course, even the most stunning pattern is of no avail if the fish's body shape and skin quality are inferior.

A SOCIABLE HOBBY

A few hobbies can be successfully conducted without making any direct contact with other people, but Koi keeping is not among them. Admittedly, a certain amount of knowledge can be gleaned from books, magazines and lately the Internet, but a Koi pond viewed only by its owner is like the proverbial rose blooming in the desert. Koi people desire and benefit from interaction with like-minded souls, if only to defend themselves against the charge that they spend inordinate amounts of time and sums of money on something that is essentially pointless. Such accusations are normally made by non Koi-keeping partners!

Koi shows are as much social gatherings as they are an opportunity to pit one's fish against the competition, while lifetime friendships can be forged at Koi clubs. An outsider looking into the Koi hobby could be forgiven for thinking it elitist, even snobbish, and patronised only by the very rich. The reality is quite different – far from there being a structured and impenetrable hierarchy, everyone involved with Koi, from whatever walk of life, can contribute something useful.

KOI CLUBS

In Britain we are fortunate – this being a small island, nobody is too far away from the meeting place of their local Koi club. There are two major organisations, the BKKS (British Koi Keepers Society) and the Northern and Southern chapters of the ZNA (Zen Nippon Airinkai), but most members also pay a small subscription fee to their local affiliated body or section. There are, besides, a number of successful independent Koi clubs owing allegiance only to themselves.

In the United States, because of the distances involved, it is more difficult to meet fellow hobbyists and so the major Koi clubs rely heavily on their regular shows and conventions to develop the social side. Members will travel literally thousands of miles to attend, even though bringing their fish with them is quite impractical.

Shared appreciation of Koi is the force that binds clubs together, but it goes much deeper than merely comparing one's prized fish with those of other members. If a Koi falls sick, there is usually someone available to advise on treatment; if equipment fails, there will be a standby pump on willing loan until a replacement can be bought.

Most Koi clubs will have their elected officials to manage the finances, organise guest speakers, run raffles and liaise with other clubs on exchange visits. These take place in the summer months, and typically involve members travelling together to view showpiece ponds of all sizes and degrees of sophistication. Such events afford us the opportunity to gather fresh ideas on all things Koi-related, but they are also an excuse for having a few drinks around the barbecue and enjoying a brief respite from worrying about our own Koi.

A FISHY LOVE AFFAIR

A heartening aspect of Koi keeping is that the degree of care shown to the fish has little to do with the quality of the collection or the complexity of the pond in which they swim. For example, only a minority can bear to sell on their first acquisitions to make room for better-quality fish, which is why ponds tend to contain an eclectic mix of the good, the bad and the indescribable.

The aquatics industry responds, sometimes cynically, to this caring attitude with a host of Koi-related products that do not always come under the heading of 'essential' but are bought, rightly or misguidedly, to improve our fishes' quality of life. So Koi that will never see a show vat are still fed pellets costing three or four times as much as those strictly necessary to meet their basic nutritional needs; montmorillonite clay additives provide the minerals and trace elements absent from purified tapwater; and every year thousands of gallons of expensive proprietary medications are tipped unnecessarily into ponds to 'prevent' outbreaks of disease and parasites that would probably never occur in the first place.

From all this, we can see that 'Koi appreciation' is a phrase with several very distinct shades of meaning. At top level, it is the ability to distinguish excellent fish from the also-rans, and admire the subtleties that mark out a major show-winner from Koi that appear, at first sight, to be on an equal footing with it. Such appreciation can be purely aesthetic, but it helps if you love Koi rather than admire them merely as things of beauty.

At club level, competition can still be extremely fierce. But, even when Koi are not from the top echelon, the difference between a trophy and a minor placing can hinge on the way fish are brought on after purchase. Koi that achieve their maximum growth potential in heated, uncrowded ponds with impeccable water quality are just as likely to do well as better-quality fish that do not enjoy this degree of care and so regress rather than move forward.

Finally (and this covers the great majority of Koi keepers), there are those who appreciate their fish purely for the pleasure they bring. They keep Koi in ponds alongside their goldfish, orfe and rudd, and are not bothered at all about pedigrees or bloodlines; they enjoy watching random spawnings, and, if any fry survive predation, they are proud of their unplanned 'home-breds'. We all started like this, and, while it is tempting to decry the people who are happy to stay with their hobby at this basic level, we should acknowledge that they still derive immense satisfaction from it. One day they may yet acquire a Koi that is streets ahead of the others in their pond, and then the delayed spark will kindle the fires of obsession!

24 SHOWING KOI

The decision as to whether or not to show your Koi is a deeply personal one; against the satisfaction of seeing your fish competing against others in size and variety, and perhaps even returning home a Grand Champion, has to be weighed the stress it may suffer from transportation and its spell in a show vat. There is also the remote possibility, irrespective of the style of show, that your fish may pick up an infection from other Koi.

There can be little doubt, though, that Koi shows have increased public awareness of our hobby and encouraged many more people to take it up. In addition to the competition itself, most larger shows will have dealers in attendance selling Koi and dry goods. Entertainment will be laid on for the children which, together with a craft fair and stands selling Koi-related products such as statuary and Bonsai, ensures that even family members with little or no interest in the fish will enjoy their day out.

RAISING STANDARDS
The show circuit has certainly improved the overall standard of fish exported from Japan, as many Koi are now purchased with the express purpose of being exhibited by their owners. Sometimes they do not even get to swim in their home pond before show day – the dealer keeps them at his own premises and then brings them along and enters them on the purchaser's behalf, a practice few fair-minded folk agree with. But whatever route they take to the show vat, once the very best examples of the various varieties have been put on public display, it is hard for ordinary hobbyists to settle for less – though it must be said that the depth of one's pocket can seriously inhibit this ambition!

Shows thus act as a benchmark for excellence and push the hobby forward, in terms of both fish and fish-related equipment such as pumps, filters, foods and medications. They are attended by hardcore enthusiasts and beginners alike, and many people have started out in Koi keeping as a result of seeing a show signposted and going to have a look on a whim, out of sheer curiosity.

Effectively, show fish mean Koi from Japan, though there are exceptions, as Israel now produces some fine examples in specific varieties – notably Shiro Bekko, Shiro Utsuri and Ogon. But all the best 'Koi keepers' Koi' – Kohaku, Sanke and Showa – are still Japanese-bred and are likely to remain so for the foreseeable future.

PREPARATIONS FOR THE SHOW
Even the highest-grade Koi will stand little chance if the owner does not take steps to bring it into peak condition in the weeks

leading up to a show. It goes without saying that water quality in the home pond should be impeccable, and food of a quality to maximise growth and optimise condition.

As the show date nears, colour-enhancing food can be fed to improve the intensity of the red markings, while essential minerals similar to those found in breeders' mud ponds can be supplied in montmorillonite clay preparations. When first added to the pond, these clays temporarily cloud the water, but they improve skin lustre and general vigour.

For a few days prior to a show, Koi should not be fed – this minimises the waste they will excrete in transit and in the vat, though the fish still have a tendency to graze on blanketweed if their normal pellet rations are withheld! Feeding until the last minute is frowned upon, as nobody wants their fish to share a vat with Koi that are excreting copious ammonia-producing droppings.

DISEASED FISH
It is pointless taking a Koi to a show if it is obviously diseased, or carrying parasites visible to the naked eye – this brings immediate disqualification. The benching team will also exclude Koi that appear sluggish or swim with clamped fins, as well as those that exhibit signs of carp pox, or have bloated or emaciated bodies. Small splits in the fins, or the odd scale damaged in transit will be allowed, but anything else that indicates a Koi could have a problem, infectious or otherwise, means the fish will not compete. In borderline cases, the opinion of the senior judge is always sought.

AVOIDING STRESS
In fairness to the owners, relatively few Koi are disqualified, because the sort of person who takes the trouble to enter a show is usually well aware of what is required of the fish, and will not subject them to pointless

Benching fish at Koi shows demands skill, speed and confident handling techniques.
Photo: Nick Fletcher.

journeys. Unfortunately (and this can be gauged only by trial and error), some Koi simply do not travel well. The usual sign of stress is a reddening of the white areas, brought about by haemorrhaging of the tiny capillary blood vessels under the skin. Such Koi are best left to be admired in their home pond.

Even seasoned travellers are not shown at every opportunity; a thoughtful owner realises that fish take time to recover their equilibrium and so will 'rest' them between outings, perhaps entering them into just two or three shows a year.

TRAVEL EQUIPMENT
It is essential to have the right equipment to transport Koi to and from shows. This will consist of heavy-duty polybags of a size matched to the fish; a portable valved oxygen cylinder to inflate the space above the water; elastic bands to secure the bags; a stress-relieving agent to add to the transit water; large polystyrene boxes into which the bags are placed to minimise temperature fluctuations; and, of course, suitable nets/bowls to transfer Koi from home pond to bag.

The boxes containing fish should be placed

on a firm level surface in the car or van where they cannot slide or be thrown about, and larger fish should travel sideways on, so that sudden braking will not damage noses or tail fins.

INSURANCE

It is worth inquiring about insurance if you are regularly transporting valuable Koi – premiums may be high, but these have to be measured against the cost of replacing fish, should the vehicle break down in a remote area or be involved in an accident.

SHOWS IN THE UK

Four key words describe shows in the UK: 'Open', 'Closed', 'English', and 'Japanese'. An open show is simply one into which any Koi keeper can enter fish, whereas closed shows are restricted to members of the organising society or section. In both cases, the public are usually admitted at some stage.

'English' or 'Japanese' indicates the different ways the Koi are housed for the show's duration. In Japanese-style shows, entrants do not have a vat exclusively for their own fish, but all Koi in the 13 varieties and six sizes go into communal vats.

The first stage of judging is to select first and second in each size and variety (theoretically, that would mean 156 Koi, but in practice there are usually gaps, as some varieties/sizes are not well represented). Once judged, these Koi are moved into new vats from which first, second and third in all six sizes are selected. From these are picked Best Baby, Adult and Mature Champion (categories based on size), and the Grand Champion (overall winner). At the discretion of the show committee, other awards may be made – for Best Jumbo, Best Home-bred Koi and Best Tategoi.

The job of judging a Japanese-style show is made relatively straightforward because like can be compared against like, since fish of a given size/variety swim together – the benching team, by contrast, are run off their feet moving fish around!

English-style shows, still the norm in the UK, first became popular (if that is the right word) following a scare over 'SVC' in the 1980s. Spring Viraemia of Carp is a notifiable disease which almost certainly reached Britain via unlicensed imports of common and mirror carp from Continental Europe which then came into contact with ornamental fish. The likelihood of SVC ever affecting Koi, particularly high-grade Koi, was, and still is, remote, but 'better safe than sorry' was a natural reaction. On the other hand, given that Koi are netted in and out of vats and subject to handling, even in English-style shows, there is still some risk of disease transmission, albeit less acute.

Mindful of this, Koi owners usually give their fish a short-term 'dip' once they are back home – potassium permanganate will deal with protozoan parasites and is also a mild bactericide.

English-style shows in which every competitor has his/her own vat mean hard work for the judges, who have to retain mental pictures of every single Koi (and comparable fish can often be 30 yards apart from one another). The judging process takes longer than in a Japanese-style show, and more vats have to be provided, which often means entry is by invitation only – this can lead to some ill-feeling from those who may feel their fish are worthy of inclusion.

There is no minimum entry requirement, so in theory one vat could contain two Size 1 baby Koi and the next half a dozen Size 6 fish. In addition to the Koi-holding vats, others must also be provided to hold replacement water, since, in the course of a one or two-day show, several partial water changes will have to be made. Hospital vats are essential in the case of two-day shows, since, if a Koi is disqualified for whatever reason, it must still be properly housed until it can travel home with its pond-mates.

SHOW PROCEDURE

BENCHING
On arrival at a show, fish are 'benched'; this means they are categorised according to size and variety, and it is at this stage that any disqualifications are made on grounds of poor health or abnormal physiology. To watch a skilled benching team at work is an education. The Koi arrive in plastic bags which should be floated in a vat, unopened, for about 30 minutes to equalise water temperatures. While this is going on, documentation is filled in and entry fees collected.

MEASURING
The Koi are then transferred into a shallow, floating, blue measuring bowl which has the various size categories marked on a scale (these calibrations are always checked for accuracy before the show).

EXAMINATION
Next, the head of benching looks the Koi over thoroughly, running his hands along the body and over the finnage to check for raised scales, anchor worm, broken fin rays etc. Particular attention is paid to the underside of the Koi, since (especially in larger, heavier examples) this is an area the owner can omit to properly examine before deciding whether the fish is fit to be shown.

IDENTIFICATION
If the benching team passes the Koi as healthy, it must now be identified; some shows attract hundreds of entries. At the 1998 National (Japanese-style), a hollow plastic rod holding laminated numbered raffle tickets was placed beside each fish as it was photographed, to act as a cross-reference.

Identification pictures always used to be taken with a Polaroid camera, although the trend is increasingly towards digital photography, which is speedier and gives a clearer image.

From the measuring bowl, the Koi are gently transferred to double plastic bags with enough water to cover their backs and are carried – always by two benching helpers – to their show vats. The instruction will be something like: "Size four Kohaku, vat seven."

The photographs are displayed on boards beside these vats – they serve to indicate which Koi each vat contains, and to inform the viewing public as to the varieties. For security reasons, the owner's name is usually erased. The photographs and documentation come into play again at the show's end, when de-benching takes place and hobbyists reclaim their Koi. At Japanese-style events it is sometimes quite difficult to match the right people to the right fish, especially single-coloured varieties such as Ogons. No two Koi are exactly alike, but it can get difficult telling apart equally-sized Hikarimuji.

CLASSIFICATION
Size and variety classification of Koi varies from country to country and from show to show. The governing body in Britain, the BKKS, recognises 10 classes of non-metallic fish -– these are Kohaku, Taisho Sanke, Showa Sanke, Utsurimono, Bekko, Tancho, Koromo, Asagi/Shusui, Kin Gin Rin and Kawarimono. Three further classes are for metallic fish – Hikari Utsuri, Hikarimuji and Hikarimoyo – making 13 in all.

The six UK size classifications (still measured in inches) are: Size One, 1 to 8 ins; Size Two, 8 to 12 ins; Size Three, 12 to 16 ins; Size Four, 16 to 20 ins; Size Five, 20 to 24 ins; Size Six, 24 ins and over. Except for Size One, it can be seen that the classifications move in four-inch stages. This can be unfortunate in the case of a Koi in (for example) Size 4 that scrapes in at a fraction over 16 ins long, as it is then competing against Koi nudging 20 ins. All other factors being equal, the larger fish will be preferred.

In contrast, at the All Japan Show held annually in Tokyo, there are 15 size categories, in the five largest of which male and female Koi are judged separately. There is only a 5-cm (two-inch) difference between categories. However, the All Japan is matched nowhere else in the world in terms of size and prestige, and fees for entering Koi are high in order to finance this show on the grand scale.

COMPARING KOI

Back to the UK. Visitors often wonder how the judges make their choice; since no two Koi are the same, how can fish fairly be compared against one another? The beginner tends to be drawn to a Koi because it has an attractive pattern, but this is only part of the picture. Body shape, skin quality and deportment are far more critical, and only if the judges are satisfied on these counts does pattern come into play in the decision-making process.

A well-made Koi should be neither thin nor obese, with finnage balanced to its size. Starting at the head, a common fault is a snout that is too pointed, while other Koi can be found with a foreshortened profile that makes them look like the bonnet of an old-fashioned bull-nosed Morris. The judges will try to view the Koi head-on, to make sure there is no lateral displacement of the jaw – and, of course, the mouth must be free from any deformities stemming from old injuries or congenital defects. Most of these will have been picked up at benching stage.

The eyes must be clear, neither sunken nor protruding, and the gill covers (opercula) complete and closing flush with the skull.

Over- or undersized pectoral fins can destroy the grace of an otherwise accomplished Koi. Ogons frequently have fins too small to balance their bodies. The leading edges of these paired fins should be uninterrupted by 'stepping'.

You frequently see Koi that are pinched in just behind the head. This should not be confused with the lean look of newly imported fish that have been starved before shipment, as no amount of good feeding will improve an inherently weak body shape.

The body of a Koi should broaden from the shoulders to a point level with the leading edge of the dorsal fin, and then taper evenly towards the wrist of the tail (the caudal peduncle). Fish that have not been kept in sufficiently deep ponds, or females carrying spawn, can exhibit an uneven taper when viewed from above, and this will go against them.

The back contour of a good Koi should be gently convex, not flat, balancing out a rounded and even (but not rotund) belly profile. In Doitsu Koi, particularly, there is a tendency towards the fish equivalent of a 'beer belly', resulting in a short and squat appearance that will be marked down.

Fullness of body shape becomes more evident as the Koi grows, and so fish in the smaller sizes are not expected to be scaled-down versions of their larger brethren. Also, the body shape of Koi depends to some degree on their bloodline (for example, Matsunosuke Sanke tend to be relatively slim, the result of reintroducing Magoi – wild carp – genes to encourage greater ultimate body length). Mature female Koi develop an imposing presence, as they are naturally broader in the beam than males. This is why most adult and mature Champions tend to be female. Like for like, female Koi are therefore more sought-after than males, and this is reflected in the price they command.

Grand Champion Tancho.

Photo: Steve Roberts.

SKIN QUALITY

Skin quality is something that can be appreciated only by viewing many high-grade Koi and comparing them against less accomplished examples. The words 'depth', 'clarity' and 'shine' are applicable to white skin in particular: the skin should be free of shimis (random spots of black, not to be confused with true sumi) and look as though it has been lacquered. In good Go-Sanke (Kohaku, Sanke and Showa), the scales should be almost invisible below the pigmented areas, which should be even and deep. Kiwa and Sashi (where the edges of pigmented scales border on to white skin) should be crisp, not blurred, faded or messy.

In metallic Koi, the lustre of the skin and fins should be uniform, and, in Ogons, a clear, blemish-free head is essential.

Good skin quality can be appreciated only by viewing the Koi closely in an inspection bowl in good, natural daylight – photographs or videos cannot convey the subtleties. Unfortunately, some Koi with normally excellent skin do not travel at all well to shows, and, as mentioned earlier, exhibit a stress-related reddening of the white areas. Skin quality, like all other attributes of a good Koi, can only be judged on the day.

DEPORTMENT

Deportment is best described as the way a Koi conducts itself and moves around the show vat. The fish should swim evenly, using its paired fins in equal measure without excessive body movement to give forward propulsion. It should maintain equilibrium and not rest with head down or tail up. In larger sizes, Koi should swim effortlessly and majestically, as good deportment is one of the attributes of a quality Jumbo.

PATTERN

Pattern, fairly obviously, is most important on Go-Sanke and does not come into play at all on single-coloured Koi. There used to be well-defined guidelines – for example, head markings on a Kohaku were not expected to extend down over the eyes, and traditional 'stepped' patterns were favoured over the one-offs. Pattern symmetry was tacitly appreciated, and overall the fish were judged according to how closely they approached the unattainable ideal.

These days there is a much more relaxed approach to pattern criteria, to the extent that, if all other factors are equal, a Grand Champion is more likely to have a distinctive and unique pattern, especially in the head area. Rather than symmetry, the judges are looking for balance. This does not mean that the pigmented areas either side of the dorsal should be evenly spaced or be of the same size relative to one another, but that the overall impression must be pleasing to the eye.

Many Koi, especially Showa, are 'head heavy' – in other words, they are excellent Koi from snout to midway down the body, but the patterning then falls away. Typically, such Showa have insufficient hi (red) to

Grand Champion Kohaku (size 5).

Photo: Steve Roberts.

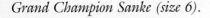

Grand Champion Sanke (size 6).

Photo: Steve Roberts.

sustain interest from nose to tail.

The permissible distribution of the three colours forming the pattern in Sanke and Showa is nowadays far less rigid than it used to be. The 'ideal' Showa was once a fish in which the red, black and white were present in equal amounts, while old-fashioned Sanke had 'tortoiseshell' sumi making up a large percentage of the pattern. Now, though, we have 'Kindai Showa' in which the white predominates, and Sanke whose sumi markings are sparse, merely serving to emphasise the red on a white ground. These two varieties, once clearly distinguishable, can now cause real confusion, even at judging level, and there have been cases where a fish is benched as a Sanke one year and a Showa the next – both decisions being correct at the time.

WATER MAINTENANCE

It is a testing time for Koi owners as they wait for their fish to be viewed, and speculation as to who has done well, or not so well, runs rife. But, while the judging teams are doing their rounds, the welfare of the Koi still has to be considered.

Droppings are regularly vacuumed from the vats, airstones are checked, the sometimes over-enthusiastic public are diplomatically asked not to put their hands in the water or otherwise disturb the fish, and – most

247

Champion Utsurimono (size 4).

Photo: Steve Roberts.

importantly – regular water quality tests are continually carried out and partial changes made where necessary, topping up from storage vats. Ammonia levels are especially critical. Digital testing equipment for ammonia, nitrite, dissolved oxygen, pH and conductivity gives virtually instant read-outs, and often companies specialising in this technology will offer their services at shows.

JUDGES

The judges are all seasoned Koi keepers who have undergone long-term training in variety identification, Koi appreciation and show procedure. Senior judges and trainees attend the larger shows together, as there is no substitute for hands-on experience, but only full judges make the final decisions.

Processing of the results, even computer-aided, takes some time – further increasing the tension. And when the awards are finally posted on to the vat boards there is inevitably a heady mixture of triumph and disappointment.

PRIZES

The prize-giving that follows, at least in the

UK, is a celebratory ceremony but not in any way an opportunity for financial gain. The trophies and special awards are treasured purely for what they represent. However, Koi dealers present at shows are understandably happy if the fish they supply do well – this attracts more customers. Sometimes, winning Koi later change hands privately among serious collectors, their value enhanced by the awards they have picked up.

GOING HOME

For Koi owners, de-benching after the show is the least favourite element. The fish have stood or fallen on their merits, and now getting them home is a priority. Having everyone clamouring for their Koi and causing vehicle congestion on the showground is not the way to go about it. The best show organisers call exhibitors in order into the central ring and the de-benching team try to ensure that the fish leave in as good a condition as they first arrived, double-bagged with oxygen.

PHOTOGRAPHIC COMPETITIONS

Some Koi owners are understandably

reluctant to take their fish around the country, yet would still like them to be judged, at least against those of friends. For such people, the photographic competition is an ideal compromise. Usually organised at club (section) level, it involves a team chosen from within the organisation travelling to home ponds and judging the Koi there and then. Each fish needs bowling for only a few minutes while the judges make their notes and take a photograph (often someone is there with a video-recorder, the tape forming the basis of a lively club evening at a later date).

A photographic record of all Koi entered gives a chance for ordinary club members to test their skills against those of the judges at a future get-together. There is rarely a consensus!

THE FUTURE

Many Koi keepers manage to enjoy their hobby with no element of competition. But, for those who do compete, there is ample opportunity – wherever in the world they live – to confirm that their Koi selection and husbandry skills are resulting in fish of which they can be justly proud.

Koi shows of the future could see changes in the benching categories, as varieties once popular fall out of favour. For example, Bekko and Asagi/Shusui presently have their own classes but are always under-represented, while there is no separate class for Doitsu-scaled Koi which are gaining in stature year on year. What will not change is the dedication shown behind the scenes by the organisers, whose efforts are not always fully appreciated.

Typically, when exhibitors have got their fish safely home, the helpers will still have days of hard labour ahead, dismantling marquees, emptying vats and returning the show venue to its original condition. There may then be a few weeks' respite before the organisers convene their first meeting to decide where and when next year's event will take place, and on whose shoulders the numerous voluntary tasks will fall!

SHOWING KOI IN THE US
Pamela Spindola

Showing Koi in the US is a very similar affair to how it is done in the UK (see above). In the US, Koi shows range from small invitational backyard judgings to open shows set in large public areas as shopping malls, hotels or parks. Most of these shows are produced by Koi clubs desiring to promote the hobby and club membership. However, in recent years, dealer associations have also begun to sponsor Koi competitions. A Koi show is a time for fellow hobbyists to enjoy the camaraderie and friendly competition.

However, these events are not just beauty contests for Koi. During the day, experts lecture on various aspects of the hobby, dealers and breeders display their latest shipment of Koi, ranging in size and qualities, and commercial vendors display the most up-to-date equipment for the pond. This well-organised event provides opportunities for the newcomer and veteran Koi enthusiast to learn more about the selection of Koi and their optimal care.

The judges for the Koi show are very knowledgeable of the standards and criteria of the varieties of Koi classification. Often, teams of judges, and judges in-training will officiate at a show, all of whom have undergone a rigorous certification process under the auspices of the Associated Koi Clubs of America, known as AKCA, or Zen Nippon Airinkai, known as ZNA of Japan.

The show site has a configuration of large blue tanks, usually measuring about six feet in diameter and three feet in height, each with a generous supply of aeration. Upon arrival at the show, the Koi are acclimatised to the water temperature, measured, carefully inspected and placed in appropriate tanks according to the size and variety. Club members, usually dressed in matching skirts and jackets, work like a trained army classifying and distributing the fish.

At some shows, pictures of each entrant's fish are taken to ensure that they return home with their rightful owner. The entry fee is determined by the number of fish entered. The host club decides on size increments for the entries and the varieties to be judged. There are 14 varieties; however, in a small show, sometimes the categories are combined such as combining all Gin Rin. There is no standard for size range. Some shows begin at under seven inches (17.5 cm) and have three-inch increments (7.5 cm), others may start at eight to eleven inches (20.5-28 cm). It is the club's decision.

During the show, the judges select the most outstanding fish of each variety and size range based on the body shape, colour, pattern and overall quality. Many judges use the show as a teaching forum, explaining their rationale for the selections. This added information has become quite popular to hobbyists and makes the show educational.

The winning fish are moved to their new tanks. The first-placed fish of a size range are then judged for Best in Size. Many times, a Best Baby, Best Young, Best Mature is also selected. From this selection comes the Grand Champion and, at times, a runner-up Grand Champion. An unusual and sometimes complicated concept of 'move-ups' is also carried out during the judging process. When there is a vacancy because a fish has won a higher award, a re-judging needs to take place to fill the empty slot. In this way, there is a true hierarchy of awards.

The owners claim their awards by filling out a form which is then put into the computer. Sometimes, more than one person claims the winning fish. The issue is usually resolved because an entrant has mistaken the size range. If not, the Show Chairman resolves the issue quickly by checking the entry forms and the accompanying photos. Experience has proved that usually these minor conflicts are resolved amicably by the parties involved.

The trophies are given out either at an afternoon ceremony or an award banquet in the evening. In addition to the officially judged awards, it has been a growing custom for visiting participants from other clubs to award a Friendship trophy to their favourite fish. One of the highlights of the dinner banquet is a slide show of the day's events and the winning fish. As the judge talks about his selections, the guests can view the fish larger than life.

The end of the show is a frenetic but organised exercise. Owners with net and tub in hand, and with a friend to help, go from tank to tank to collect their Koi. Onlookers may ask, "How do you know which one is yours?" The reply is, "You know your own dog or cat, don't you?"

25 JUDGING KOI

Putting together a successful Koi show involves great effort on the part of the organisers and those bringing fish for exhibition. But without a knowledgeable team of judges officiating on the day, all that effort would go to waste – because the main competitive element of the show would lack credibility. On the shoulders of these people rests a huge responsibility to carry out their duties impartially, fairly and in a dignified manner, all in the face of the inevitable verbal flak from owners of Koi which have not fared as well as expected.

Because no two Koi are alike, and because their appreciation can be subjective (everyone has their favourite variety), the judges could so easily find themselves on a hiding to nothing. Their standing in the eyes of the Koi-keeping public remains as high as it is only because each member of the team undergoes, or has undergone, a thorough and lengthy training programme.

Most Koi shows are run under the banner of a recognised governing body – in Britain the two largest are the British Koi Keepers Society (BKKS) and the Northern and Southern chapters of ZNA (Zen Nippon Airinkai). Their methodology differs in several respects, including size and variety classification, though the judges from both organisations are cast in very much the same mould.

REQUIREMENTS FOR JUDGES

What makes an ordinary Koi keeper decide to become a judge? It is a combination of factors. It may be that, having enjoyed all the benefits of Koi society membership, he or she now wishes to put something back into the hobby. Perhaps that person would like to gain a deeper insight into Koi appreciation by learning alongside the experts, or even to expand the social side of the hobby.

It is much easier to list the reasons why someone would not want to take up judging. To do it properly involves considerable personal sacrifice. With shows held in Britain every weekend from April to October, there is a heavy demand on a judge's free time. Thousands of miles of car travel are involved, reimbursed only at cost. Irrespective of the weather, the official has to arrive punctually at shows, smartly dressed and prepared to spend several hours on his or her feet. If the show organisation is less than perfect, much of that time can be passed doing very little while benching errors are corrected and judging sheets are amended.

Not surprisingly, then, potential judges are not exactly queuing up to be taken on. But then, if the induction and training process were too simple and painless, the standard of candidates would not be so high.

In the BKKS, its Judging and Standards Committee (JSC) is responsible for judging colour vision, and have an innate appreciation of the beauty of Koi which will be honed as the training programme, very much a 'hands-on' experience, progresses.

TRAINING AND EXAMINATION

The induction process begins with a trainee seminar held in late autumn, when the hectic show programme is finished for another year. This 'baptism of fire' straightaway eliminates some candidates, all of whom must complete three examinations over the day. The first is a written paper to test basic knowledge and comprehension of material sent to them in advance. Most topics relating to Koi keeping are covered, including health care, water quality, Japanese terminology and the BKKS show rules and guidelines.

After a discussion of this written paper (the questions are asked again around the table), stage two is a test on the classification of Koi. It is obvious that any potential judge must know the benching categories and any current amendments to them, and the test is conducted on slides flashed on a screen for just 30 seconds.

Another discussion follows, at which point some candidates are looking quite discouraged. Where, for example, should a Kage Showa be benched? These fish used to be in Kawarimono (and in the ZNA they still are). But the BKKS has decided, because of some confusion over what exactly constitutes 'Kage', that all such fish should be benched Showa.

A slide showing a Gin Rin Bekko is another potential trap. Is the fish benched Kin-Gin Rin or Bekko? Candidates are told that only Go-Sanke (Kohaku, Sanke, Showa and the 'honorary' Shiro Utsuri) are eligible for the Kin-Gin Rin category, all the rest with the characteristic sparkling gold or silver scales being benched in another class – e.g. a Gin Rin Chagoi will be in Kawarimono.

The final part of this pleasant ordeal is the

Judging is under way. If one fish is lifted in a net, the others must be too, so that a fair, impartial decision can be reached.

Photo: Nick Fletcher.

matters relating to the Society's shows, and also for administering the recruitment and training programme. The only official requirement for candidates is that they are current BKKS members who do not have a trade interest in the buying and selling of Koi – this rule is plainly there to nip in the bud any accusation of bias.

Unofficially, the would-be judge must be able to drive, must possess good eyesight and

Judging Koi

Showa or hi Utsuri? White is visible, so it's a Showa – one of the easier benching decisions.

Photo: Nick Fletcher.

judging of paired Koi slides (which is the better fish, A or B, and why?). This provokes lively comment, because there is not always full consensus, even among the examiners! Skin quality is impossible to evaluate from a slide, but body shape and pattern are usually able to be judged.

After some encouraging final words from the chairman of the JSC (unsuccessful candidates can always re-apply next year), the hopefuls go out into the night not knowing whether they have attained the required 70 per cent pass rate. They will be notified in due course by post.

SHOW EXPERIENCE

The envelope arrives, and it contains an official trainee badge! Success – but this is only the start of a long learning curve. The following spring, the trainee will be sent details of the first shows he or she is expected to attend. These can be anywhere in the country, on a Saturday or Sunday, and sometimes both.

Each trainee is taken under the wing of a senior judge, who acts as both mentor and assessor. Depending on the size of the show, two or more such teams will be present.

Perhaps benching is still taking place when the trainee arrives. First instincts are to go and view the proceedings, but this is not allowed – only when every fish has been classified according to size and variety and transferred to the appropriate show vats can judging begin. The senior judge will already have asked the organisers about any special awards to be made (such as 'Best Koi by a Junior' or 'Best Tategoi'), whether there is to be a dealers' class, and whether the eventual Grand Champion is to be eligible for other prizes too.

The usual way to split the judging workload is for each team to be responsible for certain size categories in all varieties. In the case of two teams, the first could judge Sizes One and Three, the other Sizes Two and Four. If one team finishes before the other, the remaining benching sheets can then be shared out to save time.

Typically, the senior judge will first ask the trainee to identify the fish in each vat – this is partly to test his comprehension, partly as a double-check to ensure that every Koi has been properly benched. Errors do occur – for example, mix-ups between Hikari Utsuri and Hikarimoyo or, at a more basic level, Sanke and Showa. Occasionally, the problem relates to size, and, if the senior judge suspects that a Size Three has just edged into Size Four, he will ask for it to be re-measured. In Koi shows, at least, size does matter; in the example given, it would be to the advantage of the fish to remain a big Size Three rather than compete against Koi that could be almost four inches longer. All fish are measured from nose to the tips of the caudal fin, or 'total length'.

JUDGING CRITERIA

In a Japanese-style show, the trainee will be viewing like against like and, if there are several Size Two Kohaku in one vat, he or she will probably be asked to take the least meritorious fish out of the running. This is where the judging criteria come into play – body shape and skin quality being given a higher priority than pattern. This can surprise the casual observer.

"Why do you think none of these Koi should be in the first three?" might be the next question. The trainee's answer is being mentally evaluated by the senior judge, who may well disagree strongly with the choice but is still interested in the reasoning behind it. "Look again," he may say. "The body shape on the one you think should be placed third is not all that imposing, and the pattern disguises the fact that the skin quality could be better."

The way the dialogue is conducted is important – it must be diplomatic, as the owner of the Koi under discussion could well be listening. So the fish's positive attributes are listed as well, while any demerits are played down. Often, spectators will try to ask questions, but they are politely told to wait until judging is completed before raising their point. What the judges will not do before the official results are announced is to give any indication of how a particular fish might have fared.

Sometimes Koi will need to be netted into a floating basket or bowl for closer examination. The judges should not be involved in this handling, the job falling to appointed stewards – and if two fish are being evaluated against one another, both or neither must be bowled to give them an equal opportunity to show what they are made of. The larger the Koi, the greater the possibility of it being damaged or stressed during handling, and so any fish over Size 5 is merely lifted in a net closer to the water's surface, never clear of it.

TEAM DECISIONS

The whole judging team can convene to discuss these larger fish, which usually make up only a small percentage of the total number entered in the show. Everyone's opinion is again sought, the judges vote among themselves, but the senior judge present has the final say – this ruling also applies to any dispute relating to classification or the fitness of a Koi to be shown.

Next task is to choose overall 'Best in Size' in the six categories, usually a first and a second in each. In Japanese-style shows this is not usually too difficult, but it can be a leg-aching and mind-stretching experience if the show is run along English lines. The same criteria are used as before, but, in addition, the judges take into consideration the relative difficulty in obtaining excellent examples in the 13 varieties. This is why if a Kohaku and an Ogon were equal on body shape, deportment, skin quality and size, the Kohaku would edge it; being a patterned fish, it would be reckoned superior, as pattern is another dimension to consider. Although Hariwake are two-coloured fish, they are not 'patterned' in the judging sense of the word.

It is often said that a good big Koi will always beat a good smaller Koi. With the exception of Size 1 (1 inch-8 ins) and Size 6 in a BKKS show (which can be anything over 24 inches), there is only a potential four-inch size difference in each category, but

Judging Koi

Champion (Sizes 3 and 4); Mature Champion (Sizes 5 and 6); and Grand Champion. In theory, the top fish can be of any size, but in almost every case a Size 5 or 6 Koi is chosen. Quite simply, the bigger a fish grows, the harder it is to keep looking good, and this effort is recognised. Grand Champions are almost exclusively Go-Sanke, for reasons already mentioned.

To speed the judging throughout the day, sheets are handed to stewards as they are completed and the behind-the-scenes team beavers away to correlate the results. Much of this work is now done on computer which, in theory at least, means greater speed and accuracy.

JUDGING KOI IN THE US
Pamela Spindola

Koi-judging in the US differs little from that in the UK. The qualification criteria are different, however. With the tremendous growth of Koi clubs sponsoring shows across the nation in the early 1990s, the need arose for qualified Koi judges. Up until this time, there were only a handful of USA ZNA-certified local judges and it is not always easy to arrange for a judge from Japan. In 1992, Associated Koi Clubs of America formed a Judges Certification Committee headed by three of the most esteemed Koi hobbyists in the country. This committee wrote the By-laws, established the judging, etiquette and integrity, created an AKCA judging style, and organised an on-going educational programme which included training and feedback. They also answer the requests for judges and make the assignments of head judges and candidate judges for the many shows.

An AKCA judge candidate must have been a member of an affiliate club for at least three years and be a hobbyist, not a professional. He must demonstrate a thorough knowledge

This Sanke shows Tsubo sumi (black on white) and Kasane sumi (black on red) – a stunning fish.   *Photo: Nick Fletcher.*

body bulk ('volume') can distort the picture. Only if two equally good fish are being judged against one another will the larger one automatically get the judges' vote.

Often, very large Koi have reached that size at the expense of skin quality; they may be showing signs of Hikkui, a non-malignant but unsightly type of skin cancer affecting the red pigment, or they may just be over the hill. The Koi keeper's best ploy then is to keep growing the fish on in the hope that it may be a future Jumbo prizewinner!

Once 'Best in Size' is decided, the four major awards are considered: Baby Champion (from Sizes 1 and 2); Adult of Koi-keeping and be willing to help others. For a minimum of three years, the candidate must have had a Koi pond and have cared for and raised Koi. He must have entered a minimum of three Koi shows approved and sanctioned by AKCA. Only one of these shows may be the member's own club.

To become certified, the candidate must judge a minimum of five AKCA-affiliated shows or three AKCA and two ZNA-affiliated shows. The head judge is to provide a written assessment of the candidate's performance after the show. The candidate must attend at least one annual training session at the AKCA Seminar and complete a lengthy written examination testing the individual's knowledge of Koi show experience, procedures and judging ability.

During the annual training, the candidates officiate at a mock Koi show and perform the judging exercise in front of a large audience on closed circuit television. All candidates are carefully studied for their expertise and knowledge of Koi, their ability to be decisive and their eloquence in explaining their selections in a diplomatic way.

At a sanctioned Koi show, there may be assistant judges and candidate judges, helping the head judge. In shows with hundreds of fish entries, the judges are placed in teams, usually each assigned to a specific size category. Since most of the shows have become educational, the head judge will talk to the onlookers about the variety of Koi being judged and what attributes are desirable. The good points are always noticed and mentioned first. All Koi to be judged are put into the judging tub so that each entrant knows his fish has not been overloooked. The Koi are always checked for health. Then the judging process includes review of the body conformation, the colour, the pattern, and the elegance or quality of the fish. During the judging process, the assistant judges and candidate judges offer their opinions and vote. The head judge has the last say, weighing all the input. After the judging, the judges feel content knowing that they judged fairly and to the best of their ability.